HOW TO MAKE PROFITS WITH SERVICE CONTRACTS

HOW TO MAKE PROFITS WITH SERVICE CONTRACTS

Michael R. Rizzo

American Management Association

Library of Congress Cataloging-in-Publication Data

Rizzo, Michael R.
    How to make profits with service contracts.

    Includes index.
    1. Service industries—Management. 2. Contracts for
work and labor. I. Title.
HD9980.5.R59   1987   658   86-47590
ISBN 0-8144-5807-6

Printing number

10 9 8 7 6 5 4 3

Acknowledgments

Writing a book is an exciting adventure. It provides the author with a forum to convey ideas that have been pent up in his mind—ideas that he feels will benefit others if he could share them.

In developing the manuscript, an author pursues new concepts and meets new people. Talking to the individuals in the companies profiled in Part Two of this book was an exhilarating, informative experience for me. I interviewed and was enriched by those who were making successful contract programs happen.

I extend my thanks for the time and support given to me by Joseph Cleary and Arthur Zuckerman of the Xerox Corporation; by Chuck Meola, Edward McLaughlin, and James Abate of Canon U.S.A., Inc.; by Stephen Rolla of A-Copy, Inc.; by John Winberg of NCR Corporation; by Jay Lee of Adesco, Inc.; by G. Wes Perry of Marsh & McLennan Group Associates; and by the American Arbitration Association.

A book such as this is the result of exposure to and support from many individuals. It is the culmination of a lifetime of experience. To all those colleagues, friends, and acquaintances who have made this book a reality—thank you.

Foreword

This book is composed of two parts. The first takes you through the steps involved in establishing a service contract program. The second provides you with profiles of companies that enjoy successful service contract programs. There are worksheets and Appendixes to provide practical guidance.

Each chapter in the first part covers a major topic in developing service contracts. You have two basic options. You can start with Chapter 1 and follow the topics as they lead toward building the service contract program (The arrangement is like a recipe outlining how each ingredient is added to achieve a successful result.); or you can select those chapters of interest. Since each chapter covers a complete aspect of a service contract program, you should have no difficulty reading and applying the information it contains. Regardless of which way you choose to read this book, it is suggested that you at least skim each chapter. The companies in the second part of this book were selected not only for the quality of their service programs, but because they provide the reader with a variety of approaches used by various companies in developing successful service contract programs.

Do enjoy the book, and best wishes for success in your service contract program.

Introduction

The service industry today is a multibillion dollar a year business. In fact, single industries count annual service revenues in the billions of dollars.

In any business there is an element of risk. As a rule, the service business is labor intensive, making the risk all the greater. Service managers must keep their technicians profitably occupied at all times if they are to enjoy successful operations. The seasonal and cyclical nature of the service business creates problems for managers in fully utilizing personnel during slow periods. Throughout the year, service managers are dependent on telephone calls from customers requesting service. What prompts a customer to call a particular servicing organization depends on a number of factors, which may include a listing in the Yellow Pages or a recommendation from a friend. This means that the success of the service firm is tied to factors over which it has little or no control.

This book is designed to help service managers change those circumstances. As you move from chapter to chapter, you'll generate ideas not only about how to develop your own new service contract program, but how to strengthen an existing program. Additionally, you will readily see how many of the concepts presented will help you improve the volume and profitability of time and material service programs.

This book is designed to give service managers the tools to take hold of their businesses, to actively seek out customers, and to create the desired volume of service sales, rather than wait for that volume to appear. The book will aid service firms in their desire to control their own destinies.

The pages that follow are filled with a wide range of perspectives, from "Why do it?" to "How do you go about doing it?" The book's purpose is to provide service managers with a how-to guide, but it is also directed at stimulating the creative processes within the servicing organization. In the final analysis, a book cannot make your servicing organization more successful; you must do it. It is hoped that what this book will do is stimulate your thinking and give you the guidance and assistance that will help you achieve success.

Contents

Part I: Service Contract Programs   1

 1   Why Have Service Contracts?   3
 2   Types of Service Arrangements   10
 3   Types of Service Contracts   21
 4   The Insured Service Contract   31
 5   Pricing Service Contracts   38
 6   Writing the Service Contract   93
 7   Selling Service Contracts   120
 8   Contract Administration   165
 9   Service Business Ethics   194
10   Controlling Service Parts and Materials   198
11   Third-Party Service   208

Part II: Corporate Profiles   215

A   Xerox Americare   217
B   Marsh & McLennan Group Associates   226
C   NCR Corporation   231
D   Adesco, Inc.   239
E   A-Copy, Inc.   247
F   Canon U.S.A., Inc.   259

Part III: Appendixes

Appendix One: Worksheets   273

Appendix Two: Sample Contracts and Brochures   283

Appendix Three: Magnuson-Moss Warranty Act (including
Act's Appendixes B and C)   301

Appendix Four: Florida Service Warranty Kit (including
Chapter 634 of the State Law)   323

Index   361

Part I
Service Contract Programs

1
Why Have Service Contracts?

"You can't make money selling service." Seth Johnson sat in his office as he reflected on that statement. He had heard it so often from other service managers. As Seth reviewed the financial statement of his service operation, he began to accept the premise that it was difficult to make money selling service. From year to year he struggled to break even. The road was bumpy, with marginal profits one year and small losses in other years.

As service manager of the fictitious American Control Technologies, Inc. (ACT), Seth had the responsibility of running the entire corporate service operation. ACT produces and sells fully integrated safety systems for industrial, commercial, and consumer applications. The industrial and commercial products are sold through ACT's own sales force directly to the user. An independent dealer organization was established to sell the consumer products. Seth was responsible for ensuring that adequate service is provided to the customer, whether it be an industrial, commercial, or consumer account.

Service for the commercial and industrial customers is administered through a network of service centers located throughout the United States. Each center is staffed by a regional service manager and a group of service technicians whose number varies at each center depending on the amount of anticipated service work. In looking at each region's service history, Seth recognized that the expected service volume wasn't always realized, or at least it wasn't realized on the days, weeks, or even—on occasion—the months that the regional managers thought it would occur. This was costing money. Senior management insisted that service be rendered within a few hours of receipt of a customer's call. They felt that this prompt response was necessary to maintain the customer's perception of product integrity. This fast response meant that an adequate number of technicians had to be on hand during peak demand periods, which also resulted in high levels of unapplied labor (labor that is not billable to the customer) during slack periods.

Seth's problem was further compounded by his attempt to ensure that the dealer network maintain an adequate number of service technicians to properly service its customers. Though the agreement stipulated that each dealer was to maintain a staff of at least three adequately trained technicians, it was common knowledge that most of the dealers had only one or two technicians on their payrolls. In fact, many had none at all. This resulted in numerous complaints to corporate headquarters, and Seth was directed to rectify the situation. He was sympathetic to the small dealer, who felt that the three-technician requirement was burdensome, but he recognized that it was necessary if each was to respond to a customer's need promptly.

Seth had to come up with a solution to the problem of his own organization's marginal operation and the dilemma faced by his dealers. He decided that the best attack on what appeared to be an insurmountable quandary was to list the problems and then see if profitable solutions could be found to them. Seth made his list and titled it:

Goals for Profit

1. Fully utilize service technicians' time—improve productivity.
2. Respond promptly to a customer's call for service.
3. Improve scheduling procedures so as to plan each technician's activity rather than react to a customer's needs.
4. Improve cash flow.
5. Improve working capital.
6. Control cost of labor and parts more effectively.
7. Meet the corporate goal for service, which enhances product image.
8. Improve value of product to customer.
9. Help company sell more products.

10. Develop a plan for profit.
11. Assist the dealers in running profitable service operations by solving for them many of the same problems as listed above.
12. Improve collection of accounts receivable for service work.

Seth studied the list for some time. Then a solution came to him that would provide a basis for meeting all his goals. The answer was in the issuance of service contracts. Seth reasoned that the service contract would solve his corporate and dealer problems as well as provide the customers with additional benefits they were not receiving under the current time and material service program. To be sure he was right, Seth decided to list the benefits these service contracts would offer the company:

Benefits of Service Contracts to the Servicing Organization

1. Service contracts help stabilize manpower utilization by allowing the service manager to plan for, rather than react to, customer needs.
2. Contracts provide improved scheduling through better knowledge of work load.
3. With service contracts, there is full utilization of manpower, which helps advance productivity levels.
4. Because contract fees are paid prior to rendering service, they:

   A. sustain a positive cash flow.
   B. improve working capital.
   C. reduce collection problems.
   D. improve profits through investment of contract fees.
   E. provide cash necessary to purchase parts and supplies in economical quantities as well as allow acceptance of cash discounts.

5. The product's image is improved by preventing major failures, since scheduled maintenance and needed repairs are rendered in a timely manner.
6. Customer satisfaction with product performance and service will lead to additional product purchases.
7. The contracts display the manufacturer's, the dealer's, or both's confidence in the product.

8. The contracts fulfill the manufacturer's obligation to the customer by ensuring the product's maximum use and life.
9. The contracts provide a means of gathering data on product performance.
10. The contracts help in planning for profits.
11. The contracts reduce customer complaints, thereby reducing the cost of handling these complaints.
12. Service personnel will become aware of customers' expansion plans, providing preferred leads for additional sales.

Seth then compiled another list showing the benefits that a contract program would offer the customers:

Benefits of a Service Contract to Customers

Commercial and Industrial Customers

1. Permits accurate budgeting of maintenance and service expenditures by providing the customer with a fixed cost for the contract period.
2. Reduces or eliminates the need for:

   A. service personnel.
   B. specialized diagnostic equipment.
   C. repair tools.
   D. parts inventories.
   E. overtime.

3. Decreases down time by providing trained technicians in the quantity needed to do the work quickly.
4. Eliminates the customer's concern with scheduling service personnel, since it becomes the responsibility of the servicing organization.
5. Reduces maintenance and repair costs, since the contract fee is based on estimated average repair costs and the major repair risk is spread over many contracts.
6. Offers preferred response to calls for service over those received from time and material customers.

Consumers

1. Provides simplified budgeting.
2. Eliminates unplanned major repair expenses.

3. Improves the value and life of their investments.
4. Reduces apprehension in the purchase of a new product on the market.
5. Offers peace of mind and reduced anxiety after the product is purchased by assuring that any failures will be repaired at no additional risk.

In reviewing the list of benefits to the servicing organization, Seth began to comprehend the far-reaching effects of the contract program. He realized that the service contract enhances the perception of good service by meeting a customer's repair and maintenance requirements with a payment not directly related to a particular problem. Since customers "buy" the contract, they eliminate the frustration of having to pay a repair bill when the product fails. The contract is sold to customers at a low-stress time, usually when they have happily purchased the item. Thus, customers are usually pleased that they have bought the contract, especially if the product fails. This lends a positive image to the product or, at the very least, minimizes the feeling of "adding insult to injury" that normally comes with the repair bill.

Another plus that the contract offers is that the servicing organization can observe the use or misuse of a product. Seth could see that, by providing scheduled maintenance or repair visits, the service contract offers his technicians the opportunity to guide the user in the proper operation of the equipment. This guidance would help reduce future failures and add to the product's life.

It became clear that the service contract program provides the servicing organization with the means to plan for workforce needs and utilization, to schedule work loads more easily, to predict and control profits, to improve productivity, and to enhance the operational knowledge and repair history for each product. Additionally, the service contract program helps increase income through the sale to the customer of replacement equipment (for worn-out units), peripherals (accessories), and new products.

From the customer's standpoint, the service contract can not only save money in maintenance and repair costs, but provide the peace of mind that the purchase will be properly serviced and there will be no problem of whom to call when service is needed.

There are potential disadvantages of a service contract program to both the servicing organization and the customer. Seth knew that there must be some liabilities. He decided to list the possible shortcomings, first to his company:

*Potential Liabilities of Service Contracts to the
Servicing Organization*

1. Company could experience a failure rate higher than anticipated, making the cost of fulfilling the contract more expensive
   than planned.
2. Company might not be able to market the program successfully.
3. There might be difficulty in collecting contract fees from customers prior to rendering service.
4. Company could incur a higher rate of service calls than anticipated if customer demands service on nuisance items. (For example, customer advises that unit won't run; technician finds
   wall plug pulled out or a switch that has not been turned on.)
5. There could be possible legal problems from suits filed by a
   customer or because of a failure to meet federal or local statutes.

Seth then listed the possible shortcomings of a service contract
from the customer's point of view:

Potential Liabilities of Purchasing a Service Contract

1. Customers do not experience failures, thus may feel that they
   paid for contracts they did not need.
2. The servicing organization fails to fulfill the terms of the contract by not rendering the services agreed upon or by not exe-
   cuting them in a timely manner.
3. The servicing organization goes out of business without making provisions for fulfilling the service agreements. Customers
   therefore have lost their investments.
4. The contract price is excessive in relation to the potential failure liability.

An overpriced contract can be taken to the extreme, such as when
the customer is sold a maintenance contract for a product that does not
require routine maintenance—a television set, for example. Another
instance is when the customer is convinced to purchase an agreement
on a product with a very low failure rate, at a price that covers the cost
of repairs beyond the normal life of the product, let alone the term of
the contract. We see this often with inexpensive products. The seller

offers a five-year warranty on a product that costs, say, $7. To have the item repaired under the terms of the warranty the customer must return the item with a $10 fee to cover "postage and handling." Obviously, it is cheaper to purchase a new item. In a similar fashion, through high-pressure sales techniques the customer is sold a service contract at an exorbitant price for services that most likely will never be needed.

In selling a service contract, the servicing organization is providing the customer with a form of insurance. The customer is exchanging the risk of paying a small premium, and the potential of no tangible return, for the peace of mind of having the costs met for a major repair. If the customer deals with an ethical servicing organization and sees the advantages outweighing the disadvantages, then the service contract offers a good value. Similarly, the servicing organization must be confident in its pricing and contract structure to the extent that it has covered its potential liability adequately. If the firm does this and the customer understands why he or she is buying a contract and the extent of the coverage for the fee being paid, then both parties win. A good contract program, therefore, should benefit both parties to the contract—a truly win-win situation.

2

Types of Service Arrangements

In reviewing the types of service arrangements offered, Seth concluded that they fall into three basic categories: warranty, time and material, and contract service. He also realized that the risks or costs of service can range from being borne totally by the supplier to being absorbed by the customer; alternatively, the risk can be shared to varying degrees by both parties. Seth studied the various service arrangements and came up with the following information.

Warranty Service

Most warranties provide the customer with the assurance that the product will be repaired free of charge during a specified time period. The cost of routine required maintenance can be included as part of the manufacturer's warranty or paid by the customer.

Warranties are service contracts for which the organization offering the warranty contractually agrees to provide labor and/or parts to the customer at no additional cost for a specified period of time. It is common for a manufacturer to assume the parts and labor costs of fulfilling its warranty obligation. However, variations from this basic premise do exist. In many industries, products are sold through distributors, dealers, or both, and it is the practice for the manufacturer to replace defective parts, whereas the cost of labor to diagnose the problem, install the replacement part, and make any necessary adjustments, is the responsibility of the distributor or dealer. It is important to remember that whether the cost of fulfilling the warranty is paid for entirely by the manufacturer or is shared by the manufacturer and the dealer, it should be included in the price the customer pays for the product. This is necessary if the sale is to be a profitable one.

The organization issuing the warranty should establish the type and extent of coverage. Often, however, a manufacturer may encourage or require a dealer to provide a specific warranty, even though the dealer must assume all or part of the cost of fulfilling that obligation. These terms are usually covered in the agreement between the manufacturer and the dealer. These costs usually are not a burden for the dealer if they have been included in the selling price of the product.

There are a number of factors that influence the type and extent of warranties offered to a customer. These factors are described in the following paragraphs.

1. *Marketing Goals.* Determine what the company hopes to achieve in the marketplace. It may be to position the product against a specific competitor, and to demonstrate that its item is of higher quality or presents a better value. The perception in the customer's mind is that if the manufacturer is willing to commit to a strong, long-term warranty, it must have confidence in the reliability of the product. The strategy may also take the form that if both the manufacturer's and the competitor's products are of equal quality and have the same performance characteristics, a strong, long-term warranty helps offer the customer a greater perception of value, thereby differentiating the products.

Conversely, a product with a strong position in the marketplace may not demand a strong warranty, since the product is so widely accepted by the potential customers that additional investment in an improved warranty would not significantly increase sales.

2. *Competition.* Study the warranties offered by your competitors to compare your warranty and marketing goals to theirs. In many industries it is common for all manufacturers to offer the same warranty and to differentiate their products by emphasizing product features. As mentioned previously, other companies use the warranty to improve the position of their product in relation to competition. Interpreting

the competitor's strategy will help you determine the extent and type of warranty that should be offered for your product.

3. *Customer Acceptance of Product.* The reputation of a company manufacturing or selling a product, or both, will influence its warranty requirements. A new product from a well-established, reputable organization may not need a strong warranty because the customer will base the purchase on the manufacturer's reputation. If a manufacturer with no track record in a particular product line and with a poor quality history introduces a new product, then it may be necessary to offer a strong warranty to build the perception of quality. It is important to remember that a strong warranty may not, in itself, cure a weak perception of the product in the marketplace. But when combined with good product features, quality control in manufacturing, and creative marketing strategy, the strong warranty can contribute to the overall success of a particular product.

4. *Position in Product's Life Cycle.* A product goes through various stages of acceptance in the marketplace. Initially a company may introduce the product to those individuals most likely to influence its success. It may, depending on the nature of the product, be shown to buyers for retail establishments, engineers who make specifications, trade magazines, and so on. Once these individuals have accepted the product by buying it or fitting it to their specifications, then other advertising and promotional programs are used to attract the attention of the ultimate consumers. Depending on the attractiveness of the product, sales may develop slowly or quickly. Once established, the product will grow to some point, and then sales will level off. New, improved products or changes in lifestyle, poor quality, and so on may lead to loss of interest in the product and result in a drop in sales to the point that the item is no longer profitable.

A product's warranty can be used to display a company's confidence in the new product by offering full labor and parts coverage for an extended period of time. The warranty may also be used to reestablish customer confidence in a product whose sales are declining because of an image of poor reliability or a perception of high repair costs. Warranties may again be used to differentiate a product from competing products, especially when the sales of all similar items on the market have leveled off and all the manufacturers are still trying to grow in a shrinking market. Under these conditions, the only way to grow is to get a bigger share of the pie—that is, the marketplace—at the expense of the competition. This situation is quite different from that of a market in which demand is high for a given product, and all the manufacturers have difficulty meeting the needs of the consumers. If the demand for the product is leveling off or declining, a stronger warranty (longer, more complete coverage) may provide the needed surge. Conversely, if the demand is strong and the market is growing, a minimum competitive warranty may be all that is required.

5. *Initial Cost of the Product.* The extent of warranty coverage depends on the cost of the product. To sell an item costing a couple of dollars usually will not demand a long-term warranty; other benefits of the product most likely will outweigh the impact of a short-term warranty. For an expensive item, however, the warranty may prove significant. If a wristwatch is purchased for $3, the customer is more interested in its keeping time accurately than its having a long warranty period. Should it fail, the purchaser would be more inclined to throw it away and buy a new one than to go through the trouble of returning it for repair. On the other hand, if a customer invests $500 for a watch, there would be more concern about the extent of warranty coverage in order to derive full value from the investment.

Fulfilling the Warranty Obligation

Once you determine the span of warranty coverage, then you must fulfill the obligation specified in the warranty. If the manufacturer is making the repairs with company-furnished technicians and parts, at either company service centers or in the customer's home or business, then complete responsibility and control remain in the manufacturer's hands. If, however, the service is to be rendered by independent dealers or other servicing organizations, the degree of control that the manufacturer has over the quality of that service is diluted. Just how diluted that responsibility is depends on the training and assistance that the manufacturer provides the servicing facilities as well as the extent of any control mechanisms the manufacturer institutes to ensure quality workmanship and customer satisfaction.

The approaches a manufacturer can take with dealers are varied. Some options that can be considered in fulfilling the warranty obligation through dealers can include:

1. Reimbursing dealers at their full rates for labor and parts on warranty work performed. This adds to the manufacturer's administrative expense, since monitoring time and rate labor

charges can prove burdensome. If these charges are not monitored, overcharges can result.

2. Paying dealers a fixed dollar amount for labor on given repairs,
   plus furnishing required replacement parts. This arrangement
   is not as attractive for dealers unless the labor allowance adequately covers the dealers' costs. Because the replacement
   parts are supplied by the manufacturer, dealers do not earn any
   profits on the parts furnished to customers. From the manufacturer's standpoint, this method affords greater control over
   costs of labor and parts. It also reduces administrative expense
   by eliminating the need to monitor dealers' labor costs.

3. The manufacturer can offer dealers the replacement parts only,
   with dealers absorbing all the labor costs associated with warranty work. In this situation the manufacturer's exposure to
   liability and administrative costs are reduced and the dealers'
   risks increased.

4. The extreme situation places all the warranty burden on dealers. In this case dealers absorb the cost of all labor and parts in
   fulfilling the warranty.

The greater the burden on dealers, the less control a manufacturer
has on the quality of service. It may be argued that the manufacturer
can terminate an agreement with a dealer because of poor performance, but that requires documentation over a period of time. The
positive approach is to motivate the dealers, through good relations,
proper training, and adequate support, to do a good job. In working
with independent servicing organizations, it is generally necessary to
provide full reimbursement or offer a fixed-fee program, since their
sole source of revenue is from service work. On the other hand, the
dealer (or manufacturer) servicing a product can use the sale of the
product to absorb the warranty expenses.

Warranty Reserves

Ultimately, the customer should pay the cost of the warranty. If a
profit is to be earned on the sale of a product, the anticipated expenses
of fulfilling the warranty should be spread equally over the number of
units to be sold during a given period of time. If, for example, a company plans to sell 1,000 units over a period of one year, and past history
has shown that warranty work for that product averaged $10,000 for

each 1,000 units sold, then $10 should be added to the cost of each product planned for sale.

$$\frac{\$10,000 \text{ repair cost}}{1,000 \text{ units}} = \$10 \text{ cost per unit}$$

This example is a simplification and does not consider factors such as seasonality of failures, customer application, and so forth, which can affect the cost of warranty fulfillment and a company's cash flow. Numerous formulas have been developed in an attempt to calculate warranty reserves accurately. Owing to variations in failure rates that result from the uniqueness of each product and its application, these formulas can at best serve as a guide. Failure to include warranty costs in the price of a product will result in diminished profits, perhaps even in losses.

The actual procedure to determine the warranty costs for a given number of units (for example, $10,000 per 1,000 units in the previous example) is similar to that used to price service contracts. This procedure is covered in greater detail in Chapter 5, Pricing Service Contracts.

For purposes of this discussion, let's continue with the presentation. The money in the cost of each product that is allocated for warranty labor and parts (for example, the $10 in the previous example) should be entered into a separate account as each product is sold. For example, if 500 units of the product are sold, then $5,000 should be set aside to cover warranty expenses:

$$500 \times \$10 = \$5,000$$

This money, placed in what is called a Warranty Reserve Account, is then used to pay for any warranty claims. As warranty work is performed, the cost of parts, labor, and administrative expense is deducted from this account. This procedure allows you to monitor warranty costs. The amount of money (or lack thereof) in the Warranty Reserve Account provides an immediate indication as to whether too little, too much, or the correct amount is being added to the cost of the product to meet warranty expenses. This method of accounting avoids the problem of profitably marketing a product whose cost does not include the warranty expenses, and it does not burden the service operation with the cost of labor and materials.

If the wholesaler, distributor, or dealer is expected to assume all or part of the warranty costs, it must in turn add that cost on to the resale price of the product. Similarly, it should set up a Warranty Reserve Account to control its expenses and ensure that it has allocated sufficient funds to satisfy its warranty burden. The manufacturer can assist the dealer in determining the amount of money to reserve for such warranty work by publishing data on failure history and estimated times required to make each type of repair. The dealer should request this information if it is not volunteered.

Profits from Warranties

Warranties can, in some instances, generate profits. This is usually true when it is the customer's obligation to perform maintenance or have it performed at specified periods. If the item requires this maintenance to keep the warranty in force, then the customer most often will have the manufacturer or its authorized dealer perform that needed service. Since the maintenance work is normally sold at profitable levels, income is earned. The customer's fulfillment of this maintenance requirement adds to the servicing organization's total profits. Even if the customer, a dealer, or another authorized outlet performs this maintenance, the manufacturer reaps the rewards through the sale of the parts and supplies needed to perform the maintenance.

Time and Material Service

Once a warranty has expired, the customer must normally pay for repairs. If the product fails to function properly, a servicing organization is usually called to make the necessary repairs or adjustments. The customer is billed, at some established hourly rate, for the time spent by the technician in making the repair or adjustment. In addition, the servicing organization's established selling price for any parts or materials used in making the repair is added to the bill. This form of service is called Time and Material service. The customer pays for the service as it is rendered. For example, let's assume a consumer purchases a washing machine that carries a one-year warranty on parts and labor. During the warranty period the authorized servicing organization will respond to service calls from the customer and make the necessary repairs or adjustments at no charge. However, once the warranty expires, the customer will be billed for every repair or adjustment that is made on the washing machine by that servicing company.

Recent Trends in Service Assistance

In the past, if customers called a servicing organization to ask for advice on how they might make a repair or adjustment themselves, they often would be given that advice without charge, assuming the problem was simple. The servicing organization would do this in the hope that the customers would call them to perform the more difficult repairs. Today, depending on the type of product and the user of that product, we are seeing two trends emerging.

The first trend is that some companies are charging for telephone consultation. This is becoming prevalent in the personal computer industry, where a customer may be charged $100 an hour or more to discuss an operational problem. The technician will guide the customer through various tests and procedures to zero in on the cause of the difficulty and then advise how to make the necessary corrections. The reason this type of service is popular in the computer industry is that many difficulties are not related to a malfunction of the hardware but rather are customer errors. If the technician determines that the nature of the problem is hardware-related, then the customer is advised that a technician must make the necessary repairs, and arrangements are made to have a technician visit the customer or have the customer bring the unit to a repair facility.

The second trend is that some companies actively promote free telephone consultation. Whereas in the past the servicing organization would assist customers if they should happen to call, today manufacturers and distributors of certain types of products are aware that many customers would prefer to make their own repairs if they could get some advice on how to do it. By promoting free telephone assistance, manufacturers sell more parts and more products. They sell more parts by advising the customers what parts are required to make the repairs, and by providing the customers with the manufacturer's part number. Customers are reluctant to purchase a generic part for fear that it will not work, thus the manufacturer, through rendering telephone assistance, has ensured a profitable parts sale. The manufacturer or distributor also sells more products because the do-it-yourself person is inclined to purchase a product that he or she knows will have parts readily available and whose manufacturer will provide free advice. If a program such as this is established, it is important that customers have a convenient source for the needed parts. Many industries attempt to restrict the distribution of parts to established repair facilities and are reluctant to sell to consumers directly; if such a policy exists, it will negate the strategy of telephone assistance.

The strategy that is chosen depends on the nature of the product and the ability and comfort customers have in making their own repairs. As stated previously, the computer industry often charges for advice, since the solution to most difficulties does not result in a parts sale. Also, if a part must be replaced, the average computer owner would be reluctant to attempt the repair. On the other hand, the home appliance industry has found that a significant number of its customers will make their own repairs on their washing machines, clothes dryers, and so on. Many of these companies are making their parts readily available through retailers and parts outlets. Some firms are packaging parts attractively, indicating the level of difficulty involved, as well as listing the tools needed to make the repair. In this way customers can determine for themselves, prior to purchasing the part, whether they feel they can handle the repair. These manufacturers also enclose detailed repair instructions in the package along with a toll-free number, should a difficulty arise. Companies that offer several options do so in an effort to capture all the service and parts sales opportunities. These strategies can be employed by both large and small servicing organizations. A small dealer, for example, can set up a do-it-yourself area at the service center where customers can come for parts and advice. It is important, however, to determine if the product being repaired lends itself to being done safely and easily by the nonprofessional, and if there are customers who will be interested in making their own repairs.

Advantages and Disadvantages of Time and Material Sales

Time and Material service presents the lowest risk service option for a servicing organization. The servicing firm will provide needed repair services for the customer and will bill or collect for those services immediately. Because the customer is charged for the services as they are done, there is little risk of incurring costs that are not paid for by the customer. Servicing firms who lose money on Time and Material work normally will do so because of poor management or because they have incorrectly priced their labor or parts, or both. (For assistance in the pricing of parts and labor, see Chapter 5.)

With Time and Material service, customers decide when and if the firm will be chosen to perform maintenance or repair jobs. Thus, they may choose one firm at one time and a different one on another occasion. A Time and Material arrangement presents possible liabilities for both the customer and the servicing company. From the customer's viewpoint, the servicing firm may have a policy in which its contract customers get first priority on service calls. This is a common practice, since the servicing organization has a contractual obligation to respond promptly to these customers. Also, Time and Material customers will very often be charged a higher rate for labor and parts as partial compensation for the servicing firm's added costs that result from the uncertain demand for its services.

Time and Material service presents a number of problems for the servicing organization. Planning for the optimum number of service technicians, dispatchers, and vehicles needed to respond promptly to the customers' service requirements becomes at best difficult, since a service manager does not know how many calls nor the type of call (maintenance or repair) that will be received on any given day. The service manager is faced with making difficult decisions, such as whether to keep a large number of technicians on the payroll or maintain a limited number of service personnel for maximum efficiency but let the customer wait for service. Similarly, by not knowing the type or nature of the service calls that will be received, the parts manager has difficulty establishing adequate inventory levels while still turning the inventory with acceptable frequency.

Contract Service

A service contract is an agreement between a servicing organization and a customer to perform specific repair or maintenance functions, for a consideration, during a designated time period. The designated time period is usually one year but may be longer or shorter. The consideration most often takes the form of a cash payment. In reality, service contracts are insurance policies. The customer is assured that specified services will be rendered for a set price during the term of the agreement. Just as a medical insurance policy pays specified doctor and hospital bills if a policyholder becomes ill, the service contract covers the costs of restoring a product to operating condition should it fail to function properly. Just as a health insurance policy permits the individual to control the medical costs, so the service contract helps the holder of the agreement to control the maintenance and repair costs.

The servicing organization benefits from the service contract program through greater scheduling control, optimum use of manpower, long-range income, improved cash flow, and increased profits. The marketing function benefits through added leads for new and replacement sales generated through customer satisfaction derived from an effective contract program. From the corporation's viewpoint, the service contract program generates goodwill with customers, fosters long-term growth, and increases the corporate working capital.

3

Types of Service Contracts

Questions were buzzing around in Seth's mind as the prospect and excitement of establishing a service contract program began to take hold. How do I go about pricing the contract, selling the advantages to the customer, administering the program? "Slow down, Seth," he said out loud. "Take one step at a time. First things first." Seth thought about how before he could price or administer a contract program he'd have to decide what type of contract or contracts to offer. He began investigating possible contract options, and found that the forms and variations are limited only by an individual's imagination.

Seth determined that the key to designing a successful service contract program is to assess the needs of the customers who will buy the contracts and then ensure that the contracts fulfill those customers' requirements. He found that contracts have several basic forms: Maintenance Only, Full Repair and Maintenance, and Repair Only. From these three basic forms are developed the specific service agreements that meet the product's and customers' needs.

Maintenance Only Contracts

Maintenance Only contracts are designed to ensure that the products under contract receive the manufacturer's recommended periodic maintenance in a timely, professional manner. By purchasing such a contract, the customer is assured that the product is receiving the preventive maintenance necessary to fulfill warranty requirements. The customer also gains a sense of security by knowing that the product will function with minimum repair expense and down time. Additionally, the contract adds to the value of the item purchased, since the customer knows that proper maintenance will extend the product's useful life. This confidence is further enhanced by the knowledge that the work is being done properly by trained technicians. The Maintenance Only contract relieves commercial and industrial customers not only of having to hire competent technicians to service the products, but also of needing to schedule those technicians' time. The contract minimizes the investment in specialized test equipment, tools, and parts. Generally, the servicing organization provides the customer with preferred repair service, which can include special rates as well as priority scheduling. In addition, because the equipment is serviced at regular intervals, the servicing technician can observe potential problems as they develop and take corrective action.

The Maintenance Only contract also provides several benefits for the servicing organization:

1. *Profitable Business with Minimum Risk.* Costs of labor, parts, and material can be computed easily to establish contract prices. Since all costs are known, the risk of unforeseen expenses is minimal.
2. *Effective Scheduling of Service Personnel.* Scheduled maintenance can be planned well in advance for optimum utilization of service personnel. With seasonal products, slack periods can be filled by performing maintenance tasks, thereby keeping service technicians productive at all times.
3. *Repair Service Business.* If the service technicians are doing the maintenance on the equipment, most customers will also have them perform any needed repairs. (This is also advantageous to the customer, since the technician servicing the product will be familiar with its characteristics and, as such, can normally complete the repairs much more quickly and at a lower cost.) This added service business results in additional profits.
4. *Replacement Sales.* If a unit has outlived its useful life, the servicing company is in a preferred position (assuming the cus-

tomer is satisfied with past performance) to provide the replacement unit.

5. *Add-on Sales.* The servicing organization is in a unique position to recommend peripheral equipment that will improve the product's performance, enhancing the customer's satisfaction. Add-on sales can range from a simple modification to extensive improvements.

Service personnel are in an unparalleled position to sell additional products or improvements. They have an advantage over sales personnel in that the customer is aware that a salesperson is there to sell something, but when a service person makes a recommendation, the general feeling is that since the technician has nothing to gain, the added item will truly prove beneficial. Service personnel should be trained in customer relations as well as in how to sell additional equipment and services. It may even be wise to pay a small commission on sales that service personnel initiate to encourage them to be conscious of these opportunities.

Purchasing a Maintenance Only contract makes sense from the customer's viewpoint if the contract provides good value and if the product truly requires a preventive maintenance program. If the customer is charged a fee that does not relate to the services performed, then the contract is not a good buy. For example, the customer may be able to get those services performed on a time and material basis at a lower cost. This does not mean, however, that the servicing firm cannot charge more for a service contract than for the equivalent time and material service. Remember that with a contract, the burden of maintaining customer service records and scheduling maintenance visits rests with the servicing organization. The cost of keeping these records may be added fairly to the cost of the contract.

Customers have the option of performing preventive maintenance themselves, assuming they are competent to do so, have the proper tools and instruments, and are willing to take the time to do it. Often when customers evaluate the cost of their own time, they find it less expensive to have a qualified servicing firm perform the maintenance. If there is a sizable do-it-yourself market, it is often wise for the servicing firm to sell the maintenance items (filters, lubricants, belts, and so forth) to the customer. If the servicing firm can't get the service work, at least it can sell the parts and materials and develop a good relationship with the customer. This good relationship can lead to future repair business.

The potential liabilities of Maintenance Only contracts faced by the servicing firm involve not pricing the contract properly to cover costs adequately and dealing with customers who are not satisfied with the quality of your workmanship (assuming that your servicing organization does fine work).

The first potential liability can be averted through careful contract costing and monitoring. If you find a contract is costing more than you anticipated, adjust the price of future contracts to cover those increased costs. (Review Chapter 8, Contract Administration, to gather some ideas on how to monitor service contracts.) The second potential liability requires you to analyze why you are getting numerous callbacks. It may be because of bad workmanship or poor customer relations. It may also be that the customer can't be satisfied, no matter what is done. Take corrective action if bad workmanship or poor customer relations are the cause to ensure that these problems are eliminated. The only solution to dealing with an unfair customer is to try to resolve your difficulties, if possible, declare the contract void if the customer has violated its terms, or not renew the contract at the end of the period.

Full Repair and Maintenance Contracts

When offering a Full Repair and Maintenance contract, the servicing company provides the scheduled maintenance as outlined for a Maintenance Only contract, plus provides parts and labor for needed repairs.

The advantages of this type of contract to the customer are:

1. *Simplified Budgeting.* The customer can budget accurately for repair and maintenance costs because the contract price is all-inclusive. The servicing organization agrees to perform all maintenance and repairs for a specified period of time for a fixed price.
2. *Personnel Reductions.* For commercial and industrial customers, the Full Repair and Maintenance contract reduces or eliminates the need for not only maintenance personnel, but also repair and supervisory employees. The service contract also eliminates the need to review invoices for specific repairs, time and material charges, and so on, since all costs are normally covered by the contract.

3. *Quality Workmanship.* The customer is assured of quality workmanship because the servicing organization has the trained personnel and tools to perform the needed maintenance and repairs. Since service is what the servicing company has to sell, it has a vested interest in good performance.
4. *Fast Response to Service Calls.* Generally, contract customers get preferential response to repair calls over noncontract customers, since the servicing company wants to renew the contract at its expiration. As such, a key element is providing fast, quality service.
5. *Peace of Mind.* Customers develop greater confidence in their purchases because they know that someone else has taken on the responsibility for and expense of the proper function and performance of the product. This is particularly true of major consumer products or newly introduced products of any type.

The advantages of Full Repair and Maintenance contracts to the servicing organization are as follows:

1. *Greater Profits.* Performing both maintenance and repair services results in higher sales with commensurately higher profit margins.
2. *Scheduling Flexibility.* Having both maintenance and repair commitments eases the task of scheduling personnel.
3. *Facilitated Manpower Planning.* The Full Repair and Maintenance contract helps in planning workforce requirements more accurately. This is particularly true for the difficult job of planning for the repair portion of the service business. This planning is further simplified if data have been compiled as to the type, nature, and frequency of repair required for each type of product. The data permit you to calculate the number of repair hours needed in a given time period, and also allow you to determine inventory levels.
4. *Add-on Sales.* This type of contract also provides entrée for replacement and add-on sales.

The potential liabilities of this type of service contract are similar to those outlined for Maintenance Only contracts. The repair portion of this contract interjects added risk for both the servicing organization and the customers.

The service contract will state the number of preventive mainte-nance visits the servicing firm will make during the contract period and what will be accomplished during each visit. Thus, customers will have a relatively easy means of determining the value of this portion of their contracts. For the repair portion, customers do not know what the potential failure rate is and will find it difficult to assess accurately the value of this part of their contracts. The customers generally will weigh the replacement value of their products and their potential lives against the price of the contracts. What will primarily influence their decisions is the reputation of the servicing organization. If the firm has a reputation for good service in a timely manner, at a fair price, then customers will be inclined to purchase the contracts. If the servicing organization is not reputable and the customers take the contracts, then they can experience numerous difficulties beyond poor service. Because customers are "locked in" to the servicing organization, they are reluctant to call another organization, since they paid for the con-tracts and are concerned that they would not get their fees refunded. The company or individual who does not have a contract can withhold payment and make the servicing firm concerned about collection. Of course, anyone who has purchased a service contract can call another firm to repair the item and settle the contract dispute in court, but since most servicing organizations are in business to build long-term cus-tomer relationships, these incidents are not frequent.

From the customer's standpoint, the additional areas of potential liability involve the loss of use of a product, either because the servic-ing firm didn't respond to the repair call or because it was unable to make the needed repair—if, for example, the technician was incompe-tent or the company didn't maintain an adequate parts stock. The con-sumer who purchases a Full Repair and Maintenance contract for a washing machine may face the inconvenience of having dirty clothes pile up in the hamper when the repair is not made promptly or, worse yet, have the added inconvenience and expense of bringing the clothes to the launderette. For commercial or industrial customers, the loss of production can prove extremely costly.

From the viewpoint of the servicing firm, the potential liabilities of this contract are related to incorrectly pricing the contract and con-trolling expenditures. Limited or inaccurate data can result in a pro-jected failure rate lower than experienced, leading to higher fulfill-ment costs and lower profits. Also, deficiencies in quality control during the manufacturing process can result in higher repair rates than past history indicated. The servicing organization is faced with a higher potential liability on the repair portion of this contract, but this risk is reduced by pricing the contract accurately and by being attuned to variations in quality. Work closely with manufacturing, if your company makes its own products, or with your suppliers, if you purchase products from outside sources. Variations in quality control may require you to raise prices for a short time but, more important, you should assist in determining the cause of a quality deficiency and have it corrected. Another alternative that reduces risk is to insure the service contract. This option is discussed in Chapter 4, The Insured Service Contract.

Repair Only Contracts

A Repair Only contract covers the replacement or repair of specified components of a product for an established period of time. It does not cover required maintenance. An example of a Repair Only contract is the typical service contract sold for an automobile. The company issuing the contract arranges to have needed repairs made by a local dealer or other repair shop. Owners of such vehicles, however, must have them maintained (lubricated, oil changed, filters replaced, and so forth) at their own expense. The service contract often states that unless the owner has the required maintenance performed, in a timely manner (usually according to the schedule published by the manufacturer), the contract becomes void.

Many products do not require periodic maintenance. Items such as televisions and dishwashers generally do not need regularly scheduled lubrication or adjustments, so the only agreement that can be offered on such products is a Repair Only contract.

The Repair Only contract offers the highest relative risk to the servicing firm of all the contracts that can be offered. This is because of the uncertainty with regard to the number of failures that might be experienced during the contract period. However, the risk can be reduced by gathering relevant data and employing accurate analysis. How the data are gathered and analyzed is discussed in Chapters 5 and 8, Pricing Service Contracts and Contract Administration, respectively.

Though its risk factor is the highest among the three basic contracts discussed, the Repair Only contract is the most common type offered, particularly for consumer products. If the Repair Only contract is priced fairly, it offers customers a high degree of security from unexpected major repair expenses. Customers can budget maintenance costs reasonably accurately. They can review the manufacturer's published standard maintenance recommendations and secure estimates from servicing firms for maintenance costs. These costs may increase slightly over time, owing to inflation, but the variance normally will be minor. Budgeting the costs of repairs, however, is another matter. Customers generally have no idea if and when they will have a failure or the extent of the costs involved. A Repair Only contract, therefore, permits them to accurately budget their repair expenses for the period. This is true whether the customer is a consumer or an industrial or commercial organization. This contract replaces the peaks and valleys of repair costs with a flat annual fee covering any and all repairs. Thus, by essentially sharing the risks with other contract purchasers the customer eliminates the possibility of being faced with major repair expenses. Though they may pay a premium to secure peace of mind, many customers feel the cost is worth it, particularly when they experience a failure and can just pick up the phone, call the servicing firm, and know they will not receive a bill.

The prime liability with Repair Only contracts again is that customers will incur the expense of the contract whether or not they need the repair. Also, if the contract price is more than the fair value of the loss potential, then the contract may not be a good buy. For example, the probability that a television set will fail is very low but the contract price is high. Similarly, it doesn't make sense to buy a service contract on an inexpensive item that is very reliable. Spending $15 on a Repair Only contract for a toaster that costs $30 just does not make good sense, unless you know that the toaster has a history of spending more time in the repair shop than on the kitchen counter. If that is the case, why buy it at all? A servicing firm in its right mind wouldn't sell a contract on such a product anyway.

As long as the servicing organization uses responsible pricing procedures based on reliable data, the risk inherent in a Repair Only contract should be minimal. It is virtually always a good idea to sell maintenance along with repair, but often the products do not require maintenance, or it is not economical for the servicing firm to provide it (for example, because of vast travel distances), or customers can easily or less expensively perform the maintenance themselves. Selling Repair Only contracts should be very profitable for a servicing organization; the fact that many such organizations offer them successfully is testimony to this.

If your servicing organization is concerned about potential liabilities, it can have an insurance company take on the risk. The pros and cons of this option are discussed in the following chapter.

Variations

The types of and variations on service contracts are limited only by the imagination of those writing the contracts, the nature of the products involved, the needs of the customers, the nature of the marketplace, and the servicing organization's ability to implement the provisions of the contract.

As mentioned earlier, the Maintenance Only, Full Repair and Maintenance, or Repair Only contracts can be offered. These contracts can be modified further to provide only labor and to charge for parts or provide small parts but charge for major components. Contracts can be written to cover repairs but charge for required maintenance. All units at one address can be placed under one contract for one fee, or they can be charged on a per-unit basis. Deductibles can be employed up to some initial amount (for example, the customer pays the first $100 of required repairs, then is fully covered), or a deductible can be applied to each service call.

A variation that can be very effective, particularly in consumer markets, is to offer a rebate for not placing an emergency call. For example, if customers place no emergency calls during the contract period, $50 is credited to their contract renewal or is rebated at the end of the contract period. Crediting $50 to the contract renewal is the better option for the servicing firm, since it encourages renewal. If customers do place emergency calls, $10 is deducted from their rebates for each call made. If the average number of emergency calls per unit is, say, five, and it costs the servicing company, on average, $30 per call, each call *not* made improves the company's profitability by $20 after giving the customers the rebates. This arrangement is profitable to the servicing organization and to the customers. It encourages customers to at least check if equipment is plugged in, turned on, and so on. Customers are also more receptive to telephone consultation and to self-corrective action before requesting a service technician.

Service contracts also can be issued on a cost-plus basis. In this type of contract a basic labor and parts rate is established, with customers paying a fixed percentage for profit on billed amounts. Another variation of this is a cost-plus-fixed-fee contract. In this arrangement, customers pay a fixed fee representing a guaranteed profit plus labor, parts, and administrative costs. These latter types of contracts generally are employed in larger, experimental projects in which there is little history on which to base a contract price.

Another contract variation is the wrap-around contract. This contract piggybacks on another contract or warranty. It is designed to extend the customer's amount of coverage. For example, assume a manufacturer's warranty does not cover certain components or may cover the components for only 90 days and then just major components for the remaining nine months of a one-year warranty. The manufacturer, local dealer, or independent servicing agency may offer customers a wrap-around contract that covers the parts and labor on repairs of any components not covered by the warranty during that same period. In this way customers are fully protected for the year with a contract that rounds out or wraps around the manufacturer's basic warranty. Opportunities abound for selling this type of contract whenever manufacturers, to develop the perception of a quality product, provide long-term limited warranties. Yet these warranties may be very limited, in that they may exclude many components from coverage or may cover just parts and not the labor to replace them.

Many servicing companies offer a choice of contracts. This allows customers to weigh the extent of coverage and the amount of risk against the amount they want to spend. When the servicing organization offers multiple plans, its service sales personnel can select plans that meet the customers' aspirations and budgets.

In the final analysis, when establishing a service contract program, you must look at the product, the market, the customer base, and the competition. With this knowledge, you can develop a service contract program that is marketable and profitable.

4

The Insured Service Contract

Seth was aware that for some products the service contracts would be sold through his dealer organization while for others, his company would offer contracts directly to customers. He was also aware of the financial risk that he and his dealers would face. Though the risk would be small if he priced and marketed the service contract properly, Seth wondered if the smaller dealers would be willing to take any risks at all for fear that an excessive failure rate might put them out of business. He knew that his organization would sell a large number of service contracts and thus spread out the cost of repairing troublesome units. The small dealers that may sell only a few contracts, however, could be severely injured if they sold contracts on units that had high failure rates. The small servicing organizations would not have the contract sales volume to absorb the costs of repairing those units.

Seth realized that the financial risks inherent in service contract sales can be alleviated by selling large numbers of contracts, since an abnormally high failure rate on a few units can be spread over all the contracts. Thus the cost of failures would be absorbed by the revenues received from contracts on those products that do not fail. For example, if a servicing firm sells 100 contracts for $100 each, it will have a total income of $10,000. If two units have major failures that cost $1,000 each to repair, the firm can absorb this bad experience, assuming the rest of the units require repairs totaling less than the $8,000 remaining. If, on the other hand, a small dealer sells only ten service contracts at $100 each, the total revenue would be $1,000. If there is a major failure as just described, that dealer would lose money; if there were several $1,000 failures, the dealer would be in serious financial trouble. These statistics confirmed Seth's analysis that the more contracts sold, the lower the risk from unexpected failures.

Since the pricing of the contract is based on product history, flawed data, changes in manufacturing techniques, slippage in quality control (both within the company's manufacturing operations as well as in those of vendors), and product modifications all impact on the future repair experience with those products. Thus, changes can take place that the service manager may not know about, which cause the actual repair experience to differ from that indicated by the careful analysis of the product history. Repair rates that exceed estimates can seriously affect the profitability of the servicing organization; indeed, in severe cases, they can affect the solvency of the company.

An Insured Service Contract Solves Many Problems

Many servicing firms are not capable of taking, or are not willing to take, the risks associated with offering contract programs. Additionally, manufacturers that depend on distributors or dealers to service their products may wish to encourage these outlets to offer service contracts. Many dealers or distributors are concerned about the potential liability of service contracts and, as such, look to the manufacturers for assistance. Manufacturers who fund a service contract program that is sold through distributors and dealers may want a way to eliminate the burden of processing and paying maintenance costs, repair claims, or both.

Service contract insurance offers a solution to all the problems just mentioned. For a fixed fee on a given product, an insurance company will assume the risk of maintenance and repair costs as well as handle the processing of claims and reimbursements. The insurance agreement stipulates what is and is not covered, the length of the agreement, the allowable markup on parts, the labor charges that will be paid, and so on. The insurance company outlines the specifics of the service contract for each product it covers, including the cost of the particular contract.

For a given premium, the insurance company reimburses the servicing firm for the maintenance or repairs performed on an insured unit. It normally pays for labor, parts, and materials. Labor is usually paid at the servicing company's standard rates; parts and materials are paid at rates that range from 25 to 100 percent above the servicing firm's cost—or, in many cases, at the list price published by the parts manufacturer.

Policies can be purchased for new or existing products. On a product that has been in service for some time, the insurance company often stipulates that coverage will not go into effect until 30 to 60 days after the contract is issued. This minimizes the chances of customers purchasing insurance after they have become aware of a major problem, since most customers will not or cannot wait this long for a repair. Some insurance companies may require the servicing organization to inspect the item and bring it up to acceptable operating standards before they issue the agreement. Customers are normally charged for these inspections as well as any needed repairs.

The contracts also can have other limitations and restrictions. The insurance company can, for example, limit its total liability to a maximum dollar amount or limit its liability for each occurrence. It may also exclude major components from coverage or include them at an additional premium. Many insurance companies do not insure a product for its first year in service. They offer extended service contracts that start with the second year a product is in service and that run one, two, three, or more years, with the premium reflecting the degree of risk faced by the insurance company. Some insurance companies will not insure a product in its first year to minimize the risk of a poorly designed product or substandard quality control. The assumption is that if a product is flawed, the problems appear during its first year.

When seeking contract insurance, inform the insurance company of the type and extent of coverage you desire, so that it can quote accurately on a policy that will fulfill your servicing firm's needs. Check state regulations governing the sale of such policies. Some states may require that the servicing firm, the sales personnel, or both be licensed. They also may prohibit a servicing company from marking up the premium when selling the contract to customers. It is important to check local regulations to guarantee compliance with the law—whether or not the contract is insured.

Insured service contracts minimize the risks of service contracts. Because the insurance company pays the servicing organization for services performed for the customer, collection problems are eliminated. Insurance companies are regulated closely in most states, thus there is little risk to a servicing company of not receiving a justified reimbursement. The servicing firm has the further advantages of being paid at regular labor rates plus enjoying a fair markup on parts and materials. In many instances you can make a profit by marking up the insurance company's premium when selling the policy to the customer. (Again, remember that some states may prohibit this practice.)

When offering an insured service contract, a servicing firm usually is exchanging some potential profit for a greater degree of security. It is obvious that the insurance company plans to make a profit on the program—a profit that most often comes from the servicing firm's gross margins. This presents an additional potential problem: finding an insurance company that will insure a contract at a marketable premium.

The insured contract also offers customers an added degree of security (particularly if the contract is sold through independent dealers), since they know that the contract is backed by an insurance company. This is especially true of contracts with new servicing companies that have not established their viability in the marketplace. Contracts can include a clause to guarantee that the provisions of the contract will be fulfilled by another servicing organization if the issuing company cannot do so.

In most states the servicing firm has the option not to disclose whether the service contract is insured, since the insurance is purchased for self-protection. However, as mentioned earlier, many firms use it as a sales tool, making customers aware of the added protection provided by a major insurance firm.

Factors To Be Considered

Before you contact an insurance company to discuss the feasibility of an insured service contract program, prepare for the questions that will be asked and the negotiations that will ensue. It may be wise to engage an insurance brokerage firm specializing in this area to assist and advise your servicing organization.

Key questions that are likely to be asked by the insurance company are:

1. What type of contract do you desire—Maintenance Only, Full Repair and Maintenance, Repair Only, and so on?
2. What is the nature of the products you wish to insure?
3. How are these products used?
4. Who uses them?
5. Are there any components that are not to be covered by the insured service contract?
6. Who will be offering the contracts—wholesaler, dealer, servicing company, manufacturer?
7. What must the cost be to meet the competitive demands of the marketplace?
8. What are the current labor rates?
9. How much of a markup, if any, will be required on parts?
10. What is the repair history of each component?
11. How much time is needed to repair or replace each component?
12. What is the average travel time to each customer?
13. How often will each unit require inspection and maintenance?
14. What materials or parts are used in maintaining the product?
15. How long will the maintenance procedure take?
16. Will the contract be sold at a profit by the servicing outlet—for example, a dealer?
17. If so, in what states will the contracts be sold? (Some states have restrictions on how an insured contract can be sold.)
18. Will reimbursement requests be sent directly to the insurance carrier or processed through the sponsoring company?
19. Who will be rendering the service? (The servicing organization may be different from the one selling the contract.)

The insurance broker, insurance company, or both will want to discuss your servicing organization's needs as well as carefully assess its risk. The questions may seem overwhelming at first, but they are all things service managers must ask themselves, whether an insurance carrier will be used or not. The time it takes to complete negotiations depends on how knowledgeable the insurance carrier is of the particular industry and of the product line. Understand that the nature of a product and its application influence the willingness of an insurance company to accept the service contract risk. There may be instances in which it is difficult, if not impossible, to find a company willing to insure a contract for a given product or product line. The only way to find out if one will insure at a competitive rate is to contact several insurance companies, either through a broker or directly.

Though the insurance company generally would like you to have all the answers to the questions just listed, most firms realize that all servicing organizations do not have all the answers. Thus, don't shy away from the insured contract option just because your data are limited or even nonexistent. There is a good possibility that you can find an insurance carrier willing to develop a program for you regardless of your situation.

Again it is crucial to keep in mind that insuring the service contract eliminates the risks associated with providing service for a fixed fee. The insured contract offers additional profits by allowing the seller to mark up the insurance company's premium where it is legal to do so. The sale of an insured contract guarantees that the servicing organization will get paid for all services performed under the contract according to its terms. An additional advantage is that the selling organization (distributor, dealer, or other) can use the fact that the contract is insured by a major firm as further evidence that the contract will be fulfilled. This adds to customer confidence in the contract as well as to the value of the purchase.

In exchange for the security that an insured contract offers, the servicing organization sacrifices a strong cash flow, since the major portion—if not all—of the contract price goes to the insurance company. In addition, some profit is sacrificed because the insurance company includes a profit margin in its price as compensation for the service it renders.

Deciding Whether to Insure Your Service Contracts

The decision by the service firm to insure a service contract program is influenced by the nature of the product, what facility will be servicing it, the financial condition of the contracts seller, and that seller's marketing objectives. If independent dealers will be servicing a manufacturer's products, then the insured contract assists those dealers without heavily burdening the manufacturer. The insured program ties the dealers closer to the manufacturer by offering them a profitable opportunity. It also ensures that the equipment will be properly maintained, resulting in satisfied customers who, in turn, lead to additional sales.

In determining whether to insure a contract program, the servicing organization must assess its ability to accept risk, the degree of risk inherent in the products to be covered by the service contract, and—quite simply—if it prefers to have another organization (that is, the insurance company) handle the actuarial factors associated with computing failure rates and their related costs. Some servicing organizations feel that their expertise lies with the repair and maintenance of equipment, and they prefer to leave the pricing and concerns with failure rates to an insurance company that has greater expertise in this area.

In the final analysis, the decision to insure depends on the servicing firm's perceptions of itself and on the business it is in, as well as the degree of risk it is willing to take. When determining if insured contracts are for you, evaluate the risks versus the potentially lower profits. Assess your willingness to add personnel to administer the program, and realize that the insurance company's premium includes fees for similar administrative costs. In either case you will be responsible for marketing the contracts, whether by your own personnel or by some independent firm such as a telemarketing organization. If you are undecided, it may prove helpful to explore the option with a broker such as Marsh & McLennan Group Associates in Chicago, Illinois. The time might be well spent, since it will help you assess the best way to meet your service contract profitability goals.

5

Pricing Service Contracts

In reviewing types of contracts, Seth realized that he had a twofold challenge. First he would have to develop and price contracts for the commercial and industrial products sold and serviced directly by his firm. Then he would have to put together a program to assist his dealers in pricing service contracts for the consumer market.

Seth recognized that many aspects of the commercial and industrial contracts were similar to the consumer contracts. Yet there were differences in the types of contracts as well as in the targeted customer base. Additionally, his role would differ: for dealers, Seth would be an advisor and counselor, whereas for the commercial and industrial market, he would have complete control over the entire service contract program.

Seth wondered if pricing a service contract was nothing more than a wild gamble. Pick a price and hope it's enough to make a profit. Then he thought more about it. If he knew the probability of a failure—the odds, if you will—then he could use those odds in pricing his contracts. In purchasing a contract, the customer is gambling that the dollar value of the services rendered will be more than the cost of the contract. In the broad sense this is true, but there is more to it than that. The customer buys the contract because the price of the contract is a reasonable premium to pay for the peace of mind it provides. It is a form of insurance. But how could Seth go about arriving at a reasonable price for the contract yet earn a fair profit in the process? He began to investigate pricing and found that it didn't have to be a wild gamble. Pricing the service contract would have an element of risk, but that risk could be minimized through effective data analysis.

Pricing Repair

To price a Repair Only or the repair portion of a Full Repair and Maintenance contract profitably, carefully study the product to be covered. The time spent in analysis will pay dividends in the long run; it's the difference between taking a wild gamble and knowing the odds of winning. The question, then, is how to go about pricing the contract so it is attractive to the customer yet controls the risk to the issuer.

The most effective way is to gather as much data as possible on the repair history of the product. Review the records to determine (1) which parts have failed in each product over the years (miles driven, hours of use, etc.) and (2) how much time it took to make each repair. This information should be further refined to determine:

1. *For each part that failed, the factors that contributed to that failure.* For example, what influence do age, actual run time, on-off cycles, environmental conditions, frequency of preventive maintenance inspections, and so forth have on the type and severity of repairs needed? If accurate data have been maintained and the data are kept in a computer data base program, analysis is greatly simplified. If not, consider purchasing a computer if one is not available and have someone go through each service order and enter the data. With the expanded capacities of microcomputers (also known as personal computers), all that may be needed is a personal computer and a good data base program. Whether you use a microcomputer or a mini- or mainframe computer depends, of course, on the amount of data to be stored and your other computer needs.

2. *The amount of time each repair takes to complete.* An average (mean) time can be used for pricing. The accuracy of average repair or replacement times will increase as more data are accumulated. Also, establishing time standards will help narrow the margin of error. (See Chapter 8, Contract Administration, for more information on establishing time standards.)

3. *Whether it is cheaper to repair or replace a component.* With labor rates in many cases representing a significant part of the total repair cost, it may be less expensive to replace a component than attempt to repair it. In some cases the service technician can replace the component in the field and then take the defective part to the service facility for repair. This is a common practice, for example, in industries that use printed circuit (PC) boards. A PC board with all its electronic components normally would require a great deal of a technician's time in the field to determine which component failed. To save time, the service technician normally swaps the defective board for a reconditioned one. The PC board that failed is returned to the shop, where it is either sent out for repair or a bench technician finds the defective component and replaces it. The PC board is then completely inspected and returned to stock for future use.

Costs of Parts and Labor

The first step in arriving at a contract price for a Repair Only contract or the repair portion of a Full Repair and Maintenance contract is to gather the data on each component in each model of the product. As mentioned previously, age factors, hours of operation, on-off cycles, revolutions, copies, and so on should be considered. See Table 5-1 for a simplified layout of a hypothetical Model 1 of Product

Table 5-1. Model 1 repair analysis—Mean hours between failures.

Age Factor	0–1 Year	1–2 Years	2–3 Years	3–4 Years	4–5 Years	Average Hours per Repair
Component						
A	250	250	75	50	50	2.0
B	500	500	500	500	500	0.5
C	800	800	600	600	600	0.8
D	2,000	2,000	2,000	2,000	2,000	2.0

Product model XYZ: Average hours' use per owner per year—1,000.

XYZ. Note that each component is analyzed to determine the average (mean) hours the unit will run between failures. For this product, age might have been a factor, so that was taken into consideration. With an automobile, for example, you might consider age as well as the odometer reading.

The next step is to review the data. For example, note in Table 5-1 that the failure rate for Product XYZ was consistent for the first two years of operation. Also note that between the second and third years, Components A and C were repaired more frequently. Looking further to between the third and fourth years and between the fourth and fifth years, you'll see that Component A required repair still more frequently but repair of other components stabilized. In pricing the contract, you would establish one price for models up to two years' old, another for those two to three years' old, and a third for those three to five years' old.

This price schedule can take the form of separate contract prices or of a base price for units less than two years' old with surcharges in dollars or percent increases over the basic contract price for subsequent years. For example, if the base contract (0–2 years) is priced at $100 and it costs $10 more for the next contract period (2–3 years) and $20 more for the third contract period (3–5 years), show either the actual dollars for each period or the percentage increase over the base price, for example, 10 percent for the first case and 20 percent for the second case. You would have three basic contracts priced at $100, $110, $120.

It is possible to have a multiplicity of surcharges. For example, it may be that for each 5,000 hours on the hour meter, the mean hours between failures decreased (that is, more frequent repairs were needed). This necessitates a surcharge for those units that have more than 5,000 hours on their meters. An additional surcharge would be added for those with over 10,000 hours on their meters, and so on. To arrive at these "hour-use" surcharges, look at the base period (0–2 years) and then determine if hours of use during that period had any influence on the time periods between repairs. If, for example, you note that after 5,000 hours of use Component A has a mean between repairs of 75 hours, it may warrant a surcharge. In fact, a two- to three-year-old unit may require replacement of Component A every 75 hours because most units that old have over 5,000 hours on them.

This type of analysis is not difficult if the information has been entered into a computer data base program. The service orders should

Table 5-2. Number of repair hours per service contract period (Product XYZ, Model 1).

Component	Repairs per Year	Hours per Repair (from Table 5-1)	Total Repair Hours
A	$\frac{1,000}{250} = 4.00$	2.0	8.00
B	$\frac{1,000}{500} = 2.00$	0.5	1.00
C	$\frac{1,000}{800} = 1.25$	0.8	1.00
D	$\frac{1,000}{2,000} = 0.50$	2.0	1.00
Total number of repairs per year:	7.75	Total repair hours: 11.00	

include data such as meter readings, parts replaced, number of service hours, serial and model numbers, and so on. This repair history can be readily entered into a data base program, and you can then analyze the repair history of a specific unit manufactured on a given date. Chapter 8, Contract Administration, shows how such data also assists a service manager in monitoring the service contract program.

Having assembled the data, your next step is to determine the average number of hours in a year that a typical customer uses the product. Assume the product is used for 1,000 hours in a year. Determine the average number of repairs that are required for each component during this 1,000-hour period. Table 5-2 shows that the average total repair time for the basic service contract is 11 hours. If a service technician (salary and benefits) costs $30 an hour, then the labor cost for the contract can be calculated:

$$\$30 \times 11 \text{ hours} = \$330 \text{ labor cost}$$

To this total, add the average cost of travel time for each call. Assume the base contract is priced for calls made within a 25-mile radius of the service center. The average travel time is calculated by dividing the number of hours all technicians spent making calls within a 25-mile radius of the service center by the number of calls they made. An analysis of travel time per call shows that a technician spends an average of 15 minutes driving from call to call.

In Table 5-2, note that an average of 7.75 repairs will be made per year. This means you must expect to make 7.75 visits, on average, to each contract customer. To calculate the number of hours these calls will require, first find the traveling time per contract:

$$7.75 \text{ calls per year} \times 15 \text{ minutes per call} =$$
$$116.25 \text{ minutes traveling per contract}$$

When you know the total number of minutes, divide by 60 to convert the quantity to hours:

$$\frac{116.25 \text{ minutes}}{60 \text{ minutes per hour}} = 1.9375 \text{ hours}$$

If the technician's labor rate is $30 per hour, you have:

$$\$30 \times 1.9375 \text{ hours} = \$58.13 \text{ travel cost}$$

Add to that the labor cost figured earlier for the total labor cost:

$$\$330 + \$58.13 = \$388.13$$

The next step is to price the total cost of the components (parts). It can be seen in Table 5-3 that the cost of each component is multiplied by the average number of times it must be replaced in a year to arrive at the total cost of replacing that component during the service contract period. You may wonder how half a Component D can be replaced. Remember that Component D will last an "average" of 2,000 hours; on some units it may fail in 50, 500, or 3,000 hours. As such, each contract carries some of the burden because it is not known which units will or will not fail early. This same reasoning is used when multiplying the repair hours by 0.5. When the repair is done, it will take two and a half hours, but not all units will require the repair during their first year of operation.

Table 5-3. Component (parts) pricing (Product XYZ, Model 1).

Component	Unit Cost	Number Required	Total
A	$ 5	$\dfrac{1{,}000}{250} = 4.00$	$ 20
B	15	$\dfrac{1{,}000}{500} = 2.00$	30
C	32	$\dfrac{1{,}000}{500} = 1.25$	40
D	50	$\dfrac{1{,}000}{2{,}000} = 0.50$	25
		Total Cost of Parts	$115

How do you determine the average hours for a product that does not have a meter on it? You can arrive at a good feel for the amount of usage in several ways. First, if the product is used in your company check how many hours a day or week it is operated. Second, survey the market. Contact customers either by mail or phone and ask them about their usage. Use your own staff for this or hire a professional research firm to conduct the survey. Third, check with the trade magazines or trade organizations. Very often they survey their readers or members on product usage. Many of these surveys also provide insights into the benefits customers look for in a service contract. Use this information to prepare your contract. Fourth, look to the state and federal governments. The federal government maintains libraries in just about every major city. These libraries contain the statistics and research various government agencies have gathered, and a call to one of these libraries may provide the information you seek for your product. Similarly, visit the library of a large university in your area; ask the reference librarian for assistance. Librarians are usually very eager to help and will provide you with both federal and state data.

Sales and Profit Goals

At this point you have calculated the labor and parts costs for the repair part of a service contract. These costs should be combined to arrive at a total cost. Next consider the allocation of overhead and, finally, add profit to the contract to arrive at a selling price. But first you must establish sales and profitability goals. To determine if your anticipated profit is realistic, evaluate your projected operating expenses for the year by preparing an income statement for the coming fiscal year. Figure 5-1 (on page 46) shows a basic Income Statement for a typical service operation. When this statement is prepared in advance, it is sometimes called a Pro Forma Income Statement. Having set your targeted service business volume and having reviewed the operating expenses of your service operation, you can arrive at a planned profit. If the service operation shares space, personnel, or both with other corporate functions, then the rent, salaries, and so forth are the service department's prorated share of these operating expenses.

If the profit shown is consistent with the department's objectives, then all is fine. If it is too low, then review the income statement to see if some operating expenses can be reduced or if the sales volume can be increased while maintaining the same level of fixed expenses. In making any adjustments that may result in increased sales and reduced expenses, keep in mind that this is not an exercise in arithmetic. Be sure the changes are realistic and achievable.

Assuming that the total dollar profit meets your objectives, the next step is to calculate this profit as a percentage of sales:

$$\frac{\$151,000}{\$588,000} = 25.7\% \text{ profit}$$

Next determine the percentage of income generated by service contracts:

$$\frac{\$500,000}{\$588,000} = .85 \text{ or } 85\%$$

The share of operating expenses to be carried by service contracts is:

$$\$437,000 \times .85 = \$371,500$$

The share of profit from service contracts is:

$$\$151,000 \times .85 = \$128,500$$

Figure 5-1. Income statement.

American Control Technology, Inc.
Service Department
Income Statement
Year Ending December 31, 19___

INCOME
Service contracts	$500,000	
Time and materials	88,000	
Total Income		$588,000

OPERATING EXPENSES
Fixed Expenses

Rent	$25,000	
Insurance	1,000	
Taxes	1,500	
Licenses	500	
Utilities	3,000	
Depreciation	6,000	
Total Fixed Expenses		37,000

Variable Expenses

Service parts	100,000	
Service wages	200,000	
Administrative salaries	50,000	
Shipping expense	1,000	
Bad debt	1,000	
Sales promotion	4,000	
Vehicle expense	40,000	
Tools and instruments	3,000	
Miscellaneous	1,000	
Total Variable Expenses		400,000
Total Operating Expenses		$437,000

NET PROFIT FROM SERVICE OPERATIONS $151,000

Note that dollar amounts have been rounded off to the nearest $500 for simplification in this example. It is recommended that you do not round off your numbers until you calculate the final price in order to avoid cumulative errors.

Look at the Pro Forma income statement: The cost of service parts is $100,000 and the cost of service labor (wages) is $200,000. Therefore parts and labor equal: $100,000 + $200,000 = $300,000 total cost of parts and labor. Since service contract sales and costs represent 85% of the total service operations costs, multiply the $300,000 by 85%. Therefore: $300,000 × .85 = $255,000. Since service contract sales is $500,000, we can find the percentage of sales represented by service contract parts and labor:

$$\frac{\$255,000}{\$500,000} = .51$$

Service contract parts and labor represent 51% of contract sales.

In a similar fashion, the percentage of sales represented by operating expenses (other than parts and labor) can be calculated:

Total operating expenses	$437,000
Total labor and parts	− 300,000
Operating expenses	$137,000

Since contract sales represent 85% of total sales, the service contract program will bear 85% of the operating expenses. Figure the service contract operating expenses this way:

$$\$137,000 \times .85 = \$116,450$$

Calculate the percentage of sales represented by operating expenses:

$$\frac{\$116,450}{\$500,000} = .233 \text{ or } 23.3\%$$

In summary:

Parts and labor	51.0% of sales
Operating expenses	23.3% of sales
Profit	25.7% of sales
Total	100.0%

The next step is to determine the total cost of parts and labor for each contract to be offered. For example:

> *Model 1*
>
> | | |
> |---|---|
> | Labor cost (including travel) | $388.13 |
> | Parts cost | 115.00 |
> | Total parts and labor cost | $503.13 |

Since parts and labor represent 51% of sales, the selling price of each service contract can be determined by dividing the cost of each service contract by the percentage of sales represented by parts and labor. In this example,

$$\frac{\$503.13}{.51} = \$986.53$$

Normally this figure is rounded *up* to the next highest dollar. Any amount that is rounded down will result in a loss of profit. If, for example, the above selling price came to $986.47 and it was rounded down to $986.00, the service firm would lose 47 cents on each contract sold. That may not seem like much but if 100,000 contracts were involved, the loss in profits would come to $47,000. Even if only 100 or 1000 contracts were involved, there would still be an unnecessary loss. This process is applied to each contract and model to be included in a service contract.

The next step is to look at the selling price of each service contract for each model. Determine if the proposed selling price is competitive, if the customer will perceive the price as a good value, and whether you can charge more or less for the contract. Also, give consideration to how the service contract program will affect corporate profitability and sales goals. Close cooperation with the marketing and financial departments may be necessary. For example, a lower-priced contract might help sell more products, thereby improving overall corporate profitability. It may be the best strategy for the service function to operate at a low profit level so as to help achieve higher overall corporate profits.

Once a final selling price is arrived at for each model, the next step is to determine how many service contracts will be sold for each model. Having established the quantity to be sold, the selling price, and the cost for each model's service contract, you can see if all these factors will meet the sales and profitability goals (see Table 5-4). As

Table 5-4. Service contract sales and profitability analysis.

FISCAL YEAR ENDING DECEMBER 31, _____

Model	Number of Con- tracts	Selling Price	Total Sales	Operating Expenses	Parts and Labor	Total Cost	Profit
1	100	$ 987	$ 98,700	$ 22,997	$ 50,337	$ 73,334	$ 25,366
2	50	1,075	53,750	12,524	27,413	39,937	13,813
3	200	250	50,000	11,650	25,500	37,150	12,850
4	75	400	30,000	6,990	15,300	22,290	7,710
5	220	200	44,000	10,252	22,440	32,692	11,308
6	400	100	40,000	9,320	20,400	29,720	10,280
7	285	644	183,540	42,765	93,605	136,370	47,170
TOTALS	1,330		$499,990	$116,498	$254,995	$371,493	$128,497

Notes:
Total Sales = Number of contracts × selling price
Operating Expenses = Sales × .233
Parts and Labor = Sales × .51
Total Cost = Operating expenses + parts and labor
Profit = Sales − Total Cost

indicated in this table, the established pricing will meet the sales and profit goals provided the targeted number of contracts are sold for each model. Rarely will totals match the sales and profitability figures planned for in the Pro Forma Income Statement exactly. In Table 5-5, sales of $499,990 as opposed to the $500,000 planned for on the income statement is quite acceptable. Similarly, a profit of $128,497 as opposed to the $128,500 desired from service contract sales is also very close. If the sales manager can make his projections come within a few hundred dollars of the Pro Forma Income Statement goals he is doing very well. It is always a question of scale: with larger total sales goals, larger dollar variations are acceptable and vice versa with smaller sales goals. With a goal of say $100,000 in sales a $5,000 shortfall is much more significant than if the projected sales were $2,000,000. Always remember that the planning process is designed to direct you toward success. Don't get bogged down debating a few dollars while missing the big picture. Careful analysis coupled with good judgment is the key to success.

The analysis can be performed effectively on a computer spread

Table 5-5. Service contract sales and profitability analysis for varying types of contracts.

Model	Target Number of Contracts to be Sold	Type of Contract	Selling Price	Total Items
1	100	Repair Only	$ 987	98,700
	50	Full Repair and Mainte-nance	1,520	76,000
	25	Repair Only site-factor charge	1,070	26,750

sheet program. The computer greatly simplifies price and quantity analysis. For example, if the selling price of Model 1 contract type A is increased three dollars to $990, a spread sheet automatically shows the effect of an increase or decrease in the selling price. The computer will change all the appropriate figures. The total sales will automatically rise to $500,290 and the profits to $128,797.

We can quickly determine what impact selling two hundred Model 1 service contracts will have on overall profitability. This can help us determine whether or not, for example, an investment in a direct mail program to sell more contracts would be worthwhile. If it is felt that the direct mail program will increase sales from one hundred to two hundred contracts and the cost of the program will be five thousand dollars, then it will pay off handsomely. The additional profit from the direct mail program is $25,366. Subtracting the $5,000 the program will cost from the $25,366 profit leaves us with a net profit of $20,366, an excellent return on investment. The net profits will most likely be greater. (Later in this chapter, there's a section on break-even analysis. It demonstrates the effects of increased sales volume on profits.)

The Service Contract Sales and Profitability Analysis illustrated in Table 5-4 was constructed for Repair Only contracts. If the servicing organization offers Full Repair and Maintenance contracts in addition to the Repair Only contracts, then the organization can add these to the analysis. For example, another column may be added to the analysis to reflect each type of contract being offered (see Table 5-5).

In this way you have a consolidated view of the sales and profit goals for each type of contract for each product model. The table can be refined further to accommodate those contracts that would involve surcharges. (See Other Factors Influencing Price, discussed later in this chapter.) For example, the number of Repair Only contracts with a site-factor surcharge can be listed on a separate line in the table. (See third line in Table 5-5.) The analysis can include as much or as little information as you desire. It should be refined to the degree necessary to control the service contract program effectively and meet targeted sales and profitability goals. As an option, set up a separate analysis for each model number or for each type of contract. These separate analyses can help you review the progress on each model or permit you to see which type of contract is most profitable. A good data base program lets you rearrange this information so you can look at any and all variations you choose.

Study the sales and profitability analysis on at least a monthly basis. In looking at Table 5-4, note that 200 contracts need to be sold on Model 3 products during the year. This means that an average of 17 Model 3 contracts must be sold each month. By reviewing the sales progress monthly, you can see whether targeted goals are being met. If, say, only 10 contracts for Model 3 are being sold each month, then you know that the annual contract sales and profitability goals are not going to be achieved. Review the service contract sales progress for all models to see if others are exceeding anticipated sales objectives, and analyze the reasons why contract sales for some products are falling behind while others are exceeding goals. With this knowledge you can then take corrective action.

By reviewing the sales and profitability analysis on a regular basis, you also avoid a last-minute panic response to poor sales or profits. You can deal with problems early in the year and thus redirect the organization's efforts to ensure that profit goals are realized by the end of the fiscal year. You can, for example, use a telemarketing or direct mail program to boost sales on a contract with poor performance. Optionally, you might direct greater effort to a contract on another model that is doing well. For example, sales on Model 2 can be increased to compensate for a shortfall in sales on Model 1.

Appendix One contains worksheets to help you price your repair contracts. The worksheets can be readily adapted as a guide for pricing maintenance contracts as well.

Pricing Maintenance

Pricing a Maintenance Only contract or the maintenance portion of a Full Repair and Maintenance contract is a lot simpler and more risk-free than pricing a repair contract.

To price the maintenance, determine:

1. The number of maintenance calls to be made for a particular model product each year.
2. The maintenance operations to be performed on each call.
3. The time each operation will normally take.
4. The parts and materials to be used on each call.

If the Model 1 product previously discussed requires four maintenance inspections a year, and each maintenance call requires a given number of operations, here's how to price this portion of the contract.

Let's assume that the company's engineering department has determined that the unit must be lubricated four times a year, the filters and belts must be changed twice a year, and Component W must be replaced every 1,000 hours. Set up a table listing the labor hours, the hourly cost, and the total cost. Similarly, list the parts and materials and their costs. Table 5-6 illustrates this. Using the $30 an hour labor rate, calculate the labor cost. Similarly, using unit costs for parts and material, calculate the total cost for parts and materials. Determine the travel time based on an average for a given radius from the service facility—for example, trips within 25 miles take an average of 15 minutes. Remember, however, that this is an average time. With a high density of service calls, a technician may have to only travel 5 minutes between some calls and perhaps as long as 45 minutes between others. The data base will give the average traveling time per call. The cost of fuel and maintenance for the service vehicle is covered in the operating expenses as shown on the income statement.

The total cost of maintenance on this model for this application is $291. This cost must be converted to a selling price to cover the overhead and profit. Assuming the operating costs and profit objectives are the same for maintenance as for repair, the selling price of the contract is calculated as follows:

$$\frac{\$291}{.51} = 570.59, \quad \text{or} \quad \$571 \text{ selling price}$$

Table 5-6. Maintenance cost analysis.

Call	Actions	Hours	Labor Cost	Parts and Materials	Cost	Parts and Materials Cost	Total Cost
1	Lubricate	1.00	$30.00	Lubricant	$ 1.00	$ 1.00	
	Travel	0.25	7.50				
	Total labor		$37.50	Total parts		$ 1.00	$ 38.50
2	Lubricate	1.00	$30.00	Lubricant	$ 1.00	$ 1.00	
	Replace:						
	1 filter	0.50	15.00	1 filter	5.00	5.00	
	2 belts	1.00	30.00	2 belts	3.00	6.00	
	Travel	0.25	7.50				
	Total labor		$82.50	Total parts		$12.00	94.50
3	Lubricate	1.00	$30.00	Lubricant	$ 1.00	$ 1.00	
	Travel	0.25	7.50				
	Total labor		$37.50	Total parts		$ 1.00	38.50
4	Lubricate	1.00	$30.00	Lubricant	$ 1.00	$ 1.00	
	Replace:						
	1 filter	0.50	15.00	1 filter	5.00	5.00	
	2 belts	1.00	30.00	2 belts	3.00	6.00	
	1 part W	0.50	15.00	1 part W	10.00	10.00	
	Travel	0.25	7.50				
	Total labor		$97.50	Total parts		$22.00	119.50
	Total Maintenance Cost						$291.00

In determining the final selling price, use techniques similar to those for pricing repair, namely, market conditions, customers' perceived values, and an understanding of the role of maintenance in meeting corporate and service department goals for marketing, sales, and profitability. In a Full Repair and Maintenance contract, make every reasonable effort to combine repair and maintenance calls. This will help increase profits because if maintenance is performed during a repair call, access time to the inside of the unit is saved as well as the travel time of a separate maintenance call. If the maintenance pricing is part of a Full Repair and Maintenance contract, then it is added to the repair portion to arrive at a total contract price. For example, for Model 1, the contract selling price would be:

$$\$987 \;\; + \qquad 571 \qquad = \;\$1,558$$

repair	maintenance	contract
selling	selling	selling
price	price	price

This pricing method just described is the one most used by major servicing organizations to price their service contracts. It is easy and reasonably accurate. Though complex formulas have been devised to improve accuracy, they most likely will discourage all but the most mathematically oriented service manager.

Other Factors Influencing Price

In addition to the previous guidelines for pricing the maintenance contract, consider each of the following factors.

Multiplicity of Units. Depending on the nature or type of products being serviced, there may be a number of units at one location. These units may be a single model or a variety of models. In pricing the Maintenance Only or the maintenance portion of a Full Repair and Maintenance contract, consider the cost savings that might be realized if maintenance is done on a number of units at the same time at the same location. The travel and administrative time saved can result in significant savings. These savings can add to the profitability of the contract program or can be used to price the service contract more competitively.

Job-Site Factors. In pricing the service contract, give consideration to any difficulties the product's location may present. There may be some special problems, including accessibility of equipment for service, adverse environmental factors (for example, unit must be serviced outdoors in winter), restricted or elevated work areas, hazardous work atmospheres, and so on.

Location Factors. Determine whether there are particular difficulties in reaching the location, such as a need to travel over rough terrain (for example, to service electronic equipment on isolated units such as transmission towers) or to service units in a foreign country.

Travel Factors. As indicated previously, the basic contract price may be written for a set travel distance of up to, say, 25 miles from the service facility. Add a surcharge for other distances, for example, 25 to 50 miles, 50 to 75 miles, and so on. This surcharge would include the cost of extra travel time and additional service vehicle operating expenses.

Contract Surcharges

Surcharges for each applicable factor should be established as either a dollar amount or a percentage added to the basic contract price. For example, if a basic service contract sells for $100 and there is a 15 percent surcharge for units located outdoors and a 10 percent surcharge for units located anywhere from 25 to 50 miles from the service office, then pricing this contract would be as follows:

Basic service contract	$100
Job-site factor $100 × .15 =	15
Travel factor $100 × .10 =	10
TOTAL CONTRACT PRICE	$125

To determine the amount of a surcharge, simply go into the data base program and select those service calls that employed that particular factor. Compare the added cost to similar calls that did not include this additional restriction. For example, if it normally takes one hour to perform a given repair under normal conditions, but one and a half hours because of a job-site factor, the cost of the additional half hour's labor should be added to the contract price when that factor is present. If you prefer to use a percentage, then simply get the average total cost for a given repair and calculate the average total cost for a similar repair accomplished with one of the added-cost factors. Take the dollar difference and multiply this difference times the anticipated number of times the repair must be accomplished under these adverse conditions. Divide this result by the basic contract price to arrive at the percentage to add to the service contract selling price.

Let's take an example. Assume that a given repair at a particular installation must be performed outdoors an average of twice a year. Also assume that the basic cost of parts and labor for this repair is $50. When performed outdoors, the job costs $60. If the basic contract costs $200, then:

$$\$60 - \$50 = \$10 \text{ added cost per service call}$$
$$\$10 \times 2 = \$20 \text{ added cost for two service calls}$$

$$\frac{20}{200} = .1 \text{ or } 10\%$$

A surcharge of 10 percent would be added to the basic contract price.

If the contract selling price was $250 (that is, a 20 percent profit on sales), then the added-cost factor must be increased to include its share of overhead and profit in calculating the percentage. For example:

$$\frac{\$20}{0.8} = \$25 \text{ dollar surcharge}$$

$$\frac{25}{250} = .1, \text{ or } 10 \text{ percent surcharge}$$

If in error the cost of the surcharge were divided by the selling price, the surcharge would be too low:

$$\frac{20}{250} = .08, \text{ or } 8\% \text{ (instead of the correct } 10\% \text{ factor)}$$

To use the old adage, keep apples with apples. The contract sales price is:

$$250 \times 1.10 = \$275$$

Or, if you prefer:

$$\$250 + \$25 = \$275$$

Contract Pre-Inspection

Quite often an opportunity comes along, through either direct marketing efforts or a servicing organization's reputation for good service, to sell a contract to a firm that has previously had its equipment serviced elsewhere. A lack of knowledge concerning the condition of the product to be serviced can add significant risk to the contract with this type of customer.

To minimize this risk, a servicing organization should establish a policy for such situations. The policy generally should require that the servicing organization be permitted to inspect equipment being brought under contract. Customers normally are charged a flat fee for these inspections, with the fees based on average time and costs involved. The customers are then advised of the time and material costs required to bring the unit up to operating standards. If permission is granted, the technicians make the necessary repairs and the servicing organization enters into the contract with a properly functioning unit. If customers choose not to have the repairs done, then they have to pay only the flat fees, in exchange for which they have estimates on the needed repairs. The pre-inspection helps keep the servicing organization from being saddled with a unit that requires repairs which exceed the cost of the contract, especially at the beginning of the agreement.

If the equipment has been serviced on a regular time and material basis by the servicing organization from whom the contract will be purchased, then pre-inspection most likely is not necessary. The servicing organization should have adequate knowledge and data on the particular unit to determine if the contract will present a higher risk than other units of comparable age and usage. Remember that if the equipment has been repaired and maintained on a regular basis by your organization, then refusing to issue a contract may cause the customer to question the quality of your firm's past performance on the unit, assuming, of course, that contracts are being offered on other units of similar age and usage.

When establishing the policy on pre-inspection requirements, consider several other factors:

1. *The value of the product.* If the replacement value of a product is relatively small, then the pre-inspection may cost more than the entire price of the service contract—or of the product, for that matter. An inexpensive, highly reliable product may carry a low contract price because the potential failure rate is small and the unit does not require regular maintenance. It would be difficult, for example, to charge a $40 inspection fee on an appliance that sells for $300 and carries a contract price of $75. The customer will look at the cost of the contract as $115 ($40 + $75 = $115). When compared to the replacement cost of the product, $115 to place the item under a service contract may not be worth the price. If the risk to the servicing organization is relatively small (in the extreme situation the product could be replaced at a wholesale cost that, in most cases, is substantially less than the retail

cost); maintenance—or the lack thereof—is not a factor (the unit does not require any) in determining component failure rates and the contract sale is highly profitable. All these factors suggest a strategy that eliminates the need for pre-inspection. To avoid the situation in which a customer has a defective unit and purchases the service contract after a failure has occurred, you can stipulate a waiting period of 30 or 60 days before the contract takes effect. The long waiting period is inconvenient for customers with defective units, since they will not be able to use the item during the waiting period.

2. *Is the contract to be insured?* As part of its agreement with the servicing organization, the insurance company may dictate whether a pre-inspection is required.

3. *Exclusions in the contract.* If the most expensive or difficult items to be repaired are excluded from the agreement, then the servicing organization's risk is minimized, possibly precluding the need for pre-inspection.

In reviewing the question of pre-inspection, consider the factors just mentioned, always balancing the risk to the servicing organization and its profitability with the saleability of the contract if an inspection is required.

An Alternative Contract Pricing Technique

The method outlined earlier to price service contracts produces the best results because it is based on specific data. But many service managers may not have kept accurate records or may feel it is too costly to review past service invoices and enter the facts into a computer data base. Others may wish to have a method that permits them to easily calculate the contract sales volume needed to meet certain profit objectives or to determine the profitable utilization of a specific number of service technicians. This alternative method provides the service manager with the necessary flexibility to do these things as well as be able to review the contract program from various perspectives.

The following example, using four technicians to handle the service contract work on a given product, shows the way you can work toward establishing a contract price. First consider the steps to take in determining the necessary sales volume so as to achieve a desired profit.

Step 1. Review the Known Factors and Goals

You know that each technician works 40 hours per week. Each receives two weeks' paid vacation and 12 paid holidays and is allotted five sick days. The technicians are paid an average of $25 per hour including benefits. They average four hours a week in unapplied labor (time not directly billable to customer, for example, coffee breaks, filling out reports, and so on).

You also know that the desired profit before taxes is 25 percent of sales. The total dollar cost of parts and materials spent repairing the product during the past year was $100,000. The total labor cost incurred repairing the product during the past year was $300,000. Note, however, that the number of units repaired is not critical as long as the figures are derived from a substantial number of units to ensure a broad base. Deriving this information from a small base—for example, a dozen units—may result in distorted, erroneous data because these few units may have had repair needs that were above or below normal. The labor figures should also be derived from the same units as were the parts and material costs.

The overhead attributable to service contracts on products is as follows:

1. Labor overhead expenses (those overhead expenses directly attributable to labor) were $50,000.
2. Parts and materials overhead (those overhead expenses directly attributable to parts and materials storage and control) was $20,000.
3. General and administrative overhead (those overhead items not directly attributable to either labor or parts and materials) was $30,000.

Step 2. Calculate the Labor Cost

First find the number of hours the technicians work. Each technician is paid for 2,080 hours per year, or 40 hours × 52 weeks. Then, in terms of the total gross labor hours, multiply times 4:

4 technicians × 2,080 hours per year = 8,320 hours

Then determine the number of productive hours:

Productive hours = gross labor hours − nonbillable hours

To determine the number of nonbillable hours, figure the total paid time not spent working:

2 weeks' vacation (10 days × 8 hours)	= 80 hours
12 paid holidays (12 holidays × 8 hours)	= 96 hours
5 sick days (5 sick days × 8 hours)	= 40 hours
4 hours per week unapplied labor (4 hours × 52 weeks)*	= 208 hours
Total nonbillable hours per technician	= 424 hours

Therefore, the total nonbillable hours for 4 technicians are:

4 technicians × 424 hours = 1,696 hours

To figure the total productive hours, subtract the total nonbillable hours from the total gross labor hours:

$$\begin{array}{r} 8,320 \\ -1,696 \\ \hline 6,624 \text{ total productive hours} \end{array}$$

In this example, it is assumed that all technicians receive the same amount of vacation time, holidays, sick time, and so on. If this is not the case, then just calculate the amount of nonbillable time allocated to each technician and total it. For example, assume Technician 1 has three weeks' vacation; this total nonbillable time add up to 464 hours (424 + 40 hours' extra vacation). Assume Technicians 2 and 3 have the amount of nonbillable time as figured earlier—424 hours. Assume Technician 4 has five weeks' vacation. This nonbillable time is 504 hours (424 + 80 hours' extra vacation). Therefore, the total nonbillable time for all technicians is:

464 + 424 + 424 + 504 = 1,816 hours

* Vacation, holidays, and so on are part of the 52-week period. In this example, the total unapplied labor for all technicians was divided by 52 weeks to arrive at a weekly average. Therefore, multiply by 52 to arrive at annual unapplied labor per technician.

On occasion, you may wish to use a technician part of the time on service contract work, and the rest of the time on time and material work. For example, 50 percent of a technician's time is spent on service contract work; to arrive at the number of productive hours, simply multiply the technician's total hours by one-half and the nonbillable hours by one-half.

Let's return to the example of the four technicians. Once you have calculated the total productive hours, you can determine the labor cost. Simply follow this formula:

Total productive hours × average wage = total labor cost

Thus, in the example:

6,624 hours × $25 = $165,600

To determine the average wage, add up the hourly wages of all the technicians and then divide by 4. If each of the technicians is receiving different hourly wages and each's productive time also varies, it is simpler to calculate the labor cost for each individual, then add up the individual labor costs to arrive at the total labor cost.

Step 3. Calculate the Parts and Material Cost

You should know the total cost of parts and materials, even if you keep no records of the total costs for individual components. If service records are not available, ask the company's financial personnel or the accountant to identify these costs. In the extreme when records are so poor that data are not available, don't lose hope of pricing the service contract. Randomly select 10 to 20 percent of all the service orders for the product under consideration. Total the parts and material costs on these orders as well as the labor costs. Place the labor costs over the parts and material costs to arrive at a labor to parts and material ratio (L/PM).

Using the ratio, calculate the parts and material cost. In Step 2, the labor cost (the four technicians) was calculated at $165,600. If the service order survey shows that the average labor cost runs three times the dollar cost of parts, you have a 3 : 1 ratio:

$$\frac{\$300,000}{\$100,000}$$

Therefore, the parts and material cost can be calculated as follows:

$$\frac{1}{3} = \$165,600 = \$55,200 \text{ total parts and material}$$

Calculate the labor to parts and material ratio even when all costs are known, since it is used in upcoming steps.

Step 4. Calculate the Total Costs

The total costs consist of the sum of the total labor cost, total parts and material costs, and the total forecasted overhead for contract sales. In preparing the income statement, you should separate those overhead expenses—both variable and fixed—that are attributable to labor from those that are ascribable to parts and materials. Those items that cannot be assigned to either should be placed in a third category: General and Administrative (G&A) expenses. To further distinguish service contract overhead expenses from time and material overhead, establish a ratio between the number of technicians allocated to each function. The costs can then be prorated along these lines. This method is particularly useful in allocating fixed overhead expenses. Normally it is relatively easy to allocate the variable expenses to each function, since the expenses will vary with respective contract and time and material sales volume.

In our example, the service manager has determined that the following are the overhead expenses (see Step 1):

Labor overhead	$ 50,000
Parts and materials overhead	20,000
General and admin. overhead	30,000
TOTAL	$100,000

Therefore, the formula is:

Labor cost + parts and material cost + total overhead = total cost

For greatest accuracy, derive the overhead figures from the anticipated expenses for the time period in which the contracts will be sold (usually the upcoming year). Using the formula, calculate the total cost:

$$\$165,600 + \$55,200 + \$100,000 = \$320,800 \text{ total cost}$$

Step 5. Calculate Total Contract Sales Necessary to Meet Profit Objectives

To calculate total sales, use the following formula:

$$\text{Total sales} = \frac{\text{Total cost}}{1 - \dfrac{\%\text{ profit before taxes}}{100}}$$

Because the desired before-tax profit is 25 percent, the total sales figured as follows:

$$\frac{\$320{,}800}{1 - .25} \quad or \quad \frac{\$320{,}800}{0.75}$$

$$\text{Total sales} = \$427{,}733$$

If the servicing organization is to achieve a profit before taxes of at least 25 percent of sales, fully utilizing four service technicians, then it must secure \$427,733 in service contract business.

Step 6. Determine Labor Rate to be Used in Pricing Service Contracts

To price the labor for a service contract, you must determine the portion of General and Administrative expenses and the portion of profit to be carried by labor. Previously, the labor to parts and material ratio (L/PM) was calculated. Using this ratio, allocate the General and Administrative expenses and profit as follows:

$$\frac{\text{L}}{\text{PM}} = 3:1$$

Since labor represents three portions and parts and materials represents one portion of the total labor picture, you have a total four portions. Therefore, labor represents three-fourths of the total cost. To allocate the General and Administrative (G&A) expenses to labor, take three-fourths of this expense:

$$\frac{3}{4} \times 30{,}000 = \$22{,}500$$

Similarly, apportion the profit to labor. Profit represents 25 percent of sales; thus to find total profit:

$$.25 \times 427{,}733 = \$106{,}933$$

The profit to be earned from labor is:

$$\frac{3}{4} \times \$106{,}933 = \$80{,}200$$

Having calculated the G&A and the profit assignable to labor, proceed to find the total labor burden:

Labor cost	$165,600
Labor overhead	50,000
G&A assignable to labor	22,500
Profit to be generated by labor	80,200
TOTAL	$318,300

Next, divide this total labor burden by the labor cost to find the labor multiplier:

$$\frac{\$318{,}300}{\$165{,}600} = 1.922 \text{ labor multiplier}$$

Using this multiplier, determine the billable labor rate:

$$\begin{array}{ccccc}
\$25 & \times & 1.922 & = & \$48.053 \\
\text{Hourly labor rate} & & \text{Labor Multiplier} & & \text{Billable labor rate}
\end{array}$$

An alternative and perhaps simpler way of finding the billable labor rate is to divide the total labor burden by the productive hours.

$$\frac{\$318{,}300}{6{,}624} = \$48.053$$

If you chose to round off your pricing for labor, *always* round off your figures upward and not downward. If in the example above the service firm decided to round down the hourly labor rate to the nearest dollar, then the charge would be $48 per hour and the company would lose $.053 on each hour billed. For example

$$6,624 \times \$0.053 = \$351.07 \text{ in profits would be lost}$$

If the service firm had 100,000 billable hours, the loss in profits would be more dramatic:

$$100,000 \times \$0.053 = \$53,000.00 \text{ lost profits}$$

Though it may be easy to look at the hourly rate and say you'll take off the five cents, that small quantity, when multiplied by the total annual hours consumed, can result in a sizable amount of money lost. Remember it all comes out of profits because the costs must be met no matter what the hourly rate. All that remains is profits and any reductions in selling price will result in a dollar-for-dollar, penny-for-penny lower profit.

Step 7. Determine Parts and Materials Rate to be Charged

Parts and material rates are calculated in a manner similar to that for labor. The G&A and profit assignable to parts and materials must be calculated. Using the labor to parts and material ratio, you'll note that one-fourth is assignable to parts and materials (remember three-fourths was previously assigned to labor). First calculate the G&A assignable to parts and materials:

$$\frac{1}{4} \times \$30,000 = \$7,500$$

Next calculate the profit assignable to parts and materials:

$$\frac{1}{4} \times \$106,933 = \$26,733$$

Then, calculate the total parts and materials burden:

Parts and material cost	$55,200
Parts and material overhead	20,000
G&A assignable to parts and materials	7,500
Profit assignable to parts and materials	26,733
TOTAL	$109,433

Divide the total parts and material burden by the parts and material cost to get the parts and material multiplier:

$$\frac{\$109,433}{\$55,200} = 1.9825$$

If all parts and material costs are multiplied by 1.983, then the profit objectives will be met if the parts and materials sales volume equals the total parts and materials burden of $109,367. Check your calculations:

Billable labor hours 6624 × $48.053 =	$318,303
Parts and materials cost $55,200 × 1.9825 =	109,433
SALES TOTAL	$427,736
TOTAL CONTRACT SALES GOAL	$427,733

The calculations check out. The $3 difference results from rounding off numbers. If the difference were several hundred dollars, then the calculations would have to be rechecked for errors. It should be clear that the labor burden represents the total labor sales required to meet the profit objectives to be derived from labor. Similarly, the parts and material burden represents the sales volume to be generated by parts and materials to meet its profit objectives. The sum of the labor and the parts and material burden gives you the total service contract sales goal.

Refining Parts and Material Pricing

You can refine the pricing of parts and material by breaking them down into cost groupings. Factors that influence the determination of these groupings include the cost to process an order for an item, the cost to inventory it, competitive pricing, the frequency in turnover of an item, and its purchase price. For example, you may determine that the groupings should include items costing less than $1, $1.01–$5, $5.01–$25, $25.01–$100, and over $100. Once you set up groupings, you can establish multipliers for each grouping.

Next, formulate the prices and verify whether they are competitive and profitable. The multipliers are a tool, and should not be used arbitrarily. The final price on each item should reflect your profitability goals and the market conditions. An item that is relatively expensive and does not turn over frequently may have to be sold at a higher price than other items in the same cost category which turn over more frequently. For example, it costs about the same amount to process an order for a ten-cent washer as for a $500 motor. If you use the 1.98 parts and material multiplier established previously, then the washer will sell for twenty cents ($0.10 × 1.98), and the motor for $990 ($500 × 1.98). Thus, a ten-cent profit is made on the washer and a $490 profit on the motor. If washers turn over more frequently and motors turn over very slowly, this may be proper pricing. The customer, on the other hand, may freely accept paying thirty cents for a washer but balk at spending nearly $1,000 for a motor. Accurate pricing to reflect genuine costs is also important in ascertaining the true profitability of each service contract. If the parts pricing you use to calculate the selling price of the contract or to assess the cost of fulfilling the contract is too high or too low, then you cannot make an accurate assessment of the contract program.

Another point that should be reviewed concerns the common practice of doubling parts and material costs to establish selling prices. An example shows how blindly using such a practice can be costly to the servicing organization.

If a part is purchased for $10, using the rule of thumb it would be sold for $20. But if the buyer for the servicing company is able to obtain the part for $8, by either purchasing a larger quantity or using another source, then the part would be sold for $16. In the first instance, the company realized a profit of $10; in the second case, the profit was only $8. This means the company makes $2 less, even though the buyer expended effort to purchase the part at a lower price.

In pricing labor and parts and material, use the methods outlined to arrive at selling prices. Once the prices have been established, review them to ensure that they are competitive. If they're too high or too low, determine the reason and, if justified, make the necessary adjustments. Then recalculate your profits based on the planned volume to ensure profit objectives will be met.

On time and material sales, avoid offering low labor rates with the hope of making up the difference on parts. Some companies use this technique because they know most customers compare hourly labor rates. Customers, however, become aware that the parts prices are very high, and they don't call that servicing organization again. More important, low labor rates hinder the servicing organization's ability to sell those customers service contracts.

Once you have established labor and parts prices, continually monitor them to ensure that they remain viable.

Pricing the Contract

Having established the billable labor rate and the selling prices for parts and materials, you can now price the service contract.

If your servicing organization is an independent third-party organization, a dealership, a distributor, or so on, ask the manufacturer of the product for data on the failure rates of components.

Gathering service life data is extremely important. Manufacturers do this to ensure the viability of their products in the marketplace, since only through the accumulation and analysis of such data can they determine which components need improvement and how many units of each part to stock. Most manufacturers can also provide information on recommended preventive maintenance intervals for each product, as well as the type of maintenance procedures to be employed. Having this information and establishing the costing greatly simplify the final pricing of the contract.

If, for example, the contract will cover a one-year period, then review the manufacturer's list of each component's service life. Table 5-7 is a typical chart that can be furnished by a manufacturer to facilitate service contract pricing. Using the procedure described at the beginning of this chapter (Pricing Repair), you can employ the hourly billable rates and established selling prices for parts to price the contract.

To determine how much time it will take to replace each component, ask the manufacturer for standard times or review your own service orders to gather this information. See Chapter 8, Contract Administration, for a suggested technique to establish time standards.

If the manufacturer cannot furnish data on the service life (failure rate) of the components, then select all the service invoices from a group of customers for whom the product was serviced in the past year. The number of customers selected depends on your resources to pull the invoices and review them. The more invoices reviewed, the greater the accuracy. Once the invoices are pulled and grouped by customer, review them for the nature of each call and the time it took to

Table 5-7. Expected service life of components (Model 1).

Drawing Key Number	Component Description	Component Number	Quantity in Unit	Service Life (Hours of Operation)	Remarks
1	Printed circuit board	ZX-34562-1	1	200,000	None
2	Linkage	AC-21000-7	2	75,000	Replace both at same time.
3	Belt	WT-26487-2	4	48,000	Check all belts for wear. Replace as necessary.
4	Scraper	AL-74231-0	1	20,000	May be reversed 10,000 hours per side.
5	Seal, water	SL-69472-1	1	50,000	None
6	Clutch plate	CP-72694-8	1	100,000	None
7	Clutch spring	SP-93184-2	2	100,000	Replace with clutch plate.
8	Pall	PQ-21783-1	1	200,000	None
9	Ball bearing, main shaft	BL-65291-3	2	60,000	Replace both at same time.
10	Bushing	BU-93218-1	1	250,000	None

make each repair. This information on the types of repairs can also be used to verify the manufacturer's data. When service life data are not available from the manufacturer, then the contract price must be based on failure rates indicated by your invoices and your own experience and knowledge. This latter method of arriving at failure rates is less reliable but better than making wild guesses.

Once you have the service life data and determine the hourly repair times for each repair, you can price the contract. For example, assume the product whose component service life is shown in Table 5-7 is to be placed under a service contract. It is known from the clock readings taken from the service orders that the average customer runs the unit 100,000 hours a year. It is also known that the average time it takes to replace each component (also taken from the service orders) is as follows:

Drawing Key Number	*Hours*
1	0.25
2	0.50 for both
3	0.25 each
4	0.75
5	1.00
6	2.00
7	0.25 for both springs
8	1.50
9	0.50 for both bearings
10	1.00

Next, consult Table 5-8 to find the number of times in the coming year each component will have to be replaced. Then refer to Table 5-9 to determine the number of hours' labor required to replace each component. The total labor time to replace components of the product is 16.608 hours. Multiply that by the hourly rate to arrive at the total labor cost.

16.608 hours × $48.06 hourly rate = $798.18 total labor cost.

Thus $798.18 is the labor cost to use in pricing the contract.

Multiplying the average number of repairs per year times the price for each part will give you the parts price. Table 5-10 shows the parts pricing for each component, plus the total for the contract. Note, however, that for this example, the parts prices are fictitious. In reality, you would arrive at the prices using the multiplier and refine them as outlined earlier in this chapter in the section Refining Parts and Material Pricing.

Table 5-8. Average repairs per year.

Drawing Key Number	Labor			Parts
1	$\dfrac{100,000}{200,000}$	=	0.50	0.50
2	$\dfrac{100,000}{75,000}$	=	1.33	$1.33 \times 2 = 2.66$
3	$\dfrac{100,000}{48,000} \times 4 =$		8.33	8.33
4	$\dfrac{100,000*}{10,000}$	=	10.00	$\dfrac{100,000}{20,000} = 5.00$
5	$\dfrac{100,000}{50,000}$	=	2.00	2.00
6	$\dfrac{100,000}{100,000}$	=	1.00	1.00
7	$\dfrac{100,000}{100,000}$	=	1.00	$1 \times 2 = 2.00$
8	$\dfrac{100,000}{200,000}$	=	0.50	0.50
9	$\dfrac{100,000}{60,000}$	=	1.67	$1.67 \times 2 = 3.33$
10	$\dfrac{100,000}{250,000}$	=	0.40	0.40

* NOTE: Labor is double that of part, since part is replaced only at every other failure but labor time is required to reverse as well as to replace scraper.

In summary, let's review the costs that have been calculated to determine the selling price:

Labor	$798.18
Parts	268.93
SELLING PRICE	$1,067.11

Table 5-9. Labor hours calculations.

Drawing Key Number	Average Repairs per Year		Time per Repair		Total Hours
1	0.50	×	0.25	=	0.125
2	1.33	×	0.50	=	0.665
3	8.33	×	0.25	=	2.083
4	10.00	×	0.75	=	7.500
5	2.00	×	1.00	=	2.000
6	1.00	×	2.00	=	2.000
7	1.00	×	0.25	=	0.250
8	0.50	×	1.50	=	0.750
9	1.67	×	0.50	=	0.835
10	0.40	×	1.00	=	0.400
					16.608

The service contract would be sold at $1,068 (rounding off to the next highest dollar), after you had reviewed competitive prices. Try the problem that follows to reinforce the labor and parts pricing method just outlined. (Use Worksheet 5 in Appendix One to help you price your service contract.) You can also practice the alternative pricing method in the following problem.

Table 5-10. Parts pricing.

Drawing Key Number	Average Repairs per Year		Part Price		Total Price
1	0.50	×	$ 75	=	$ 37.50
2	2.66	×	4	=	10.64
3	8.33	×	3	=	24.99
4	5.00	×	10	=	50.00
5	2.00	×	5	=	10.00
6	1.00	×	100	=	100.00
7	2.00	×	5	=	10.00
8	0.50	×	15	=	7.50
9	3.33	×	5	=	16.70
10	0.40	×	4	=	1.60
					$268.93

A Pricing Problem

The corporate plan calls for $500,000 in profits to be generated this coming year from service contract sales. The plan also calls for a return on sales of 40 percent before taxes.

Labor represents 55 percent of the total costs, while parts represent 18⅓ percent of the total costs. Service technicians each receive 3 weeks' vacation, 12 paid holidays, and 7 sick days. Nonbillable labor usually runs 78 hours per technician per year. Labor costs an average of $25 per hour; service personnel work 37½ hours per week. General and Administrative expenses are $40,000, labor overhead runs 65 percent of total overhead, and parts overhead is 15 percent of total overhead.

Determine the following and check your results. The solution follows.

1. Maximum cost of overhead if profit objectives are to be met
2. (a) Total labor cost; (b) Labor overhead
3. (a) Total parts cost; (b) Parts overhead
4. Number of service technicians required
5. Billable labor rate

Solution

You should have found the solution, using the following steps:
1. Determine the sales volume necessary to meet the profit objectives.

$$\frac{\$500,000 \text{ Profit}}{.40 \text{ Return on sales}} = \$1,250,000 \text{ sales}$$

2. Find the total cost.

$$100\% - 40\% \text{ (return on sales)} = 60\% \text{ of sales}$$
$$.6 \ (\$1,250,000) = \$750,000 \text{ total cost, } or$$
$$\$1,250,000 - 500,000 = \$750,000 \text{ total cost}$$

3. Determine the labor cost.

$$\$750,000 \times .55 = \$412,500 \text{ (answer to question 2a)}$$

4. Determine the parts cost.

$$\$750{,}000 \times 0.18\frac{1}{3} = \$137{,}500 \text{ (answer to question 3a)}$$

5. Find the overhead.

$$\text{Total cost} = \text{labor cost} + \text{parts cost} + \text{overhead}$$
$$\$750{,}000 = \$412{,}500 + \$137{,}500 + \text{overhead}$$
$$\$200{,}000 = \text{overhead (answer to question 1)}$$

$$\text{Labor overhead} = 0.65 \times \$200{,}000$$
$$= \$130{,}000 \text{ (answer to question 2b)}$$
$$\text{Parts overhead} = 0.15 \times \$200{,}000$$
$$= \$30{,}000 \text{ (answer to question 3b)}$$

6. Determine the number of service technicians required.

$$\frac{\text{Labor cost}}{\text{Average hourly labor cost}} = \text{productive hours}$$
$$\frac{\$412{,}500}{\$25} = 16{,}500 \text{ productive hours}$$

Each technician has gross hours of:

$$37.5 \text{ hours} \times 52 \text{ weeks} = 1{,}950 \text{ gross hours}$$

The total unbillable hours for each technician are:

3 weeks vacation (37.5 hours × 3)	=	112.5 hours
12 paid holidays (7.5 hours/day × 12)	=	90.0 hours
unapplied labor	=	78.0 hours
7 sick days (7.5 hours × 7)	=	52.5 hours
TOTAL		333.0 hours

Then, to find the available productive hours:

1,950 gross hours − 333 nonbillable hours = 1,617 available productive hours per technician

$$\frac{\text{Total productive hours}}{\text{Available productive hours per technician}} = \text{number of technicians}$$

$$\frac{16{,}500}{1{,}617} = 10.2 \text{ technicians required (answer to question 4)}$$

7. Determine the billable labor rate. First find the labor to parts and material ratio:

$$\$412,500 : \$137,500 = 3 : 1, \; or$$
$$\frac{55\%}{18\tfrac{1}{3}\%} = \frac{3}{1}$$

G&A assignable to labor is:

$$\frac{3}{4} \times \$40,000 = \$30,000$$

Profit to be earned from labor is:

$$\frac{3}{4} \times \$500,000 = \$375,000$$

The labor burden is:

Labor cost	$412,500
Labor overhead	130,000
G&A assignable to labor	30,000
Profit to be earned from labor	375,000
TOTAL LABOR BURDEN	$947,500

$$\text{Labor multiplier} = \frac{\text{Total labor burden}}{\text{Labor cost}}$$
$$= \frac{\$947,500}{\$412,500}$$
$$= 2.297$$
$$\$25 \times 2.297 = \$57.43 \text{ billable labor rate}$$

Rounding off to the nearest higher dollar gives $58 billable labor rate (answer to question 5). *Or,*

$$\frac{\$947,500 \; (\text{total labor burden})}{16,500 \; (\text{total productive hours})} = \$57.43$$

8. Check your results.

Parts cost	$137,500
Parts overhead	30,000
G&A assignable to parts ($\tfrac{1}{4} \times \$40,000$)	10,000
Profit to be earned from parts ($\tfrac{1}{4} \times 500,000$)	125,000
TOTAL PARTS BURDEN	$302,500

The billable labor hours are:

16,500 × 57.43 $947,595

The total sales are $1,250,095: $302,500 + 947,595 = $1,250,095.

The total sales goal (from Step 1) is $1,250,000. (There's a slight error from rounding off numbers.)

Break-Even Analysis

Once the desired service contract sales volume is established, you need to set up a way to monitor the program to ensure that the goals are being met. A simple way to do this is with a break-even chart. The chart provides the means of determining the required sales volume to meet overhead costs as well as measuring profitability at various sales volumes.

To construct a break-even chart, you must know:

1. *Fixed Expenses.* These are expenses that will be incurred whether or not any service contracts are sold. Examples of fixed expenses are rent, basic telephone charges, electricity, and depreciation.

2. *Variable Expenses.* These are expenses that change with sales volume. Examples of variable expenses are sales commissions, parts costs, and gas for service vehicles.

3. *Total Expenses.* This is the sum of the fixed expenses and the variable expenses.

4. *Sales.* This is the dollar value of the service contracts sold.

Constructing the Break-Even Chart

Figure 5-2 is a break-even chart constructed from the example that follows. Here the service manager has made these determinations:

1. The servicing organization plans to sell $500,000 worth of service contracts.
2. The fixed expenses attributable to the service contract work is $100,000.
3. The variable expenses for $500,000 in contract sales will be $250,000.

Figure 5-2. Break-even chart.

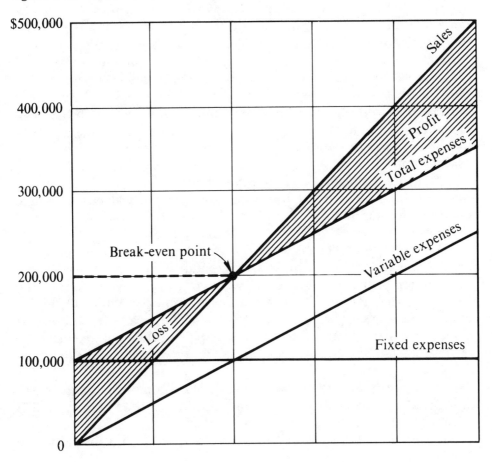

4. The total expenses are:

$$TE = FE + VE$$
$$= \$100,000 + \$250,000$$
$$= \$350,000$$

The first step is to draw a vertical and a horizontal axis (ordinate and abscissa) at some convenient size to fill the graph paper. Place the $500,000 sales figure at the top of the vertical axis and divide the rest of the vertical axis into convenient dollar amounts from 0 to $500,000. Then draw a horizontal line equal to the dollar amount of your fixed expenses ($100,000). Draw another horizontal line at the planned sales amount ($500,000). Draw a 45° diagonal line from zero (0) up to the horizontal planned sales line; where the diagonal line intersects with the planned sales line, draw a vertical line back down to the horizontal axis. (An alternative way is to draw the horizontal line from the planned sales amount, measure a distance along the horizontal axis equal to the distance from 0 to the planned sales point, then draw a vertical line from the horizontal axis until it intersects with the horizontal line previously drawn.) A square is now formed. Then draw a diagonal from zero across the square to the opposite corner; label it the "sales" line.

Plot the total expenses along the right-hand vertical axis. Draw a line from the fixed expense line at the left-hand vertical axis across the chart to the plotted point on the right-hand vertical axis; label it "total expenses."

The intersection of the sales line and the total expense line is the break-even point. If you draw a horizontal broken line through this intersection back across to the left-hand vertical axis, you can read the dollar sales necessary to break even. In this example, $200,000 in sales would be necessary just to cover expenses. The area below the break-even point that falls between the sales line and the total expense line represents loss; the area between these lines that falls above the break-even point is profit.

To monitor the variable expenses, plot the total variable expenses along the right-hand vertical axis and draw a line from zero (0) to this point. It is not necessary, however, to include the variable expense line to monitor the break-even and profitability factors, as shown in Figure 5-2.

With the break-even chart, it is easy to determine what the total expenses and profit should be at any sales volume. To do this, simply draw a horizontal line from the sales amount in question to the sales line. Then draw a vertical line at this point and read the total expenses, variable expenses, and profit. Compare these planned figures with actual performance; if goals are not being met, take corrective action.

Let's use the chart to examine an example. To determine what the profit level should be at $250,000 in sales, draw a horizontal line from the $250,000 point to the sales line. At this intersection draw a vertical line down to the horizontal axis. Now read the total expenses as $225,000, at the point where the vertical line intersects the total expense line. The profit is calculated as $25,000. Profit is Sales minus Total Expenses $(P = S - TE)$. Therefore:

$$\$250,000 - \$225,000 = \$25,000$$

The variable expense at this sales volume is $125,000.

Break-Even Point by Formula

The break-even point also can be calculated quickly by formula. Use this method when the only information you desire is the break-even point:

$$\text{Break-even point } (BEP) = \frac{\text{Fixed expenses}}{1 - \dfrac{\text{Variable expenses}}{\text{Sales}}}$$

For the example just completed:

$$BEP = \frac{100,000}{1 - \dfrac{250,000}{500,000}}$$

$$= \frac{100,000}{1 - .5}$$

$$= \$200,000$$

This, of course, is the same figure that was arrived at using the chart. The disadvantage of the formula is that performance cannot be monitored as readily as with the chart.

Computer programs are available to perform break-even analysis. You can use a basic spread sheet program to perform all the forms of analysis that can be handled with the chart method.

A Break-Even Analysis Problem

Use Figure 5-2 to test your understanding of the break-even chart, and answer the questions that follow. Note the solution.

1. What would be the profit at $250,000 in sales?
2. At what sales volume will a $50,000 profit be realized?
3. Determine the profit achieved at $100,000 in sales.
4. What must the sales volume be to break even?
5. How much profit will be earned at $400,000 in sales?

Solution:

1.

Sales	$250,000
Total expenses	− 225,000
PROFIT	$25,000

Note: This is the same problem given previously as an illustration; see Figure 5-2A.

Figure 5-2A. Graphic solution, problem 1.

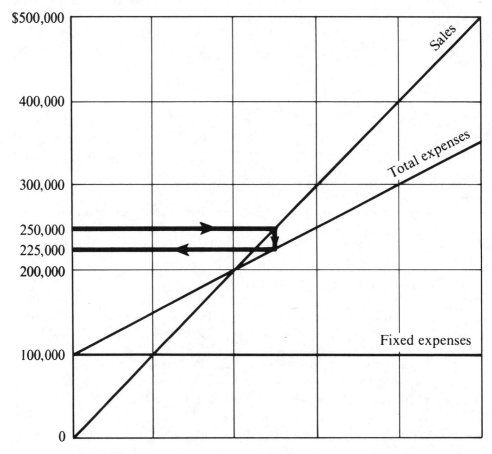

Figure 5-2B. Graphic solution, problem 2.

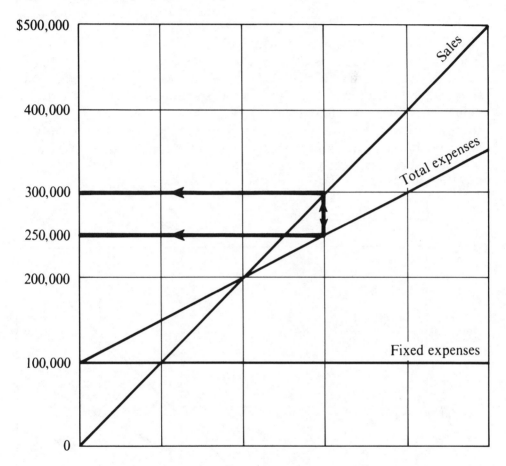

2. Look at the break-even chart and locate a $50,000 profit differential between sales and total expenses. By drawing vertical lines in the profit area you can see that, at $300,000 in sales, a $50,000 difference is apparent between sales and total expenses. See Figure 5-2B. The answer is $300,000 in sales.

3. By drawing a horizontal line from $100,000 to the sales line, you will note that, to intersect the total expense line, the vertical line must be drawn upward. Drawing this vertical line upward until it intersects with the total expense line and then horizontally to the vertical axis, you will find that the total expenses are $150,000. Therefore:

Sales	$100,000
Total expense	− 150,000
(LOSS)	−$ 50,000

Because the difference is negative, there is a $50,000 loss at $100,000 in sales. See Figure 5-2C. The answer is $50,000 loss. Also, note that this $50,000 difference falls into the loss segment of the break-even chart, verifying the calculations.

4. Look at the point where the sales and total expense lines intersect and bring a line horizontally back to the vertical axis. You will note that the break-even point is $200,000. See Figure 5-2D. The answer is $200,000 in sales volume needed to break even.

Figure 5-2C. Graphic solution, problem 3.

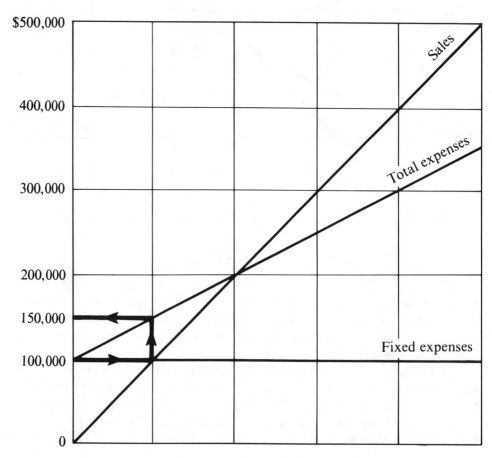

Figure 5-2D. Graphic solution, problem 4.

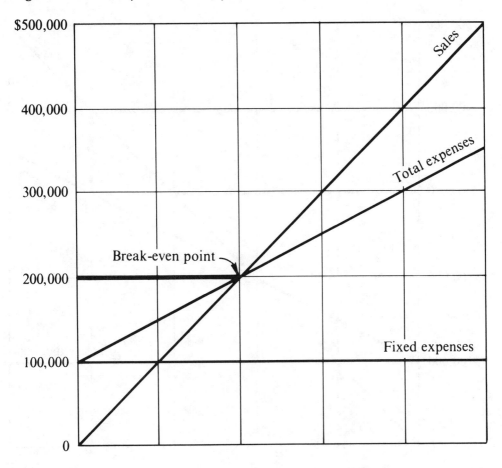

5. Draw a horizontal line from the $400,000 point on the vertical axis to the sales line. At this point, draw a vertical line downward to the total expense line. At this intersection, draw a horizontal line back to the vertical axis and read the dollar amount of $300,000:

Sales	$400,000
Total expenses	− 300,000
PROFIT	$100,000

The answer is that $100,000 in profit will be earned on $400,000 in sales. See Figure 5-2E.

Figure 5-2E.   Graphic solution, problem 5.

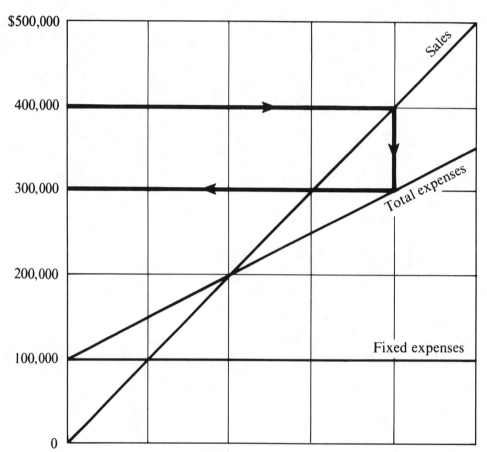

Note that when sales increase from $300,000 to $400,000, the profits increase from $50,000 to $100,000. In other words, by increasing sales by 33 percent, you increase profits 100 percent. Why?

The answer is that the fixed expenses do not increase with sales volume, therefore they become less significant with increases in volume. In fact, at the break-even point all the fixed expenses for the period of the break-even chart (say, a year) are accounted for and covered by the first $200,000 in sales. Beyond this point, profits increase at a more rapid rate than sales. This is why it is important to keep fixed expenses low, permitting your servicing organization to reach its break-even point at a lower dollar sales volume and resulting not only in greater profits but in profits earned earlier in the year.

Break-Even Analysis on the Basis of the Number of Contracts

The service manager may wish to construct a break-even chart that not only will show the dollar profit amount at a given dollar sales volume but will also identify the number of actual contracts to be sold to achieve a given level of profitability. For example, a servicing organization may determine that it has to sell $200,000 of a certain type of service contract to break even. However, this does not automatically indicate to the service manager how many contracts must be sold. He could of course divide the cost of a single contract into $200,000 and arrive at the number of service contracts that must be sold to break even. However, there is a way to incorporate into the break-even chart a means to determine the number of service contracts that have to be sold in order to break even, or to achieve a desired level of profit. Including this feature in the break-even chart eliminates additional calculations and saves time.

This method has its limitations since a break-even chart can be constructed only for a specific service contract selling at a given price because the break-even chart reflects the total cost for a specific number of units. Thus, if you try to incorporate contracts with different selling prices into one chart it will be impossible to determine what mix of contracts are represented by a given sales volume. The method does, however, permit you to analyze the break-even point in dollars and number of contracts sold for a specific service contract. Many organizations prefer to construct separate break-even charts for each type of contract offered, making it easier to distinguish between those which are profitable and those which are not. These same servicing organizations may also construct a break-even chart using the method previously described to analyze the total service contract program with regard to total dollars sold rather than the number of units sold. Thus a service firm often combines both methods in planning and controlling programs.

The Break-Even Analysis Incorporating the Number of Service Contracts

Constructing a break-even chart that incorporates the number of service contracts is very similar to the method described previously. See Figure 5-3.

Figure 5-3. Another approach to the break-even chart.

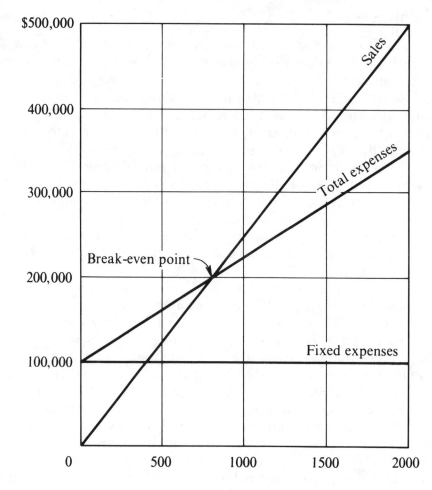

So that you may see how this method compares to the one previously described let's again assume that the servicing organization plans to sell $500,000 worth of repair contracts.

The fixed expenses will be $100,000; variable expenses $250,000; and total expenses $350,000.

Since each contract sells for $250, the total number of service contracts to be sold for $500,000 is 2,000.

$$\frac{\$500,000}{\$250} = 2,000$$

The first step is to draw a vertical and horizontal axis to fill the graph paper. Then divide the vertical axis into convenient dollar amounts between 0 and $500,000. Divide the horizontal axis in convenient contract quantities (units) from 0 to 2,000. (Note: When units are shown on the horizontal axis, it is not necessary for both axes to be equal. That is, the 0-to-$500,000 dollar amounts can be spread over 6 inches and the 0-to-2,000 units can be spread over 5, 6 or 7 inches, if desired.) Draw a horizontal line to the right from the $500,000 point on the vertical axis. Draw a vertical line upward from the 2,000 unit point on the horizontal axis. The two lines will intersect. Then draw a diagonal line from 0 to the point where the two lines intersect. This is your sales line. *The steps that follow are the same as those given for the first method (where units were not used).* Draw a horizontal line from the left-hand vertical axis at the $100,000 mark. This is the fixed expense line. Then mark a point on the right-hand vertical axis at the $350,000 level. Draw a line from this point down to the left to the point where the horizontal, fixed expense line meets the left vertical axis. This is the total expense line.

As with the first method, the intersection of the sales and total expense lines represents the break-even point. By moving down (vertically) to the horizontal axis you can find the number of service contracts that must be sold to break even. In this example, it is 800 service contracts. Therefore the servicing organization must sell 800 contracts at $250 each to break even. (See Figure 5-3.) The sales volume at break-even is $200,000.

The break-even chart constructed in this manner is used the same way as the other one. For example, to find the profit on the sale of 1,000 service contracts (Figure 5-3A), locate the 1,000 contract quantity on the horizontal axis. Then move vertically toward the sales line until it intersects the total expense line. If you draw horizontal lines from the points where the vertical line intersects the sales and total expense lines, you can read the sales and total expense figures on the vertical (left) axis. The difference between those dollar amounts is the profit ($250,000 sales − $225,000 total expenses = $25,000 profit).

If the service manager wanted to know how much of a loss would be incurred if only 600 service contracts were sold, he would draw a vertical line at the 600-unit mark (Figure 5-3B) through the sales and total expense lines. At the points of intersection, draw horizontal lines toward the vertical axis (left) and read the dollar amounts. The difference between them represents the loss. In this example, the vertical

Figure 5-3A. Graphic solution for profit.

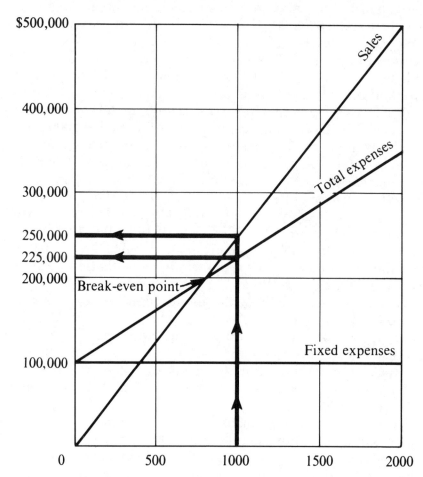

line drawn from the 600-unit amount shows sales of $150,000 and total expense at $175,000, resulting in a loss of $25,000.

In a similar way the service manager can determine the number of units that must be sold to achieve $300,000 in sales (1,200 contracts with a profit of $50,000). This is found by moving horizontally from the $300,000 point (Figure 5-3C) on the vertical axis to the sales line and drawing a vertical line downward. The figures are read as before.

Figure 5-3B. Graphic solution for loss.

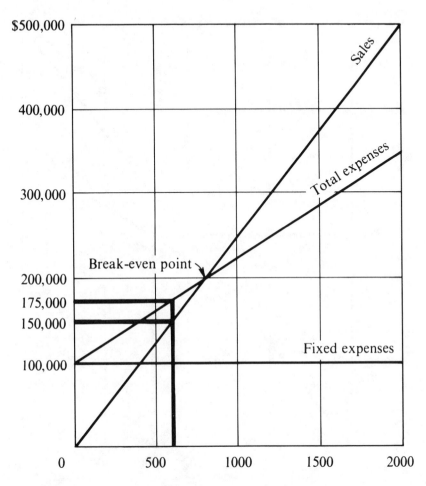

A Formula for the Number of Service Contracts Sold

As already shown, the break-even point (in dollars) can easily be calculated. If the service manager also needs a fast way to find out how many contracts must be sold to break even, that calculation can readily be made:

$$\text{Break-even point} = \frac{\text{Fixed Expenses}}{\text{Selling Price} - \text{Variable Expenses}}$$

Figure 5-3C. Graphic solution for sales.

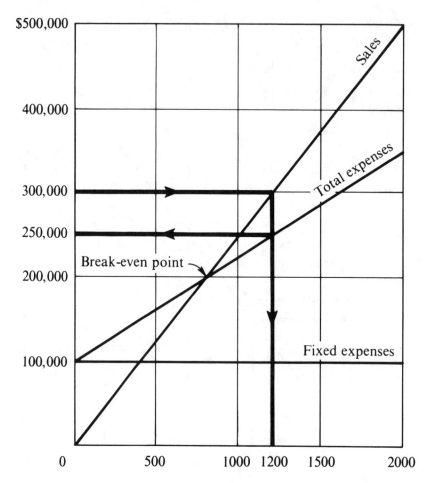

Fixed expenses = Total fixed expenses
Selling price = The selling price of each service contract
Variable expenses = The variable expense of each service contract

In the example just completed:

$$\text{Break-even Point} = \frac{\$100,000}{\$250 - \$125} = 800 \text{ service contracts}$$

The service firm must sell 800 service contracts to break even. The $250 selling price and the variable cost of each contract were determined by the service manager. In this example he plans to sell 2,000 contracts for a total sale of $500,000. Therefore:

$$\frac{\$500,000}{2000} = \$250 \text{ selling price for each contract}$$

In a similar manner the variable expense of each contract can be calculated since the total variable expense is $250,000:

$$\frac{\$250,000}{2000} = \$125 \text{ variable expense for each contract}$$

Again, this method can be used only for a service contract selling at a given price. A separate calculation must be made for service contracts at different prices, just as a different break-even chart must be constructed for each different service contract. If you use the very first method (the one without any units designated on the horizontal axis), then all types and prices of service contracts can be combined for analysis. As mentioned before, many servicing organizations use both methods in order to evaluate each type of contract as well as their total contract programs.

Other Financial Considerations

Service contracts generate a fair amount of up-front cash. It is important that this money be invested in a form that is liquid and one that provides a high rate of return. The corporate comptroller generally handles this responsibility, but the service manager should be kept informed on how the money is invested, since the profits from that investment should accrue to the service function. The return on investments from money derived from service contract sales should become part of the contract program profit structure. Liquidity is, of course, important because cash must be available to meet payroll and other expenses.

Funds received from contract sales can be substantial. The comptroller may wish to use the income to finance other operations within the company, especially in lieu of borrowing the money from a financial institution. Using the funds in this way is one of the benefits of a service contract program. However, you should be aware of this action and should be advised of what action is being taken to ensure that needed funds are readily available. Normally the financial area of the company can establish a line of credit with a bank that equals the amount of contract income. Should some of the funds be needed, the arrangements to secure them would have already been established. Failure to ensure liquidity will seriously—if not fatally—affect the entire contract program, if not the whole service function.

Seth began to comprehend fully how important good repair data were to price the service contract accurately and to minimize risk. He also became aware that, as a manufacturer, he had a responsibility to gather service life data on all parts in the products sold and serviced by his dealer organization and to convey this information to them. In fact, Seth could see the importance of using his acquired knowledge to provide the dealers with contract pricing for the various types of contracts they would offer. In this way even the small dealer, that may have difficulty using the published service data, can opt to use the standard contract pricing. Seth realized that in providing this pricing he would have to use some standard labor costs and parts markups. He understood that, by informing them of the basic pricing technique and the profit levels he used in arriving at the contract selling prices, dealers could make any needed adjustments on their own.

Seth could give dealers the option of either pricing their own contracts using the data and assistance he provided, or participating in an insured service contract program.

Seth felt comfortable with how things were going. He could now price the commercial and industrial service contracts for products that would be serviced by his direct servicing organization, as well as be able to put together a dynamic service contract program for his dealers which would bring them closer while improving his organization's national image.

6

Writing the Service Contract

Seth's service contract program was developing nicely. He determined the benefits of the contract program both for his company and for potential customers. Additionally, he understood the various types of contracts he could offer and how he could price them. Seth now turned his attention to actually writing the contracts. He knew that it was important to inform customers of what the company would and would not do under the contract. Seth also realized that he should convey what the customer's obligations would be. He recognized that writing the contract clearly and correctly would help preclude potential disagreements between the company and the customers.

In preparing to write the contract, Seth made a list of things he should do to come up with a viable document. Here's his list:

1. Review the basic elements of contract law.
2. Check both federal and state laws applying to service contracts.
3. Review existing contracts for form and content to get ideas for items to include.
4. Write the contract.
5. Review the written service contract and the entire contract program with a qualified attorney.

Having made his list, Seth began the task of developing each of the five points.

Basic Elements of Contract Law

Generally speaking, to have a legally binding contract there must be three elements present. These elements are (1) an offer, (2) an acceptance of the offer, and (3) a consideration (usually in the form of a cash payment).

The Offer

For the offer in a contract to be recognized as such, it must be a clear promise to do something for another person or a company, in return for an act or promise of some defined performance by the person or company to whom the offer was made. For the agreement to be binding, the offer must be accepted by the person or company to whom it was tendered. If the other party does not accept the offer, then a contract does not exist.

The Acceptance of the Offer

The question that may arise is, what constitutes acceptance? Acceptance can take various forms. The most common is the simple act of signing the contract. The service contract salesperson presents or mails the completed contract to the customer. The customer signs it in the appropriate place (as will be discussed later the contract should contain a place where the customer indicates his acceptance by signing) and returns it to the servicing organization.

Acceptance can be indicated in other ways, as well. For example, a repair might be required on a given piece of equipment that's not covered by a warranty or a service contract. The service manager or technician tells the customer that it will cost $100 to make that repair, and the customer says "Okay, do it." An offer and an acceptance has taken place. If, however, the customer says, "That's too much money; I'll give you only fifty dollars" and the technician, without saying a word, makes the repair, a counteroffer and acceptance have taken place. The counteroffer, which is the $50 offer made by the customer, automatically nullifies the $100 offer made by the servicing company. The servicing company does not, of course, have to accept the counteroffer, and can nullify the counteroffer by restating (countering the counteroffer) the $100 offer with, "No, I cannot accept fifty dollars. If you wish the repair made, it will cost one hundred dollars." Or the service manager can offer to do it for $75. If the customer accepts the $100 figure (or the $75, if that is offered), then an agreement has been reached.

If we return to the customer's $50 counteroffer, and the technician makes the repair without saying anything, acceptance is indicated by the action, that is, by making the repair. The servicing organization has a binding contract because the $50 counteroffer was the last offer made and was accepted through the technician's action.

Common law accepts the premise that an offer expires within a reasonable amount of time after it is made; the question is, what period of time is considered reasonable? For example, a servicing organization sends a contract to a customer. The customer says that he wishes to take some time to review its provisions. He doesn't return it. Several months later, the signed contract appears in the mail. The day after the contract is received, the dispatcher has a service call from the customer requiring a major repair on the item under contract. Under the terms of the contract, does the servicing company have to make this repair? The question that the courts may ultimately have to decide is whether the offer was still valid at the time the contract was signed. To avoid this potential problem, include an expiration date in the offer. For example, "This offer is valid only for 30 days from January 5, 19__"; or, preferably, "This offer expires on February 11, 19__." Statements such as these help eliminate misunderstandings as to how long an offer remains valid.

The Consideration

The third element generally necessary to have a binding contract is the consideration. The consideration can take many forms, the most common of which is money. The customer agrees to pay the servicing organization a given number of dollars in exchange for which the servicing company performs specified services on the product covered by the agreement. Situations can arise in which a contract can be enforced even when there is no consideration rendered. For example, if a servicing firm offers a contract to customers at no charge, and the customers accept it and rely on the servicing firm to maintain their equipment, a binding contract may exist. The courts may hold that since the customers are depending on that servicing organization to repair their products under contract, it is a valid agreement, even though a consideration is not present. This is why you often hear of someone paying $1 for an expensive piece of property or for a service. The $1 represents a consideration, and thus precludes any question of the contract's validity. Generally speaking, both parties should benefit from the contractual agreement.

Other Contract Terminology

A *breach of contract* occurs when either party to the contract violates its terms. For example, the servicing organization can be in breach of contract if it fails to respond to service calls within the time period stipulated in the contract, or if it does not perform the number of preventive maintenance inspections outlined in the contract.

Customers may be in breach of contract if they do not make payments as agreed to, either by being late with the payment or by not paying the full amount due. The injured party may sue the other party for damages.

A *contract is discharged* when both parties fulfill their obligations. For example, the servicing organization has properly rendered the services outlined in the contract during the term or life of the agreement, and the customer has paid the fees (consideration) in full, in a timely manner.

Federal and State Laws

It is important to review current federal laws, as well as the requirements of individual states in which the service contracts will be sold. Laws, on both the state and federal levels, will affect not only how your contract can be written, but how it can be sold. An in-depth review of current federal and state requirements would take volumes of books. Even if you attempted this, changes in the law between the time the material was written and the time you read it would make it incomplete and perhaps obsolete. But the following is an example of the type of legislation that you will confront when preparing service contracts. Here is an overview of the federal Magnuson-Moss Warranty Act, followed by a description of some of Florida's state requirements. The first is a federal act, affecting all organizations servicing consumer products in the United States; the Florida legislation is included as an example of strict state regulation.

Magnuson-Moss Warranty Act

Enacted in 1975, the Magnuson-Moss Warranty Act affects all consumer products manufactured after July 4 of that year. It covers the terms and enforcement procedures for written warranties and service contracts, and is enforced by the Federal Trade Commission.

There are a number of dollar amounts used in the description which follows that may prove a bit confusing unless the act is read carefully. The text of the Magnuson-Moss Act (and appendixes B and C to the Act) are reproduced in Appendix Three at the end of the book. A company is subject to the provisions if it issues a warranty on a consumer product with a retail value of more than $5. If the retail value of the product is more than $10, the manufacturer or any issuer of a warranty must state if the warranty is a "full or limited warranty" and, if limited, what those limitations are. Appendix B to the act adds to these basic rules by stating, in addition to other provisions covered later, that for any product retailing for more than $15, the seller must make the warranty available to the buyers for review prior to the sale. It is the warrantor's (usually the manufacturer) responsibility to provide the seller (usually a retailer) with copies of the warranty for every product being sold, so that the consumer can read it prior to purchasing the product. You can see that the act builds increasing restrictions as the retail price of the product increases from $5 to $15. Appendix C of the act deals with the procedures for settling disputes.

When reading the Magnuson-Moss Warranty Act, note that there appears to be a lot of repetition. As new provisions are added at each dollar threshold ($5, $10, $15), previous provisions are either repeated or expanded upon. If you are marketing a consumer product, read the act carefully and be sure you understand it. The entire Magnuson-Moss Warranty Act is reprinted in the Appendix; the discussion that follows touches on some of the highlights. A final word of caution: the act is subject to revision, and it is wise to contact the Federal Trade Commission before taking any action to ensure that you are aware of the latest statutes. Also, the Federal Trade Commission will review your proposed service contract (or warranty) and render an opinion as to its compliance. This opinion is not binding on their part but does provide guidance.

According to the Magnuson-Moss Act, a manufacturer does not have to issue a warranty at all, but if it does, the warranty must "clearly and conspicuously" indicate whether it is limited or full. The act details what constitutes a limited warranty and what constitutes a full warranty. It applies only to consumer products, and it defines what is a consumer product. Though the act is primarily concerned with written warranties, it does deal with service contracts. The service contract as outlined in the act is a "contract in writing to perform, over a fixed period of time or for a specified duration, services relating to the maintenance or repair (or both) of a consumer product." The act states that service contracts that are sold at the time the product is sold, or within 90 days thereafter, are precluded from making disclaimers of implied warranties, which many states have as part of their laws. The act also states that the service contract must "fully, clearly and conspicuously disclose its terms and conditions in simple and readily understood language." The act also requires the issuer of the service contract to extend the term of the contract if the consumer is deprived of the use of a product owing to the servicing organization's failure to effect needed repairs in a timely manner.

It is interesting to note that an insurance policy (even if it reads like a service contract) designed to protect the consumer against mechanical breakdowns or defects is covered by the act unless a state's insurance regulations supersede any of the act's provisions. This is to avoid putting the act in conflict with state insurance regulations and to indicate clearly that state insurance regulations take precedence should a question arise.

The Magnuson-Moss Warranty Act contains a list of elements designed to guide the Federal Trade Commission in drafting its regulations for the administration of the act. According to these elements, the warranty or service contract should contain the following:

1. Clear identification of the names and addresses of the warrantors.
2. Identity of the party or parties to whom the warranty is extended.
3. Products or parts covered.
4. Statement of what the warrantor will do in the event of a

defect, malfunction, or failure to conform with such written warranty; at whose expense; and for what period of time.

5. Statement of what consumers must do and expenses they must bear.

6. Exceptions and exclusions from the terms of the warranty.

7. Step-by-step procedures which consumers should take to obtain performance of any obligation under the warranty, including the identification of any person or class of persons authorized to perform the obligation set forth in the warranty.

8. Information with respect to the dispute settlement procedure offered by the warrantor and a recital, where the warranty so provides, that the purchaser may be required to resort to such procedure before pursuing any legal remedies in the courts.

9. Brief, general description of the legal remedies available to consumers.

10. Time during which the warrantor will perform any obligations under the warranty.

11. Period of time within which, after notice of a defect, malfunction, or failure to conform with the warranty, the warrantor will perform any obligations under the warranty.

12. Characteristics or properties of the products, or parts thereof, not covered by the warranty.

13. Elements of the warranty in words or phrases that would not mislead a reasonable, average consumer as to the nature or scope of the warranty.

Using this outline, the Federal Trade Commission developed a list of written warranty terms. Many of the Federal Trade Commission's terms are familiar to most consumers, since they have seen them in their written warranties (see appendix B to the Magnuson-Moss Act). Here are some important highlights (from Section 701.5):

(a) Any warrantor warranting to a consumer by means of a written warranty a consumer product actually costing the consumer more than $15.00 shall clearly and conspicuously disclose in a single document in simple and readily understood language, the following items of information:

   1. The identity of the party or parties to whom the written warranty is extended, if the enforceability of the written warranty is limited to the original consumer purchaser or is otherwise limited

to persons other than every consumer owner during the term of the warranty;

2. A clear description and identification of products, or parts, or characteristics, or components or properties covered by and where necessary for clarification, excluded from the warranty;

3. A statement of what the warrantor will do in the event of a defect, malfunction or failure to conform with the written warranty, including the items or services the warrantor will pay for or provide, and, where necessary for clarification, those which the warrantor will not pay for or provide;

4. The point in time or event on which the warranty term commences, if different from the purchase date, and the time period or other measurement of warranty duration.

5. A step-by-step explanation of the procedure which the consumer should follow in order to obtain performance of any warranty obligation, including the persons or class of persons authorized to perform warranty obligations. This includes the name(s) of the warrantor(s), together with: the mailing address(es) of the warrantor(s), and/or the name or title and the address of any employee or department of the warrantor responsible for the performance of warranty obligations, and/or a telephone number which consumers may use without charge to obtain information on warranty performance;

6. Information respecting the availability of any informal dispute settlement mechanism elected by the warrantor in compliance with Part 703 of this subchapter;

7. Any limitations on the duration of implied warranties, disclosed on the face of the warranty as provided in Section 108 of the Act, accompanied by the following statement:

Some states do not allow limitations on how long an implied warranty lasts, so the above limitation may not apply to you.

8. Any exclusions of or limitations on relief such as incidental or consequential damages, accompanied by the following statement, which may be combined with the statement required in subparagraph (7) above:

Some states do not allow the exclusion or limitation of incidental or consequential damages, so the above limitation or exclusion may not apply to you.

9. A statement in the following language:

This warranty gives you specific legal rights, and you may also have other rights which vary from state to state.

(b) Paragraph (a)(1)–(9) of this section shall not be applicable with respect to statements of general policy on emblems, seals or insignias issued by third parties promising replacement or refund if a consumer product is defective, which statements contain no representation or assurance of the quality or performance characteristics of the product; provided that (1) the disclosures required by paragraph (a)(1)–(9) are published by such third parties in each issue of a publication with a general circulation, and (2) such disclosures are provided free of charge to any consumer upon written request.

As stated earlier, the manufacturer of a consumer product does not have to issue a warranty, thus the act's provisions would not apply. Also, you might wonder about industrial or commercial purchasers of products or service contracts. Are there any laws that affect contractual relationships in these situations? The answer is yes. You should familiarize yourself with the provisions of the Uniform Commercial Code, which covers a wealth of material applicable to commercial and consumer service contracts. The Magnuson-Moss Warranty Act was designed to build on other laws, not override them. This is why you must be aware of both federal and state laws governing service contracts.

It is usually wise to issue a warranty, since many states have laws governing implied warranties. Under these implied warranties, the manufacturer may be required to perform services on a product because there is no written warranty that excludes them. Thus the lack of a written warranty may force a manufacturer to provide more extensive coverage by default, owing to state or local law. By writing a limited warranty, a manufacturer can outline the specifics of what is and is not covered. This does not necessarily guarantee that the manufacturer can avoid performing certain services; some states have regulations that override certain provisions of written warranties. Generally speaking, however, the better option is to state the coverage offered.

State Regulations

Regulations governing the sale of service contracts vary from state to state. Even the departments that have jurisdiction in this area vary somewhat. A servicing organization planning to set up a contract program in a given state should contact that state's information center for guidance. Once you've reached the correct department and received a copy of any state regulations, try to determine if any municipalities in the state have restrictions. The process may sound laborious, and to some extent it is, but the alternative is possibly to place your servicing organization in violation of government statutes.

Florida is an example of a state with specific requirements for organizations wishing to sell and administer service contracts for consumer products sold within the state. But Florida is only one such state. There is a movement throughout the United States to establish or tighten up legislation governing the writing and fulfilling of warranties and service contracts. The prudent servicing organization monitors the laws and legislative discussions related to those laws in the states that it is doing business or proposes to do business. Such companies should take an active role (and many already do) in this aspect of the legislative process.

Florida's regulations governing the sale of service contracts are likely to serve as a model for such legislation in other states. Let's briefly outline their requirements in regard to the sale of service contracts. Remember, however, that these laws may change. If you plan to sell service contracts in Florida—or in any other state—contact them for information on current legislation.

Service contracts—or as they are called in Florida, service warranties—come under the jurisdiction of the state's Department of Insurance. The company that issues the service warranty is called a Service Warranty Association. The Service Warranty Association must register with the state by completing an application as well as furnishing a copy of the certificate of incorporation, articles of incorporation, by-laws, names and residences of each director and officer (including a biography of each); copies of all service warranties to be offered and rates to be charged for each type of warranty; an outline of the organization's business history; a complete breakdown of any proposed commission structure on the sale of service contracts; most recent financial statement; a consent and agreement form; names and addresses of all affiliates and subsidiaries; copies of any contractual liability policies; an application fee; a deposit of up to $100,000 or, in lieu of a deposit, a surety bond or escrow agreement; and a list of all states in which the company is presently doing business. These requirements may seem extensive, and they are, but the state has put together a Service Warranty Kit to help you assemble the material. The kit contains all the forms necessary to secure a license plus instructions on how to complete them. Additionally, the state also encloses a copy of Chapter 634 of the Florida Statutes, which covers the regulations on warranty associations (see Appendix Four).

Once the proper documentation is filed and the fees paid, the state reviews the application. If it meets all the criteria, the application is approved. But even if a servicing organization is approved to sell service warranties, the process is not yet completed. Each sales representative who will be selling service contracts must also be licensed. Essentially, the procedure for licensing representatives involves an application and a filing fee. Once the application is approved, the representative is licensed to sell service contracts.

It is important to carefully review the statutes, since there are other requirements beyond those outlined here. For example, you must file annual reports listing the service contracts sold and their amounts. Based on this report, you must give evidence that stipulated reserves have been maintained. (A reserve is an amount of money set aside to fulfill the service warranty. The amount is determined by the projected sales volume.) If these reserves are not maintained or the reports are not filed on time, the servicing organization may be subject to additional taxes, fines, or both.

Florida is one example of a state that closely controls the service contract business to protect its citizens from unscrupulous operators. The other extreme are those states that have virtually no controls at all.

To receive a copy of the Florida Service Warranty Kit, contact: Insurance Commissioner, Department of Insurance, The Capitol, Tallahasse, Florida 32301. When writing or calling, also request an application for the State Registration for Representatives, since this is not part of the kit. The registration of representatives is handled by an area different from the one that registers companies or insurers. Both, however, are within the Department of Insurance.

Reviewing Existing Contracts

A wide variety of service contracts are available for review. Equipment located in the office, factory, or home may be covered by service contracts. Take a look at the contracts. Several examples have been included in this book (see Appendix Two). A federal or state law library will have numerous books containing service contract forms; ask the librarian for assistance in locating them. Your servicing company's attorney may be able to provide standard contract forms for your review. In the final analysis, these examples should provide guidance when you draft a service contract specifically designed to meet your servicing organization's needs.

Writing the Service Contract

The following is an outline of items to consider including in a service contract. These are suggestions; as mentioned before, you should structure the contract to meet your servicing organization's needs. For example, an automatic renewal provision or a cancellability clause may or may not be included, or they could be revised to meet your specific objectives.

A well-written contract helps preclude litigation because its provisions are easily and fully understood by both parties. Once the service contract is drafted, have it reviewed by an attorney who is well versed in contract law to ensure that it is legally correct.

It is important to construct the service contract carefully in a form that is easily understood by both parties and is legally correct. The contract should include what products are covered, who will service them, the customer's name and address, the type and extent of services to be rendered, and the responsibilities and obligations of both parties. The printed contract is the written instrument that reflects the servicing firm's agreement with the customer. As such it should cover all the points necessary to make that agreement work to their mutual satisfaction. A well-written contract serves as a reminder to both parties of the specifics of the agreement. Though it is desirable to have a legally correct contract so it will stand up in court, the main purpose of the written contract is to prevent disputes. If customers take a servicing firm to court because the verbal agreement does not coincide with the written one or because of ambiguities in the written contract, the firm's reputation is seriously affected, whether the customer is right or wrong.

Items to Include in the Service Contract

1. *Title of the Agreement.* The contract should have a title to identify the company issuing the contract (making the offer). Titles such as *ABC Preferred Service Plan* or *XYZ Comprehensive Service Agreement* help describe the nature of the contract and develop the customer's confidence in the purchase as well as state the name of the servicing organization. The company's full legal name and address should also appear. It is also a good idea to include a phone number that can be called for service or if questions arise concerning the agreement.

2. *Parties to the Agreement.* List the name of the customer, the customer's address, and the location of the equipment. The address is particularly important in commercial and industrial contracts. It is quite common for the customer's corporate headquarters to be at a location different from its branch facility, where the products may be serviced. Service contracts for consumer products may not require a provision for product location, since the product usually is located in the customer's home. This portion of the agreement will read something like the following:

This contract (agreement) is made between
_____ located at _____ and
       Customer   *Headquarters Address*
ABC Service Co., covering the equipment listed below located at

_____.
      Equipment Location

3. *Equipment Covered.* List the make, model, serial number, and installation date of the equipment covered by the agreement. If maintenance is to be part of the contract and the number of maintenance calls varies from product to product, make provision next to each listing to indicate the number of maintenance calls covered. If all the products require the same number of maintenance calls, then include a statement as to the number of such calls under the section titled "Provisions of the Service Contract." Here's an example of the listing for products with differing numbers of maintenance calls:

This agreement (contract) is applicable only to the following listed equipment:

1. ____ ____ ____ ____ ____ ____
   Product Make Model no. Serial no. Installation   No.
                                          Date   Maintenance
                                                  Inspections

2. ____ ____ ____ ____ ____ ____
   Product Make Model no. Serial no. Installation   No.
                                          Date   Maintenance
                                                  Inspections

If all the equipment is installed at the same time, such as with integrated products, the installation date for each item can be eliminated and a single separate line shown indicating the installation date.

_____
Original Installation Date

4. *Period of the Contract.* It is important that you state clearly the period of the coverage provided by the agreement. (Note that the date can include the hour of the day and you may even specify Eastern, Central, or Standard time, depending on how precise you want to be.) Use a statement such as:

This contract is effective from ＿＿＿＿＿＿＿ to ＿＿＿＿＿＿＿ .
                                                              Date   *Date*

Or include a statement to the effect:

This contract is effective for one year from ＿＿＿＿＿＿＿＿＿ .
                                                                              Date

Or:

This contract is effective for THREE YEARS from date of acceptance of this agreement by customer.

If you use this last statement, include another statement to the effect:

This contract will be void if not accepted and returned within ＿＿＿＿＿＿＿ of ＿＿＿＿＿＿＿ .
                Days   *Date*

This latter statement precludes a customer from holding the agreement and signing it at some later date, especially after a failure has occurred.

5. *Automatic Renewal.* It is generally a good idea to incorporate an automatic renewal provision because such a provision ensures continuity of service for the customer as well as facilitates an ongoing contract program for the servicing company. (Automatic renewal means you don't have to resell the contract. Most customers will just pay the renewal bill when they receive it. Some customers are apprehensive about signing a contract; an automatic renewal does not require the customer to sign again.) If, however, you have some doubts as to whether or not you wish to continue issuing the same type of contract, then you may want to eliminate this provision. In this way you avoid the problem of having to notify customers that their old service contracts are void while offering them new or amended contracts that may not be as extensive as the old ones. (The change in contracts may be

necessary because of poor product repair experience, low profits, or perhaps changes in the competitive structure.) Customers also may perceive a cancellation or rejection of the automatic renewal option as your lack of confidence in the product. Thus, customers may become alienated toward not only the product but your company as well. By not offering an automatic renewal provision, you can just not send customers new contracts at the expiration of the old ones or offer revised contracts without the stigma of cancellation or reduction in service. If you use the automatic renewal provision, it should read something like this:

> This contract shall be effective for a period of twelve (12) months commencing on _____ unless cancelled 30 days prior
> *Date*
> to the end of the contract period by either party to this agreement; this contract shall be automatically renewed for successive twelve (12) month periods at the prices, terms, and conditions in effect at the time of renewal. Either party to this agreement may cancel the contract by providing at least 30 days written notice prior to the renewal date. The customer will be provided with written notice of renewal prior to each renewal date.

When you notify the customer that the contract period is expiring and that the contract will be renewed automatically, send an invoice as well as an amendment to the contract if you are changing any of the provisions of the contract. Payment of the invoice acknowledges receipt of the notice and of any amendments. In fact, it's a good idea to write on the bill "Amendment to Service Contract Enclosed." Include an explanation of the changes and give any pertinent reasons for them so the customer understands why they are necessary.

6. *Provisions of the Service Contract.* State what the servicing firm's obligation is. For Maintenance Only contracts, such a statement may read:

> We agree, during the term of this contract, to inspect, lubricate, and clean mechanical components and replace filters and belts on the equipment listed above twice a year. Coverage under this contract shall include the cost of any lubricants, cleaning compounds, filters, belts, and service labor as may be required to perform these functions during normal working hours.

For a Full Repair and Maintenance contract, the statement should read like the sample below:

> We agree, during the term of this contract, to inspect, lubricate, and clean the mechanical components and replace filters and belts on the equipment listed above twice a year. Additionally, we will repair or replace at our option the component parts at the above-listed original address of installation, for the period of this contract, if the equipment is inoperative due to a breakdown of a component part which in our judgment fails under normal use and service. Coverage under this contract shall include the cost of all lubricants, cleaning compounds, filters, belts, and component parts as described below. Labor required to perform such services is included for services performed during normal working hours. Service rendered after normal working hours, including Saturdays, Sundays, and holidays, will be billed at the overtime rate in effect at the time the service is rendered.

You should indicate your company's normal working days and hours in the contract, as in the following example:

> Normal working hours are Monday through Friday, 8 A.M. to 5 P.M. Holidays are as follows. . . .

For the Repair Only contract, the statement should read as follows:

> We will repair or replace at our option the component parts of the above-listed equipment while it is located at the above-listed original address of installation for the period of this contract if the equipment is inoperative due to a breakdown of a component part which in our judgment fails under normal use and service. Coverage under this contract shall include the cost of component parts as described below. Labor required to perform such services is included for repairs performed during normal working hours. Service rendered after normal working hours, including weekends and holidays, will be billed at the overtime rate in effect at the time the service is rendered.

Again, you should indicate your company's normal working days and hours in the contract:

Normal working hours are Monday through Friday, 8 A.M. to 5 P.M. Holidays are as follows. . . .

7. *Definitions, Conditions, and Exclusions.* These three items can be placed together under the above title or listed as separate items. The layout you choose depends on the complexity of each topic and the format that provides the greatest clarity.

The Definitions section specifies what is and is not covered by the service contract. The following is a good example:

The components covered by this contract for the equipment described above include: drive motor, fan motor, main turning motor, heating elements, compressor, and internal controls. The contract shall not include: heat exchanger, cabinet housings, painting, trim decorations, and any wiring controls and piping external to the equipment.

The Conditions section outlines the basis of the agreement. Here is an example:

1. The only parties to this agreement are the customer named above and the ABC Service Company.

This statement clearly excludes any third party from the agreement and clarifies that only the two parties named are participants in the contract.

2. This agreement will become void if, in the opinion of ABC Service Company, the equipment covered by this contract has been subjected to negligence, misuse, vandalism, fire, lightning, accident, windstorm, dust, corrosion, or flooding, or if the equipment has been altered or tampered with in any way or operated in a manner contrary to the manufacturer's published recommendations.

The objective of a service contract is to protect the customer from unexpected expenses resulting from normal wear and tear or unexpected failure of components resulting from the product's malfunction; it does not protect from expenses resulting from external causes. Repairs needed because of the exceptions listed above normally will be covered by the customer's casualty insurance.

3. The methods, means, and time employed by ABC Service Company in fulfilling this contract shall be solely within its discretion.

In this third paragraph the servicing organization is simply stating that it will decide how and when the service will be performed. It precludes allowing the customer to tell the servicing firm how to run its business. The clause protects the firm should there be litigation because of the servicing firm's failure to follow the customer's directives.

4. Any repairs necessitated by causes not covered by this contract shall be billed to the customer at ABC Service Company's current rates for materials, parts, and labor.

This statement simply says that service not covered by the contract is to be paid for by the customer.

5. The option to repair or replace defective parts or materials is at the sole discretion of ABC Service Company.

This statement keeps the customer from demanding that a component be replaced with a new one if the servicing firm feels it can be repaired.

6. This product is to be brought to an authorized ABC Service Center for service under this contract. The costs of transporting the product to and from the authorized service center for service is the sole responsibility of the customer.

If the contract requires that the customer bring the product to the service facility, it should be so stated in the contract.

7. Any controversy or claim arising out of or relating to this contract, or the breach thereof, shall be settled by arbitration in accordance with the Commercial Arbitration Rules of the American Arbitration Association, and judgment upon the award rendered by the Arbitrator(s) may be entered in any Court having jurisdiction thereof. The terms of this contract shall be governed by laws of the state of _____ .
                                                (*Your State*)

Give consideration to incorporating a statement such as this last one for reasons to be mentioned later, in the section on qualified legal counsel. It should, of course, be reviewed by a qualified attorney to ensure that it is binding in the states where the contract will be sold.

The Exclusions section limits the liability of the servicing organization:

> 1. There shall be no liability under this contract for structural alterations to the premises, within which the equipment is installed, necessary for service, labor, parts, repair, or replacement as provided for under this contract.

Simply stated, customers should not block access to the product. If they do, it is their responsibility to remove the obstacles: their failure to do so eliminates the servicing company's obligation to perform the work.

> 2. There shall be no liability under this contract which in any way duplicates protection provided under any other existing warranty or contract.

This second clause is used when there is evidence in the industry of double dipping, that is, collecting from two sources for the same repair. The customer may, for example, collect under a casualty insurance contract and have the servicing firm perform the service at no charge under the service contract.

> 3. ABC Service Company shall not be liable for any contingent or consequential damage of any nature, such as loss of use of facilities or any other damages arising by or out of failure of a component part of the equipment, or inspection maintenance or repair of said equipment covered by this contract.
>
> If your state does not allow this exclusion, these conditions may not apply to you.

This third statement limits the servicing organization's liability for production losses or damages to other equipment owing to failure of the product being serviced. Some states prohibit an organization from absolving itself of this liability. If you operate in such a state, check your liability insurance to be sure your firm is protected. Failure to carry adequate insurance can prove devastating, should a customer sue for damages.

4. ABC Service Company shall not be liable for failure to detect conditions or circumstances necessitating repair or replacement of equipment covered by this contract.

The classic example is when a product fails shortly after the technician has serviced it. This clause is designed to limit the servicing firm's liability. It helps preclude a lawsuit based on what may be construed as negligence on the part of the service technician. The question of whether or not the technician should have detected a problem may be difficult to prove, but it can result in expensive litigation.

5. ABC Service Company shall not be liable for equipment or system performance characteristics beyond the maintenance (or repairs) of covered product components as specifically described in this contract.

This last paragraph is designed to limit liability to the repair of components specifically outlined in the contract. Its objective is to keep the servicing firm from being drawn into accepting responsibility for components excluded in the contract or into areas beyond the limits set forth in the agreement.

8. *Special Conditions.* If you don't have any, don't list any, otherwise list them. This category includes any special conditions required by the servicing organization or the customer. For example, a customer may insist that maintenance be performed only on Thursdays; it should be stated in the contract.

9. *How to Get Service.* It is a good idea to itemize the steps that the customer should take to get contract services. These steps help encourage customer satisfaction, and are required for consumer contracts, as outlined in the Magnuson-Moss Warranty Act. Here is a typical list of steps included in a contract:

To obtain service under this contract:
1. Call our service dispatcher at 1-800-228-0000, (or, for the service center nearest you, phone _____).
2. Advise the dispatcher that you have a Full Repair and Maintenance Contract.
3. Provide the dispatcher with your company name and the contract number, make, model, and serial number of the equipment requiring maintenance or repair.
4. Advise the dispatcher of the nature of your service need.

We will advise you when the service technician will arrive to perform the needed service. Should you have any questions concerning your contract coverage or services rendered, please call our service manager at the number listed above. If the question is not answered to your satisfaction, please write to our Customer Service Department, ABC Service Company, 1234 Service Avenue, Anytown, Ourstate 00000.

Similarly, for consumer products that are to be brought to a service center, include something similar to this:

To obtain service under your Five Star Service Contract:
1. Bring the product to the nearest ABC Service Center with the Quick Service Card provided with your service contract.
2. Describe the nature of the problem you are experiencing. Please bring any notes you may have describing the difficulty; they may help speed our diagnosis and repair.
We will inspect the unit and repair it immediately, if possible, or advise you when it will be ready to be picked up. Should you have any questions about your service contract or the service rendered, please discuss them with the service manager at the repair facility. If your questions are not answered or any problem not resolved to your satisfaction, contact ABC Service Contract Headquarters, 1234 Service Avenue, Anytown, Ourstate 00000.

10. *Attachments.* Should there be any additional documents, descriptions, or information that are to be part of the contract, then include a statement to that effect on the face of the contract. For example:

The following attachments are an integral part of this contract.

1. Holiday service amendment
2. Software support amendment

11. *Price of the Contract.* Include a statement indicating the price of the contract for a given period:

We agree to perform the services as described under *Provisions of the Service Contract* for a period of one year as stated under the *Period of Contract*, subject to the definitions, conditions, and exclusions outlined herein for the sum of _____.

Use numbers *and* words to list the price; for example, "one hundred dollars ($100)."

Some states presently require that a sales tax be paid. Make it clear to the customer that any taxes due are in addition to the selling price of the contract. For example:

> There shall be added to the price of this contract applicable charges for any required state or federal taxes. These would include, but are not limited to, state sales and/or use taxes.

12. *Terms of Payment.* You need to stipulate the terms of the payment. Here is an example:

> The full sum is payable in advance of the effective starting date of this contract (or "shall be paid in monthly installments of _____. Each payment is due on the tenth of the month"). Failure to make payments on time will result in termination of service.

13. *Required Statement.* The Magnuson-Moss Warranty Act requires that the following statement be included in every warranty and service contract sold with consumer products.

> This contract gives you specific legal rights, and you may also have other rights which may vary from state to state. (Magnuson-Moss Warranty Act—Consumer Products)

It is becoming common to see the statement on commercial and industrial contracts since usage sometimes overlaps. Future legislation may mandate it for all service contracts. Many servicing organizations feel that this type of notification, whether required or not, will help their case should litigation arise. It would demonstrate for the court that the customer was notified that there may be other state laws to protect his interests.

14. *Cancellability.* If you want the contract to bind both parties for the full term, then add a statement to this effect:

> This contract is noncancellable by either party except that, if the customer fails to pay the amounts due under this contract or breaches the terms of the agreement, ABC Service Company may terminate this contract upon written notice to the customer. ABC

Service Company does not waive any other legal remedies it may have.

On contracts that have an automatic renewal provision, add a statement to the effect:

The customer shall have the right to cancel this contract at the end of the contract period by providing ABC Service Company with written notice at least thirty (30) days prior to the expiration date of this contract.

15. *Signatures.* Provide space for signature by both parties:

ABC Service Company Acceptance

_____   _____   _____
   Signature   *Title*   *Date*

Customer Acceptance

_____   _____   _____
   Signature   *Title*   *Date*

Service Contracts for Consumer Products

When you write a service contract on a consumer product, remember to read the provisions of the Magnuson-Moss Warranty Act. Keep the layout and contents simple and straightforward but be sure you cover all the elements. See the suggested format for a consumer product contract (Figure 6-1).

Qualified Legal Counsel

It is important to have a qualified attorney review and approve the service contract before it is issued. The purpose of a contract is to make the terms of the agreement clear to all parties. You will help avoid litigation by having what has been agreed to presented in clear written

(text continued on p. 118)

Figure 6-1. Sample format for a service contract for a consumer product.

CONTRACT NUMBER: A12345

ABC Consumer Products Service Company
1234 Mechanic Street
Anytown, Anystate 00000

Service Contract issued to: _____

_____

_____

_____

Product Installed at: _____

_____

_____

_____

This service contract covers the products listed below:

PRODUCT	MODEL	SERIAL NUMBER	INSTALLATION DATE
_____	_____	_____	___ / ___ / ___

This contract is in force for the period listed below:

Contract Begins: _____   Contract Ends: _____

If you need service, please call (123) 555-1111. Tell our representative your contract number as listed above and give your name and address. Keep this contract handy in case we have any other questions.

Figure 6-1, continued.

Terms and Conditions Of This Service Contract

What We Will Do: In return for the full payment of the contract price, ABC Consumer Products Service Company will furnish, for the period of this contract, any parts and labor necessary to return the product listed above to working order should it fail to operate during normal usage.

What We Will Not Do: We will not make any repairs under this contract if the loss or damage was caused by (1) the product being operated under conditions for which it was not designed; (2) external causes, such as, but not limited to, fire, flood, hail, lightning, windstorm, earthquake, theft, misuse, abuse, *or* (3) the product being operated with improper or inadequate plumbing or electrical power. We will not replace any cosmetic items such as, but not limited to, sheet metal parts, trim, and plastic handles. Normal maintenance such as changing the air filters, vacuuming the interior of the unit, and cleaning the exterior of the unit are not covered. ABC Consumer Products Service Company will not be responsible for any damage, loss, or injury resulting from a delay in rendering service under this contract and in no event will we be liable for consequential damages. (*Some states do not allow the exclusion of incidental or consequential damages, so the above limitation or exclusion may not be included in all contracts.*)

Where Service Will Be Provided: Service will be provided at the location shown above or, if the contract is marked "Carry In Service" it will be repaired at one of the ABC service centers. You can find the location of the service center nearest you by calling the number listed above or 1-800-222-3333.

How to Get Service: Call the number listed above during normal business hours (Monday through Friday, 9 AM to 5 PM), except holidays. Find our telephone number in the White Pages of your local telephone directory.

If You Have An Unresolved Problem Or Need Further Help: Speak to our Manager of Customer Service by calling our main office at 1-800-222-3333 or by writing to us at ABC Consumer Products Service Company, 678 Service Road, Our Town, Our State 00000, Attention: Manager of Customer Service.

Cancellation: You may cancel this contract at any time and for any reason. In order to cancel this contract your must notify us in writing. Send your written notice of cancellation to ABC Consumer Products Service Company, 678 Service Road, Our Town, Our State 00000, Attention: Manager of Customer Service. The contract will be cancelled on the date we receive your written

Figure 6-1, continued.

notice. You will receive a prorated refund of the price you paid, based on the number of months remaining on this contract, if any. ABC Consumer Service Company will not cancel this contract during the entire period for which it is written except for nonpayment.

Renewal: This contract will not automatically be renewed. If ABC Consumer Service Company offers you a renewal contract, the price, terms and conditions may be different than those in this contract.

This document sets forth our entire agreement with you. No conditions, promises, or representations not written in this document shall change or modify the terms contained in this contract. This contract gives you specific legal rights and you may also have other rights which vary from state to state.

---

form, understood by both parties. The contract should prevent litigation and disagreement and promote customer satisfaction and harmony. It should also be legally correct, so that in the event of a lawsuit it will protect the servicing organization's interests.

In drafting the service contract, give consideration to including a statement to the effect that contract disputes will be settled by an independent organization such as the American Arbitration Association. This type of organization supplies an arbitrator who is versed in the law and is more objective than a jury might be. In lieu of such an organization, you could specify that both parties agree that disputes be heard by a judge without a jury. The reason again is to ensure objectivity and fairness. There may be laws precluding the use of such clauses, however. If you decide to include such a statement, investigate whether it is acceptable in the states where your contracts will be sold.

It may also be wise to include a statement to the effect that "any disputes arising out of this agreement shall be resolved under the laws of the State of _____." The reason for this is that if the servicing organization must go to court, it will have the dispute settled in the state where its headquarters is located. This saves the expense of having to defend a lawsuit filed in a distant state. Again, some state laws may prohibit this requirement, so be sure to check.

From this brief discussion on basic contract law, you can see that the legal aspects of writing service contracts are complex. The information in this chapter and throughout the book can serve as a guideline in drawing up service contracts; it cannot substitute for qualified legal counsel, who can guide the servicing organization in drafting and offering service contracts. Qualified legal counsel is well worth the cost. An attorney versed in current contract law can help prevent the servicing organization and its principals from becoming involved in serious litigation or criminal prosecution.

Seth now had a pretty good idea of how to write the service contract. He would prepare the necessary contracts for his commercial and industrial products. Additionally, he would draft suggested contracts for the consumer products that could be offered by his dealers.

Once the contracts were assembled, Seth would submit them to his corporate attorney for review. After discussing them with the attorney and making any necessary revisions, he would have the contracts printed. The service contract program was well on its way, and Seth felt good about it.

7

Selling Service Contracts

There is a saying in business that "Nothing happens until you sell something." Seth knew that he had to put together a marketing plan to promote and sell the service contracts if his program was to be successful.

The first step in putting together a successful marketing program was to write a plan. Why plan? Planning helps you think through what has to be done, when it has to be done, and how it is going to be done. A good plan results in fewer mistakes, thereby saving time and money.

Writing the Marketing Plan

For a plan to be effective, it must be written. A plan that isn't written down is as good as no plan at all. Seeing the ideas on paper helps you evaluate and revise those ideas in the "clear light of day." This cannot be done effectively in your mind.

Analyzing the Situation

Begin by considering the steps to take in drawing up a marketing plan.

Service Contract Marketing Plan

Outline of Steps

1. Analyze the situation.
2. Survey problems and opportunities.
3. Evaluate assumptions about the future.
4. Establish objectives.
5. List strategies to be employed.
6. Establish a timetable.
7. Prepare a budget.
8. Write the action plans.
9. Establish monitoring and control procedures.
10. Write contingency plans.

The first step in the planning process is to evaluate the servicing organization's present situation. Make a close analysis of the macro- and microenvironments in which your organization must function. In looking at the microenvironment, evaluate the competitive situation. Determine the answers to questions such as:

1. How many competitive servicing organizations offer service contracts?
2. What types of contracts do they offer?
3. How do their offerings compare with your company's offerings?
4. What types and/or size of customer do these competitors serve?
5. Are these the same customers your organization is targeting?
6. What will the customers desire in a service contract?
7. Have other organizations satisfied their customers' needs?
8. Will your contracts fulfill their needs better? In what way?
9. Are the customers paying for contracts at prices profitable to the servicing company?

By looking at the customer and competitive situations and by making a list of questions such as those just given, you can begin to get a feel for some of the problems and opportunities you'll deal with in the marketplace. The microenvironment, then, is the business atmosphere that surrounds your servicing organization. It contains the immediate problems and opportunities that you must deal with if you are to have a successful service contract program.

Also give attention to the macro-environment and its trends. The macro-environmental factors include federal and state regulations and laws; economic conditions such as inflation and the cost of borrowing money; and political events such as wars or disruptions in other parts of the world that can affect your ability to do business. Usually it is easier to understand the microenvironment and its importance to your business because it involves your competitors and customers. The macro-environment can, in some instances, seem abstract. It is difficult to understand, for example, how a disturbance in the Middle East can affect your ability to offer and fulfill a service contract. If you reflect on it, however, you can see that such a disturbance might slow or stop the flow of oil. This, in turn, can limit the availability of gasoline, thus restricting your ability to fulfill contractual obligations. All this is not so far fetched when you consider what happened in the 1970's when the flow of oil from Iran was halted. In most instances, a servicing firm cannot influence macro-environmental factors as easily as it can the microenvironment. Nevertheless, its managers must be aware of what is transpiring or may transpire so that they can be prepared to deal effectively with the situation.

Surveying Problems and Opportunities

Having assessed the microenvironment (your immediate competitors, customers, and so on) as well as the macro-environment (political, technical, societal, and economic conditions), you will see certain problems emerge. You also will become aware of opportunities to improve sales and profits, which take us to the second step.

The problems and opportunities so defined should be listed as part of your plan. Most often a problem also presents an opportunity. This is so because more than likely the competition is facing the same problem. If your servicing firm can solve that problem, you may find a new source of business and a means to increase profits.

Making Assumptions about the Future

Your analysis of the current and future states of the business environment will lead you to make a number of assumptions about the future. You may assume, after careful analysis, that the number of potential customers for service contracts will increase at a predicted rate each year in the foreseeable future. You may determine that inflation will remain at a low rate (or may feel it will accelerate rapidly). You may conclude that no new competitors will enter the market (or may see that the opportunities in the service contract market will attract additional competitors), and so on.

Establishing Objectives

Having carefully reviewed the problems and opportunities and having made your assumptions about the future, you are now ready to set your objectives for the service contract program. When you priced the contracts, you established sales goals to ensure that the profitability objectives of your organization would be met. These sales goals are incorporated into others you've established, such as a desire to secure a certain share of the service contract market. Market share is the percentage of contracts sold by one servicing firm as compared with the total service contracts sold by all the firms in the market. For example, if the total number of contracts sold to a particular type of customer is 5,000 and, of these, 1,000 were sold by your firm, then you have a 20 percent market share:

$$\frac{1000}{5000} = .20 \times 100 = 20\%$$

Set your objective to achieve a given share of the market; it will provide a means of assessing your firm's success in the marketplace. Studies have shown that, in the long run, those companies that enjoy a high market share also maintain a better return on investment than others with smaller shares of a given market. Remember that objectives must be established in quantifiable terms, such as the number of contracts to be sold, total dollars to be earned in sales and profits, and percent share of the market to be gained. By having a number or an amount to be achieved, it is easier to determine if a goal has been met or by what percentage it was not achieved. For example, if your goal was to sell $1 million in service contracts during the year and after that year was over you determined that the firm only achieved $800,000 in sales, you know that your goal was missed by $200,000, or 20 percent:

$$1,000,000 - 800,000 = 200,000$$

or:

$$\frac{\$200,000}{\$1,000,000} = .20, \text{ or } 20\%$$

Rather than having set a quantifiable objective, if you had just stated that you planned to sell a lot of service contracts, you would have no way of determining whether 50 or 50,000 was "a lot." Without measurable goals, you have no way of knowing how good "good" is and how bad "bad" is.

Listing Strategies

Once you've set your objectives, the next step is to develop the strategies that your organization will employ to meet them.

Your strategies, then, should consist of a description of what course you'll take to meet the specific objectives you have established. They should state what direction the servicing organization will go in to meet those objectives, taking maximum advantage of the previously identified opportunities and solving the known problems. The strategies may include statements that establish how the customers will be contacted and sold contracts. For example:

> We will meet our established contract sales objectives by employing the following strategy: (1) establishing a telemarketing program and (2) contacting customers who purchased our products.

The strategy here is to sell contracts by telephone, using a list of product customers. The plan could have included a direct mail or advertising program. Quite often a single strategy can be used to meet several objectives. For example, objectives for the total dollar sales, the mix, and the number of contracts to be sold can often be met with a single strategy statement.

Drawing Up a Timetable

Having established the strategy to be used, you would next set a timetable showing when each objective will be met. This timetable ensures that not only will the objective be met, but that it will be met within an acceptable time.

Preparing a Budget

An important part of your plan is the budget. You must determine the costs that will be incurred in employing these strategies. Budgeting is a process of financial planning. It is the means of assessing how much the contract marketing program will cost, as well as determining if those costs are reasonable and consistent with desired profitability levels.

Writing Action Plans

Action plans are written in our next step. Figure 7-1 is an example of such a plan. In the action plan, you get down to specifics: the actions that you will take to meet the objective. For example, your strategy may have been to establish a telemarketing program. Your action plan uses this strategy and lists all the specific actions that you must take to put that telemarketing program into action—order the phones, buy the desks, hire the telemarketing sales people, and so on. In the action plan you define who is responsible for each action and by what specific date that action must be completed.

Monitoring and Controlling

Finally, you must establish procedures to monitor and control the planned actions. Determine who will monitor the action plan to see that the deadlines are met and ensure that the strategies lead toward accomplishing the objectives. Establish a control procedure to detect problems quickly, before they seriously affect the organization's ability to achieve its goals. You or an assistant can keep track of the due dates of various aspects of the plan. Review the break-even analysis (discussed in Chapter 5) weekly at first, then monthly or quarterly as you gain confidence in the plan and in the personnel implementing it.

Contingency Planning

The marketing plan is a road map to which you should refer on a regular basis. In reviewing the plan, ask yourself: Has the environment changed? Have new problems emerged? Are the assumptions made about the future still viable? Are the strategies being used still the most effective ones, or should they be modified or completely

Figure 7-1. Sample action plan.

[COMPANY NAME]
Action Plan

DATE: _____5/7_____

PLAN MANAGER _____JANE EDWARDS_____

OBJECTIVE 1: Establish telemarketing program by 11/1/__ .

Actions	Responsibility	Date to be Completed	Date Completed
Rent 1600 sq. ft. for tele-marketing function	A. Smith	6/2	6/1
Purchase furniture	S. Samuels	6/28	6/28
Have 14 phone lines in-stalled	T. Thomson	7/12	7/14
Order computer terminals	J. Johnson	8/1	8/1
Set up computer programs	A. Albrect	9/15	9/12
Establish customer list and list upgrade system	B. Brown	10/1	10/1
Prepare telemarketing script	J. Edwards	10/1	10/1
Prepare Feature-Benefit analysis	C. Christen	9/15	9/14
Prepare Competitive Analysis	C. Christen	9/20	9/19
Hire competitive tele-marketing sales person-nel (14 persons)	J. Edwards	10/15	10/15
Train telemarketing sales personnel	P. Paulsen	10/30	10/30
Begin calling customers	J. Edwards	11/1	11/1

changed? Are the control procedures working, or are we missing dead-lines? The plan is not cast in stone. It is a living document, designed to be changed to meet changing conditions.

In writing the plan, give concern to the possibility that competitors may react in a variety of ways or that certain other elements may change. For example, you may have made the assumption that there will not be a gasoline shortage. This assumption was based on the fact that at the time there were no problems in the oil-producing countries or in the refineries. However, if an oil shortage might occur and if this occurrence could seriously affect your organization's ability to fulfill its contract obligations, then you would write a contingency plan.

A contingency plan is simply a plan written in addition to the regular marketing plan that deals with potential problems which could seriously disrupt the business. In the case of an oil shortage, for example, a servicing organization that had planned for that occurrence would be in a stronger position than its competition. A servicing firm with contingency plans develops those plans in advance, when it can think through the problem cooly, not in the heat and under the pressure of the crisis. It's the difference between planning for a possible crisis and reacting suddenly to one. Planners inevitably have the edge, since they have more time to analyze courses of action and select the most viable one.

Write separate contingency plans for each potential major problem. Put these plans aside, but update them as necessary to be put into effect should the potential problem become a reality. Most contingency plans are never used, but having them is like owning insurance (or service contracts); you'll certainly be glad you have them when they are needed.

Sell the Contract at the Time of Purchase

Every customer who has purchased a product your organization services is a potential service contract customer. The fact that customers have made a purchase, however, does not automatically ensure that they will call your firm and order a contract. Contracts must be sold aggressively. Certainly, a number of contracts are sold through referrals or customer inquiries, but normally these represent the proverbial "drop in the bucket," when compared to the full sales potential.

Those companies that both sell and service products should always try to sell the service contract when they sell the products. As a rule customers have selected your company's product after some consideration. Normally they will be happy with their purchases and in a good frame of mind. This is the ideal opportunity for the salesperson to offer a service contract. The price of the contract is usually small in relation to that of the product, therefore for a little extra money, the customer can get the peace of mind that a service contract offers. It is also an efficient time to sell the contract because the salesperson is at the customer's home or place of business anyway. Why not use the opportunity to sell the contract and increase the total sales dollars? This same strategy also applies if the product is sold through retail outlets; the customer is present, so sell the contract.

There are additional benefits to selling the contract at this time. Most products carry a warranty, so by selling the service contract along with the product, the servicing organization benefits from the extra cash during this initial, warranty period. For example, if a product comes with a one-year warranty and the customer is sold a one-year service contract that covers the product during its second year, then the servicing firm has the full use of the money during the warranty period. Many servicing organizations offer customers a discount on the contract price as an incentive at the time the product is purchased, thus increasing even more the possibility of a contract sale. Generally, the servicing firm makes up the discounted amount by investing the money during the warranty period. Customers benefit by receiving a discount, and they do not have to worry about buying a contract at a later date when the cost may be higher.

You should remember that customers must be informed when a service contract begins after the warranty expires. It is a violation of the Magnuson-Moss Warranty Act as well as of the law of virtually every state to mislead customers into thinking that the contract begins from the date of purchase. Servicing firms have been brought to court for this type of violation, and have faced severe penalties. Violations occur most often when the person selling the contract tells customers that they are getting two years' protection for, say, $30. Customers reason that it is costing them $15 a year for the contract, when in reality the cost of the first year's coverage (which is the warranty) is included in the price of the product. The contract costs the customer $30 for a one-year service contract. To comply with the law, you must separate the warranty from the contract. This is true even if you are selling a wrap-around contract. The wrap-around contract provides added coverage during the warranty period for elements not covered by the warranty. For example, a customer purchases a dishwasher, and the warranty covers the entire machine for the first year plus an extended warranty on just the motor and wash arm for the next four years. The servicing firm can offer a wrap-around contract that covers all the components not included in the four-year extended warranty period. The customer must be told that your four-year service contract covers those components *not* covered by the extended warranty for that period.

If the product salesperson cannot sell the contract when the product is sold, then the servicing division should be notified so it can place that buyer on its potential customer list. In this way the potential customer is not forgotten as a targeted account. Your marketing plan should outline the strategy that will be employed. For example, the plan may state that your strategy is to sell the contract at the time the product is sold; if the contract is not sold at that time, a note is made on a copy of the sales order and it is sent to the telemarketing group or a service salesperson to follow up.

The servicing organization's salespeople then place such names on their overall target customer list. The target customer list can be made up simply of all customers who have purchased products from the company, or can include owners of certain types of products, irrespective of the manufacturer or seller. The sections that follow explore how to develop this list to your greatest advantage.

Developing the Customer Profile

The first step in selling service agreements is to determine who your potential customers are. If your marketing plan was written properly, you have established the customer base. When you know the type of customer you are pursuing—that is, large, medium, or small companies engaged in specific industries; or a certain group of consumers, identified by age, income, and so on—you can promote the contract in such a way as to make it attractive to those potential customers.

Commercial and Industrial Products

In identifying the commercial or industrial customer, you must first establish what your servicing organization's strategy is to be. The marketing plan, again, should have shown this. Is it your strategy just to go after those companies that have purchased products from your company? If this is the case, review your sales orders for their names and addresses. If your strategy is also to sell service contracts to purchasers of competitive products, then you must identify the firms that have purchased the type of product your company sells.

How do you find these firms? The federal government is a major source of data used in identifying groups of commercial and industrial firms. The government's Standard Industrial Classification Code, or SIC code as it is most often called, categorizes all varieties of businesses. If you know the type of industry that buys the kind of products you wish to service, then you can look in the SIC code directory for that specific industry. For example, if you want to locate razor blade manufacturers, look in the directory to find the code. Armed with the SIC code (usually four digits, although some are longer), you can now proceed to identify the size of your customer base.

Where do you find the SIC code directory? You can purchase it from the federal government, or call or visit a federal library (located in major U.S. cities) or a major university library. In addition, each customer usually knows its SIC code, and many firms place it on their purchase orders. Your company could provide a place on its sales order form to write in the SIC code, thus ensuring that the salesperson selling your product will ask the customer for it. Lastly, the Dun & Bradstreet Corporation publishes SIC codes in their credit listings along with other information. Your credit department may be able to locate the SIC codes for you.

Once you match an SIC code with each customer (and your product sales department can easily be convinced to do it, since there are also many benefits from their standpoint), then you can enter the data into a computer. The computer will sort customers by SIC code, allowing you to see readily which SIC code or codes have the most customers for the type of product. For example, you may find that 80 percent of the sales of a specific model or type of product are to a given industry. Knowing this, you can focus your sales efforts on the industry with the largest contract sales potential.

This process offers a special opportunity for servicing firms geared to selling contracts to users of several brands of the same type of product. When you know the customers who have purchased a particular type of product, and you determine the SIC code of the largest group of these purchasers, then you can acquire a list of most, if not all, of the potential owners. There are numerous companies that sell lists of firms categorized by SIC code. These companies publish catalogs listing all the SIC codes and industries they have in their data base. The catalogs tell you how many firms the company has listed in the United States or in a certain geographical area. For example, if you want to know how many firms with a given SIC code are located in your state or county, the catalog of a list firm will tell you.

You can purchase the names and addresses of all the companies in your state with a given SIC code. The cost of each list varies among the list companies and also by SIC code within a list company. Generally these lists start at a few cents a name but can go much higher. You can use the lists for a direct mail sales campaign; they even provide the names and addresses on peel-off labels or provide them on a computer tape or disk for telemarketing or service sales.

Independent dealers or wholesalers should contact their product suppliers for assistance in this area. Many manufacturers have SIC codes in their data base and are willing to share the data with dealers, distributors, or wholesalers. If this is not possible, independent dealers or distributors can follow the same procedure to establish a targeted service contract customer list for the areas they serve.

Consumer Products

In the consumer market, as in the commercial and industrial market, the servicing organization must determine whether it wishes only to offer contracts to purchasers of a single brand or to service a variety of brands.

If the plan is to service only the products it sells, then you simply contact the customers who purchased the product and try to sell them service contracts. Records should be kept of certain customer characteristics. For example, you might determine that persons in a particular age group, earning an income within a certain range, living in a private home (as opposed to living in an apartment), and so on are more likely to purchase a service contract. You can focus sales and promotional efforts on these people. Sales orders and warranty cards provide excellent means for gathering such data. Also, if the product is sold by a salesperson, that salesperson may be able to ask the customer for some information.

The warranty card should be designed so as to answer the questions that the marketing and service functions have. Use multiple-choice questions that can be checked off easily by the customer. For example:

What is your age group?

☐ Under 20 years   ☐ 45–55 years
☐ 20–25 years   ☐ 55–65 years
☐ 26–35 years   ☐ over 65 years
☐ 36–45 years

The ranges given (in this example, the age groups) should be meaningful. For example, if you know that most contracts in the past have been sold to persons in the 45–55 years group and to those over 65 years old, then you should define those groups when structuring the question. If the groupings used the ranges of 40–50 and 50–60 years, the response would be spread over a 20-year period (that is, 40–60 years), whereas the customers you are interested in fall within the 10-year period of 45–55 years. The wider ranges ultimately would lead you to contact more customers (at greater expense), many of whom would not be interested in service contracts. By narrowing the spread, you target the potential customers more closely.

In addition to warranty cards and purchasing records, a servicing organization concerned with servicing a wide range of brands can contact the companies that sell consumer lists. These organizations organize their lists along demographic lines, and further break them down into geographical areas. These breakdowns permit you to zero in on the type of customer most likely to buy your service contract in the area served by your firm.

Researching the Market

We've already discussed obtaining data on potential service contract customers through input from product sales, SIC codes and commercial lists, as well as warranty cards. Although this information is extremely valuable, there may be times when you must further research the market for your contract sales, whether they be to commercial and industrial customers or to consumers. First, let's consider how to obtain information from existing sources.

The federal government provides a wealth of information on consumers, such as data on the number of persons nationwide or in a specific locality who fit certain income specifications, age groups, and so on. The government also has data on the number of persons who own their own home, have television sets, and so on. The key to researching the marketplace is to determine the questions you have about that marketplace. Once you have formulated these questions, you can call or preferably visit a government library or the library of a local college or university; a business school library is particularly useful. Give the reference librarian your list of questions. The librarian most often will locate the answers for you or at least direct you to where the answers may be found.

Gathering this kind of information is called doing secondary research. Secondary research is information that someone else has gathered. It is the least expensive form of market research (or, if you prefer, service market research). On the other hand, secondary research is published data that may not be in the exact form you desire, thus it may require some interpretation. For example, the age groupings in some secondary data may not be exactly as preferred: you may want it in the 45–55 years group, whereas the published data is in the 40–50 and 50–60 years groups.

In contrast, primary research is gathering information that has not been published elsewhere. The advantage of primary research is that you can get the answers to your questions in the exact form that you want them. The disadvantage is that such research is normally much more expensive.

Primary research lends itself to both the consumer and the industrial and commercial markets. Through primary research you can target in on not only what type of individual or company would most likely purchase a service contract, but also what elements each is looking for in the contract. Such research can be conducted via person-to-person interviews, telephone interviews, focus groups, Delphi panels, or direct mail, to name a few. The person-to-person interview is the most expensive form of primary research, in that someone either must stop individuals on the street or in a shopping mall, or go door to door or company to company asking the questions. The advantage is that the individual being interviewed can be shown the service contract, sales brochure, direct mail piece, or whatever, and his or her reaction determined immediately. The telephone interview is not as expensive, and is effective when the person being interviewed is not required to look at something (such as the service contract). In both types, you need to spend time carefully formulating the questions. Professional research firms can be of great assistance with this.

Focus groups involve gathering a group of people, usually 8–12, headed by a moderator. The group tries to answer the questions the servicing organization has developed. The cost is moderate, since participants are usually given some nominal fee for their time. The advantage is that participants listen to each other and comment on what is being said. Often this results in new ideas for selling the contracts. Sessions are recorded on audio or video tape for future analysis. The professional firms that conduct focus groups also have special rooms with one-way mirrors so that representatives of the firm can observe the proceedings without influencing the results. You can conduct a type of focus group by selecting dealers or distributors to participate in a roundtable discussion of the merits and liabilities of the proposed contract program. The ideas generated and the involvement of those who will be either selling or fulfilling the contract program (or both) help add to the program's success.

A Delphi panel is perhaps the most sophisticated of primary research processes. With a Delphi panel none of the participants meets or even knows who the other participants are. Panel members usually are considered experts in their fields (for example, members of the corporation, distributors, or independent outsiders). A questionnaire is drawn up and mailed to each member of the panel. When the replies are received, the responses are analyzed. From these responses new questions are formulated and another questionnaire is mailed. This process is repeated until all responses indicate clearly the specific features of the contract program or customer base that are important to the panelists. The objective is to get a consensus of what the panelists feel is saleable without having one influence the other.

Direct mail offers an economical way of getting information. A questionnaire is mailed to a group of potential customers. If proper questions are asked, the data gathered will help determine if the group is truly interested in a contract and what features of the contract would influence a decision to buy. The disadvantage of a direct mail questionnaire is that there is no personal contact, and the individual who receives the questionnaire doesn't have to answer it. A device that has had success, particularly with the commercial and industrial market, is to enclose a dollar bill with the questionnaire along with a note suggesting that the receiver use the dollar to buy a cup of coffee and drink it while he or she answers the questions. This method has proved itself through an increase in the number of responses received. Another lure—for commercial customers and consumers—is to offer a prize drawing to be drawn from among the names of the questionnaire respondents. Or offer individual gifts or trading stamps to those who complete the form.

When considering any kind of research, always weigh the cost of the research against the benefits to be derived. If the method selected cannot justify the cost, then perhaps you should use another means to get the desired information.

Feature-Benefit Analysis

Regardless of how you sell a service contract (person-to-person, telephone, direct mail, and so on), it is important to understand the contract's features and benefits.

A *feature* is an outstanding characteristic or quality of the contract. For example, a feature of a given contract may be that the product covered will be inspected four times a year. A salesperson will point out this feature to the customer. The customer's reaction may be, "So what will it do for me (or my company)?" People do not buy features, but rather, the benefit to them that the feature offers.

A *benefit* is the application of a feature to the customer's individual situation. How will that feature improve the life of the product or its performance? How will it save the company or individual money? Benefits tell customers how the contract helps them. Customers buy benefits, not features—an important point that you should always remember.

A person selling a contract might assume that the benefits of a given feature are obvious and that a customer will readily see them. This is a mistake made often. What is obvious to the individual selling the contract may be far from obvious to the customer. Don't assume that the benefits of a feature will be recognized easily by the customer. Unless that customer understands all the ways the service contract will help, you risk the loss of a sale. A salesperson who extolls the features of a contract but fails to convert those features into benefits the customer can recognize will not convey the true value of the offer and will elicit an "It's too expensive" response. Such a response is a signal that the customer does not see the benefits as great enough to justify the price.

You might assume that qualified sales personnel can readily identify the many features of a service contract and easily convert them to benefits for the customer. Most often this is not the case. You should prepare a feature-benefit analysis to assure that everyone involved with the sale of the contract is aware of its features and benefits. To start, review each type of contract and list the features in each. For example, your list may include the following:

1. Four inspections per year.
2. Three-hour response time to emergency calls.
3. Automatic renewal provision.
4. All components covered.
5. All labor costs included.
6. One-year contract.
7. Priority service.

List as many features as you can. Once you've done this, analyze each feature for the benefits it offers to the targeted customers. Below is an outline you can follow in assembling your analysis. (See Figure 7-2.) For example:

FEATURE: Four inspections per year.
BENEFITS: 1. Statistics show that products receiving four inspections per year last five years longer than those not inspected.
2. Plant maintenance manager does not have to remember to perform inspections; servicing firm takes this responsibility.
3. Regular inspections save customer's company money by:
    A. Giving them five years' more use of product, saving X dollars.
    B. Eliminating salaries of maintenance personnel and all benefits paid to them, saving W dollars.
    C. Having inspections performed by qualified, experienced service technicians who are thoroughly familiar with the product; because they know the product, they can perform the inspections quickly, thereby reducing down time, saving Y dollars in production losses.
    D. Preventing premature failure of components, saving repair expense and money lost in down time.

Figure 7-2. Outline for a feature-benefit analysis.

Feature-Benefit Analysis

1. FEATURE: _____

   A. BENEFIT: _____

   B. BENEFIT: _____

   C. BENEFIT: _____

2. FEATURE: _____

   A. BENEFIT: _____

   B. BENEFIT: _____

   C. BENEFIT: _____

3. FEATURE: _____

   A. BENEFIT: _____

   B. BENEFIT: _____

   C. BENEFIT: _____

4. FEATURE: _____

   A. BENEFIT: _____

   B. BENEFIT: _____

   C. BENEFIT: _____

5. FEATURE: _____

   A. BENEFIT: _____

Figure 7-2, continued.

    B. BENEFIT: _____

    C. BENEFIT: _____

6. FEATURE: _____

    A. BENEFIT: _____

    B. BENEFIT: _____

    C. BENEFIT: _____

The list should continue until all possible benefits are listed. After listing the benefits for one feature, move on to the next feature. Have your colleagues also generate a list of features and benefits, then get together and compare lists. New ideas will emerge, and you'll get an expanded list of features and benefits.

The next step is to present your feature-benefit analysis to the sales organization. Make this part of an overall training program in which the salespeople are instructed in effective sales techniques employing feature-benefit analysis.

Sales Techniques

Whether you plan to sell the service contracts over the telephone or have sales personnel visit customers at their homes or places of business, it is important that these salespeople are trained in effective sales techniques. Good selling skills do not involve deceptive practices or trickery. On the contrary, good selling methods show customers the benefits your service contracts have to offer and the value they represent. A good sale is a win-win situation in which the customer derives benefits from the purchase and the servicing organization increases its profits. Selling, then, is the art of presenting the benefits of a service contract in a manner that can be seen by customers as beneficial to them. But how does the salesperson determine which benefits will be of most value to a potential customer? Through questioning. The salesperson determines the customer's needs by asking about them. Questioning has the added benefit of ensuring that the customer is listening to what is being said. When the question is asked, the customer answers. How the question is answered indicates not only if the customer has been listening, but also if he or she understands what is being said.

In developing a list of such questions, you must determine what factors you need to know to ensure that the appropriate benefits are conveyed to the customer. Typical questions you should ask are:

1. What type of products do you have (or, if the object is to sell a contract for a product recently sold to the customer, if the records are correct)? For example, "Our records show that you recently purchased a Model AB123 washer. Is that correct?"
2. How is the product used in your business?
3. How many hours is it run a day? How many cycles does it go through? If dealing with a consumer, How many loads of clothing do you normally wash a day?
4. Do you have your own service staff?
5. How many people do you have on the payroll doing service work?
6. Do you use an outside firm to provide service? What's the firm's name?
7. Under what circumstances do you call them?
8. Do you find at times that you cannot fully utilize all your corporate service personnel?
9. Are there other times that you wish you had several more technicians because everything seems to fail at once?

Keep writing questions that outline the information you need to know. As you see, the questions get to the heart of how the customer operates. Using the questions and listening to the replies, a salesperson should perceive how service is conducted at that customer's place of business, or what the needs are of that consumer. The salesperson can determine what aspects of repair and maintenance present the most problems to the customer, and can begin to translate the benefits of the service contract into solutions for that customer. For example, a salesperson may say, "You indicated that scheduling of technicians was a major time-consuming problem. How would you like to free yourself of this problem?" By listening carefully to the customer's reply, the salesperson can list those benefits that truly solve the customer's difficulties.

Having identified the desired benefits (those that the customer has indicated are most important), the salesperson should review them with the customer. For example, he or she might say "You indicated that your major problems are (1) scheduling of personnel, (2) high overtime costs, (3) inability to hire qualified technicians at a low cost, (4) . . . ." The salesperson would conclude by saying, "Are these the areas of most concern to you? Did I miss any?" Having secured the customer's agreement to the list of key problems, the salesperson would show the customer how the benefits of the contract will solve those problems. "You indicated that scheduling of personnel is a major problem for you. A major benefit of ACT's Super Service contract is that we handle all the details of scheduling. We will schedule personnel to respond to emergency calls promptly and schedule our maintenance personnel to perform required preventive maintenance services four times a year, as recommended by the manufacturer. You will not have to worry about a thing. We handle all the scheduling. Do you think you would like that?" If scheduling is a major problem, as the customer previously indicated, the answer will be yes. If the salesperson receives anything but a yes, then he or she has not identified the problem and must ask more exploratory questions.

When the salesperson has reviewed all the customer's problems and has shown how the service contract solves those problems, it is time to see if the customer is prepared to purchase the contract. The salesperson does this by using a trial close. The trial close finds out if the customer has seen that the benefits of the contract offer a good value. The question should be phrased in a manner that the customer must indicate either acceptance or rejection. For example, "The Full Repair and Maintenance contract costs $1,000 per year; the Modified Maintenance contract costs $750 per year. Which would you prefer?" The customer will most often pick one. Regardless of which is chosen, the salesperson should lead to make a close. "Mr. Jones, you selected the Full Repair and Maintenance contract. That's an excellent choice. Let me make sure I have all the information correctly. The contract should be mailed to your attention at QXR Company, 100 Good Street, Best Town, Your State 00000. The contract will be a Full Repair and Maintenance contract for a price of $1,000, and will be effective from June 1, 19__ through May 31, 19__. May I have your check for $1,000 now so we can process the contract immediately?" When the check or purchase order is received, the salesperson thanks the customer, says "You have made an excellent purchase. I know you will be happy with the contract," then leaves. He or she does not engage in post-sale conversation. The customer is busy, and so is the salesperson.

Customer Objections

It did not go smoothly? The customer may not have seen the benefits as true benefits. A common objection takes the form of, "Your contract does offer a lot of benefits, but the price is too high."

Before a salesperson reacts to that comment by defending the price, he or she should ask the customer, "Will you tell me why you think the price is too high?" By asking this question the salesperson essentially is asking the customer to clarify the statement. In this way the true objection can be dealt with.

The customer may reply, "Your competitor WZX Service Company offered a similar contract for $25 less." Here's where knowing the competitive offerings really pays off.

"Mr. Jones, I understand what you are saying, but we offer four preventive maintenance inspections a year, whereas they offer three. We will respond to your emergency calls in four hours, whereas their contract stipulates eight hours. The extra preventive maintenance call, which is very important to the long life of the equipment, is worth more than $25 alone. Don't you agree that all these extra benefits are an extremely good value for $25?" All the customer initially saw was an equal contract for a lower price, therefore a better value from the competitor. By differentiating the contracts, the salesperson repositions the company's contract as the truly better value.

It cannot be emphasized enough how many contract sales are lost because a salesperson does not take the time to determine a customer's true objection. There is a tendency to answer the perceived objection, most often missing the real problem. In the example just presented, the customer was not really objecting to price; he failed to see the greater value for the higher price.

Establishing Customer Contact

Potential customers can be contacted via several means. The first method is *trade publications*. Advertising in trade publications is an effective way for large servicing organizations to reach industrial and commercial markets. An advertising program effectively positions the organization and develops recognition of the services offered. Though trade advertising stimulates some response, its primary benefit is to develop recognition of the firm's capabilities, easing the salesperson's selling efforts. Similarly, consumer advertising in magazines and newspapers stimulates awareness of the services offered and also informs customers as to how to get more information on those services.

The second method is *direct mail*. Direct mail is another method for reaching potential customers in the industrial and commercial and the consumer markets. This method can be used to introduce the firm and the services it offers, as well as to follow up on customers of a company's products so as to sell them a service contract. Generally an effective direct mail campaign requires multiple mailings. Three mailings usually is considered a minimum to achieve a meaningful response, though some firms are successful with only one mailing. The format of the mailing piece, its message, and how it conveys that message are also important. There are firms that, for a fee, prepare direct mail pieces as well as handle the mailing and responses. Some magazine publishers also perform these services and mail advertising pieces to their subscribers. Lastly, when invoices are sent to customers, it is sometimes helpful to enclose a brochure about your service contract program. This latter action is particularly effective in consumer markets. In the commercial or industrial areas, the invoice generally goes to accounts payable and thus the sales effort is lost. In these instances, the direct mail piece can be enclosed with instructions to forward it to maintenance or purchasing.

A technique often used to stimulate responses to direct mail is to offer something free to the respondents. For the consumer, you can offer an inexpensive but handy item. For the commercial customers (say, the chief of maintenance), offer an emergency checklist for the product or an inexpensive but useful gadget. The incentive should be something not readily available in stores and of universal interest to the targeted audience. Having a salesperson deliver the gift provides an opportunity for a contract sale. Have the salesperson call in advance and advise that he or she would like to deliver the gift and talk about the customer's service needs.

Consider using a combination of methods to contact customers. Direct mail, magazine and newspaper ads, radio, and television all offer viable options. Many firms consider television prohibitively expensive. If this is your situation, look into advertising on a cable channel. These channels often have more attractive rates.

If a direct mail piece doesn't work, the poor response may be caused by a poorly written letter or brochure. Perhaps the target audience was not properly identified, and the wrong people received the material. Professional help from an advertising or direct mail agency may prove a good investment.

Consider testing your ad or direct mail piece before launching a full-scale program. Send a direct mail piece to a limited number of potential customers and analyze the results. Similarly, mail two different direct mail advertisements to two groups of targeted customers and see which draws the better response. Newspapers, magazines, radio, and television ads can also be tested. Before advertising in multiple newspapers, try the ad in one publication and evaluate the response. But always consider the cost differential between testing a program and launching a full-scale campaign. Because of volume discounts or added costs of going into a select market, in some instances it may cost as much or more to test a program as to do it on the full-scale basis.

Methods of Selling Service Contracts

In some cases service contracts can be sold through the mail. Generally this applies to low-cost contracts whose benefits can be conveyed easily through a written statement. Potential customers cannot ask questions or raise objections. They must evaluate the merits of your offering strictly on their interpretation of what they have read. If they see the value of the contract, they will purchase it; if not, they will deal with their objections by throwing the material away. Customers can be given a means of getting further information if you include a telephone number, preferably toll-free. This method of selling contracts is low in cost compared with other methods, and can be targeted at those most likely to purchase the contract.

To sell most contracts effectively, however, you must use a method that permits the salesperson to interact with the customer, namely, person-to-person sales. But person-to-person sales is costly. Present cost estimates for commercial or industrial sales calls average in excess of $200. If the cost of the contract is in this range, or even three or four times this amount, you cannot justify having a salesperson call on the customer. On the other hand, service contracts that sell for many thousands of dollars can justify a direct sales call, since the cost of that call can easily be included in the price of the contract. Indeed, a person-to-person call may be the only way a customer will consider purchasing a contract when the price is high. For customers to make a high financial commitment, they often must carefully review the features and benefits of the contract to ensure it will provide the services and value desired. For complex, expensive contracts, therefore, the only practical way is face-to-face meetings between customers and the servicing organization's salesperson.

Telemarketing, or telephone selling, is another means of selling contracts. Telemarketing is lower in cost than person-to-person sales. The salesperson's travel cost is eliminated as well as the time spent traveling from company to company or from home to home. More contacts can be made in a day by telephone than through customer visits. What are the disadvantages? Selling by telephone is usually more expensive than direct mail. And, in contrast with person-to-person sales, telephone sales lack the advantage of face-to-face contact. You should review your options and decide which method (or combination of methods) offers the best potential return on your investment. Using a combination of methods means simply that you have to be more creative in your approach to selling service contracts. For example, you may decide to use a direct mail campaign to sell the contracts; for those targeted customers who do not purchase through direct mail, you then have a telemarketing salesperson follow up and try to sell the contract.

Telemarketing

Selling by telephone is similar in most respects to selling face to face. The individual using the telephone to speak with a customer is performing the same sales function as the person who visits a customer's home or place of business. In establishing a telemarketing program, the first thing you should consider is selecting personnel who are trained as salespeople.

In person-to-person sales, salespeople can use physical gestures to emphasize a point and can see customers' reactions to questions or statements. In telephone sales, this is not possible. On the other hand, telephone salespeople can follow a script to ensure the appropriate questions are asked in the proper order, thus guaranteeing that the important aspects of the presentation are covered. Face-to-face salespeople would have difficulty sitting in front of customers with a script in their hands.

Just as telemarketing salespeople cannot see customers' expressions, so customers cannot see salespeople. Voice and inflections become very important. How telemarketing salespeople sound, the enthusiasm they create, and the words they use to express a point are extremely important. Similarly, these salespeople must be trained to "read" the tone and inflections in a customer's voice to understand the true meaning of what is being said.

Since voice is the only means of conveying thoughts and feelings to the customer, telephone salespeople should be trained not only in good speaking techniques but also in maintaining those traits throughout the day. It is easy to start off in the morning with an expressive, enthusiastic voice, but as the day wears on, that voice can fall into a monotone. Successful telemarketing salespeople do not let this happen.

Expressive words help the listener create a mental picture. These combine with the speaker's enthusiasm to get the customer excited. How many times have you had a telephone conversation with someone and developed a mental picture of that person based on how he or she speaks on the telephone? That image may be positive or negative because of *how* something was said, often regardless of what was said. Enthusiasm can be created by training telemarketing salespeople to smile when they speak. It is difficult not to be enthusiastic when you are smiling.

To be understood and have the key points in the presentation remain with the customer, it is important that telephone salespeople speak clearly and slowly, with their voices rising and falling to create variety and emphasis. This does not mean using a "sing-song" or a wailing voice to get attention. (It may get attention, but also turn the customer off.) Salespeople must remember that customers may not be taking notes. In making the presentations, salespeople periodically may have to summarize important benefits to ensure that customers have retained the information. It may also be wise for them to ask customers if they have a pencil and paper handy to record important information.

The Script

The telemarketing script is a key element in ensuring a complete, successful presentation. By the same token, the script should not be read, lest it convey a "canned" performance. The script is a guide for salespeople to follow; flexibility is important in the presentation.

Customers are not following a script and, as such, will not adhere to the telemarketing pattern. There is the story of the salesperson who was making a presentation to a customer from a script. The customer interrupted to ask a question. After answering the question, the salesperson went back to the beginning of the script. A little while later, the customer asked another question. The salesperson answered it and went back to the beginning of the script again. This went on several times more until the salesperson in frustration said, "Will you let me finish first before you keep interrupting me with all those silly questions?" He lost the sale.

An advantage of telemarketing is, of course, that salespeople can use a script without customers being aware of one. The key is planning. Script planning parallels the steps in preparing a service marketing plan. The first step is to determine what the present situation is. You can gather much information from the marketing plan. Use questions such as, Who are the competing firms? What contracts do they offer? How do they market them? What are the prices of their contracts? How do the features and benefits of your contract compare with their contracts? What are your contracts' strengths and weaknesses (assets and liabilities, if you prefer) as compared to their contracts?

Having studied the situation analysis, your next step is to establish objectives. Will your objective be to sell a contract, or is your purpose to set up an appointment for a salesperson to visit the customer? If your objective is to sell a service contract, then which one will be emphasized in the presentation? Why? It is important to have objectives clearly stated, so that telemarketing salespeople can focus on these objectives. Wandering from subject to subject results in longer phone calls, and customers tiring of the conversation before salespeople have an opportunity to secure the sale.

Once you've established the objectives, then you can develop the script. Design and flow of the script should point toward the objectives.

The greeting or opening statement should introduce the salesperson and your company. It should be simple and clear: "Good morning. Is this Mr. Jones, Chief of Maintenance? This is Kathy Smith of ACT Company. We recently installed ten computers at your new facility in Anytown." What the telemarketing salesperson has done is identify who she is, and the firm she represents; she has also built a bridge between her firm and the customer by telling him that they share a mutual interest or bond, that is, that *her company's equipment* was installed in *his facility*. This helps generate interest and builds rapport.

If, for some reason, the person answering the phone is not Mr. Jones, then the salesperson asks to be transferred to Mr. Jones' office. What if Mr. Jones is no longer with the company? Then the salesperson asks who has replaced him, and speaks with that individual instead.

The next step is the "grabber." The grabber arouses interest so that a customer wants to hear more. A grabber statement should point out an immediate benefit to the customer. "Mr. Jones, my company has a program that can reduce your service costs by thirty percent." Or, "Mr. Jones, how would you like to save $10,000 in service costs next year?" Or, "Mr. Jones, I imagine the addition of the ten new computers has put a strain on your maintenance staff. Well, I'm calling because we have a program that will solve that problem and make your job easier." The grabber sets the stage and opens the customer's mind for the sales presentation to follow.

After a short pause to let the grabber sink in, the telemarketing salesperson proceeds with the questioning phase of the sale. Since you have prepared a feature-benefit analysis, you have the basis for the questions that can be formulated to determine the benefits desired. Questions to be asked should have been prepared in advance and included in the script. As indicated in the section on sales techniques, these exploratory questions help you find out what products the customer has and how they are presently serviced. Once the problems are identified, a salesperson can begin asking questions to target specific benefits: "You mentioned that when multiple failures occur, you do not have enough personnel to make the repair in a timely manner. This results in excessive down time for the equipment and high labor costs for overtime. Would you like to free yourself of this problem?" If the customer replies yes (and that will be the case if earlier questions pointed to this as a true concern), then the salesperson can note that.

In questioning the customer, a salesperson should keep that customer involved in the conversation by mixing questions that are both open ended and closed. And open-ended question is one that must be answered with a sentence. For example, "Mr. Jones, what do you consider to be the major problems you presently are encountering in the servicing of your equipment?" Mr. Jones cannot answer this question with just a yes or no. Closed-ended questions can be answered with one word: "Mr. Jones, are you satisfied with the amount of up time you are experiencing with your product?" Here Mr. Jones can simply say yes or no. Using all closed-ended questions gets the salesperson through the questioning phase quickly, but does not keep the customer involved. A mixture of question types keeps the customer involved and listening.

Having listened to each answer carefully, the telemarketing salesperson then generates a list of problems or needs that have been expressed by the customer. Using the feature-benefit analysis, the salesperson can tell the customer what service contracts are offered and how each will solve the customer's problem, that is, how each will benefit him. For example, "Mr. Jones, you mentioned that one of your major concerns is the cost of down time. You estimated that down time costs your company $15,000 per hour. Since you only have one technician on your staff, it will cost your company $30,000 for a two-hour repair. Under the terms of our contract, we will send at least two technicians for major repairs, thereby completing the repair in one hour and saving your company $15,000 per hour. Just think of the savings that you can enjoy over a year. With the service contract you do not have to keep a full-time technician on your payroll, which is an added savings. Don't you agree that this will save you money?" The salesperson should move on to cover all the customer's needs by describing the benefits offered by the service contracts. Each step should be a deliberate approach toward closing the sale. The objective is to set in the customer's mind how the contract will solve the problems and meet the needs—how it will make the job easier and more rewarding. In addition, the salesperson should believe firmly that the service contract will benefit that customer; if the salesperson cannot appreciate the benefits that the contract offers, then he or she will have difficulty selling it with enthusiasm.

Once the benefits have been explained and the price of the contract outlined, the salesperson should move to a trial close. If the customer raises any objections, the salesperson should handle them as outlined in the section on selling techniques. Once those objections have been dealt with, again the salesperson should attempt to close the sale, reaffirm a wise purchase, and conclude the call.

The script should list clearly all the steps that telemarketing salespeople should take. (See Figure 7-3 for an outline of a typical sales script.) The telephone salespeople should work with the script, with the feature-benefit analysis, and with a competitive analysis (see Table

(*text continued on p. 152*)

Figure 7-3. Outline for a telemarketing sales script.

Telemarketing Sales Script

1. *Objective of the Call.* Stated in clear terms so the telemarketing salesperson fully understands it. It is included along with the script so it will not be forgotten:

   "The objective of the call is to sell the customer a Full Repair and Maintenance contract."

2. *Introduction.* It should be read verbatim to ensure completeness and clarity. Say it slowly to permit comprehension:

   "Hello, is this Mr. Jones? [Pause] This is Karen Smith of ACT Service Company. We recently installed a computer at your State Street office [or at your home]. Are you satisfied with it?"

3. *The grabber.*

   "Mr. Jones how would you like to not have to worry about unexpected repair bills on your computer for the next *five* years?"

4. *Questioning.* Make a list of the questions to be asked of the customer. Exploratory questions, designed to determine the type of equipment the customer has (or to verify make and models shown in your records) are asked first. Exploratory questions are read directly from the script with a space provided below each question to write the customer's answer. Flag those replies that indicate a problem or need that the service contract can help resolve. Next, the benefit questions are asked. These are designed to gain agreement from the customer that he or she perceives a feature as a true benefit.

5. *Sell the benefits.* Having established the benefits most useful to the customer, the salesperson shows the customer how the service contract meets each of those needs.

6. *Handle objections.* In preparing the script, list all the possible objections that can be raised by the customer. For each objection, give the question that the salesperson should ask to clarify the response and get the true objection. Below that, list responses to anticipated answers to clarification questions.

   Customer: I like the provisions of your service contract, but your price is too high.
   Salesperson: Why do you think the price is too high?

Figure 7-3, continued.

Here are two anticipated responses:

    1.   **Customer:**   I can get the same contract for $20 less from XYZ Service Corporation.

       Salesperson: Yes, that's true, but don't you agree that a two-hour response time rather than a four-hour response time and our extra maintenance visit is worth $20?

    2.   **Customer:**   It costs more than I can get approved in my budget.

       Salesperson: How much can you get approved in your budget?

       Customer: $900.

       Salesperson: We have a modified repair and maintenance contract which provides excellent coverage and only costs $850. Let me tell you about it.

    The salesperson is given an effective response for every anticipated reason for an objection. Give considerable thought to every possible objection, the question to be asked in response to that objection, and the salesperson's answer to show the customer how the contract's benefits overcome the objection.

    7. *The trial close.* List a number of effective trial closes. The salesperson will then select the most appropriate one for each customer:

> 1. "Mr. Jones, would you prefer the Full Repair and Maintenance or the Repair Only contract?"
> 2. "Mr. Jones, you agreed that the Full Repair and Maintenance contract, which provides you with four maintenance inspections and unlimited repair service calls, is an excellent value at $500. In order to process your contract, let me verify your address. It's Acme Manufacturing, 123 Any Road, Anytown, 00000. Is that correct?"

    8. *The close.* Here the agreement is confirmed:

> "I will send you a Full Repair and Maintenance Contract that costs $500 to Acme Manufacturing, 123 Any Road, Anytown, 00000."

    9. *Reassuring the customer.* Here the salesperson assures the customer that he or she has made a wise purchase.

> "Mr. Jones, you have made a wise purchase and I know you will be happy with your new service contract. Should you need service or have any questions, please call Jim Smith, your personal customer service representative. His phone number is 1-800-123-4567."

Figure 7-3, continued.

10. *Say good-bye.*

"It's been a pleasure speaking with you. Have a nice day. Good-bye."

11. Hang Up.
    Go on to the next call.

Table 7-1. Competitive analysis, Repair Only contract.

Feature	Benefit	ACT Service Co.	XYZ Service Co.	QAR Co.	Jim's Service Co.
_____	_____	X		X	X
	_____	X	X	X	X
	_____	X		X	X
_____	_____	X			
	_____		X		X
	_____	X	X		
	_____	X	X		
_____	_____	X	X	X	
	_____	X		X	
_____	_____	X		X	X
	_____	X	X		
	_____	X	X	X	
	_____		X		
	_____	X		X	
_____	_____	X	X		
	_____	X		X	
	_____	X			X
	_____	X	X		

NOTE: The feature and all the benefits that feature offers are stated. Then each competitor is listed, with indications if its contract offers that feature and any of its benefits. A blank for the feature line indicates that the firm does not offer the feature in its contract. Likewise, if the firm's contract has the feature, it may still not offer all the benefits because of the provisions of its contract.

7-1 on p. 151). A competitive analysis is an evaluation of all the possible features and benefits that service contracts provide for customers. These features and benefits are listed by contract type, e.g., maintenance, repair, and so on. Each competitor is listed, including your own company. The companies are evaluated for individual features and benefits. It is important to do this objectively and not downgrade competitors and enhance your own company. Once the analysis is complete you can evaluate your position effectively. You'll be able to give knowledgeable replies to customer questions and objections and discover your own liabilities. You'll be able to take corrective action, or at least deal with the issue if the customer asks. You'll also be in a position to advise the customer of your competitors' vulnerable areas.

As mentioned earlier, salespeople should be flexible, using the script as a plan. After a while they will become very familiar with the feature-benefit analysis and the competitive analysis, as well as the script, and will be inclined to discard them. Don't allow that. Salespeople might have a tendency to skip over items or wander off the task at hand if these materials are not in front of them.

Training Telemarketing Sales Personnel

Good sales techniques are developed through practice. Once you've prepared the script, telemarketing people should read it and become comfortable with it. Establish sales situations to give them practice. Using an internal phone system, have them dial the training manager's extension and make a sales presentation. Record the conversations (with the full knowledge of the participants) so you can critique each salesperson's handling of the script, as well as evaluate voice, tone, pitch, speed, pauses, and so on. As mentioned previously, voice is very important in telemarketing because it is a means of conveying the salesperson's feelings. A high-pitched voice demonstrates lack of confidence. Speaking too quickly means important points will be lost, but talking in a deliberately slow monotone will put the customer to sleep instead. The presentation should be lively, clear, and enthusiastic, but not forced and artificial; customers perceive an approach that is not genuine. Check if salespeople pause after making an important point, especially after asking for the sale. In fact, when asking for the sale, they should remain quiet until the customer responds. Only after you or the sales trainer is satisfied, should a new salesperson attempt to try some actual calls, then you should monitor these calls and critique afterwards.

Automating Telemarketing

You can use a computer to help you establish a telemarketing program. The script can be programmed into the computer along with the feature-benefit analysis and the competitive analysis. At the strike of a key, a salesperson can have the next step of the script appear or view other information as needed.

The computer can also be programmed to dial the call, keep a record of sales calls that have not been completed (for example, if the person was out or the phone wasn't answered), and automatically dial the next person on a list of targeted accounts. Salespeople also can enter answers to questions and other information for retrieval when needed. The computer helps salespeople stay organized, minimizes clutter in their work areas, and improves productivity by saving the time it takes to look up the next number, dial it, and so on.

Another item of note is the fully automated telemarketing system. These units employ automatic dialing technology combined with a recorded script. The number is dialed and, when the phone is answered, the recording proceeds through the script, pausing at times for answers from the customer and followed by a pause for the customer to accept the offer. Because contact is between the customer and a machine, it lends itself best to selling inexpensive service contracts, mostly to the consumer market.

Compensating Telemarketing Sales Personnel

Many companies view telemarketers as customer service representatives rather than as salespeople, and compensate them accordingly. Managers who readily establish quotas for field sales personnel have trouble setting goals for telemarketers because they are guided by this misconception. Treat telemarketing sales personnel as you would the product or field service sales force. Each telemarketing salesperson should be presented with a comprehensive written compensation plan, outlining sales quotas and incentives. The plan should be clear and understandable to the salesperson; a plan that is difficult to interpret is worthless, since it will not help meet your ultimate objectives.

In setting up a compensation plan, you should list the objectives of the telemarketing program. For example, is the purpose to sell contracts or to set appointments for field sales personnel? If it is to sell contracts, which contracts do you want to sell? List them in order of preference. How many contracts do you want to sell? What dollar amount does this represent? How much profit will these contract sales generate?

Once you've defined your objectives, you can begin developing a compensation program that will direct and motivate sales personnel toward meeting those objectives. Set quotas for each telemarketing salesperson commensurate with the projected volume for those assigned accounts. Accounts should be assigned consistently by territory, type of account (size, industry, and so forth), product purchased, or another means. The advantage of giving salespeople accounts that continually fall into the same category (or combination of categories) is that each salesperson will become familiar with the nature of those accounts and, as such, will develop expertise in that area. This permits them not only to be more productive, but also to be able to detect changes in the environment that can be used in future planning.

Though a base salary is generally given, additional incentives in the form of commissions, bonuses, and awards can also be offered to those who achieve their goals. For maximum impact, pay out incentives as often as possible. Establish weekly, monthly, and quarterly quotas to maintain momentum, with an extra bonus, perhaps, for meeting the annual quota. Use imagination to create the compensation plan. If you want a particular type of contract to sell in greater volume than others, consider added incentives for selling these contracts.

Once the compensation plan is written, review it carefully to ensure that it is easy to understand and will accomplish your goals. Also determine what it will cost in return for the added business it will generate. When you are satisfied, present the plan to the sales force. In the presentation, explain how the plan works, and also provide an example of the incentives that can be earned if the salespeople sell the contracts in the desired volumes.

Once the plan is in effect, monitor it carefully to be sure it is performing as planned. If not, then adjust it as necessary. Bonuses can be added to commissions to spur sales of specific contracts. Incentives can be short- or long-term. You can also make them open-ended, and keep them in force until your objective is met.

Controlling the Telemarketing Program

To have a successful telemarketing program, you must establish methods to ensure maximum productivity from sales personnel and install control procedures to be certain the program is providing the planned results. Supply salespeople with lists of accounts to be called each day. The list can be kept on customer account cards, with the customer name, address, phone number, and products targeted for contract sales. Additionally, list any other contracts sold to the customer in the past, with comments on any complaints or compliments received. However, all this information is stored more easily in the computer. If the salespeople work with a terminal, then they can call up the appropriate data as they need it.

Customer account cards form the basis of a control system for the salespeople. As each call is made, they note on the card if a contract is sold, the date sold, the date it takes effect, the type of contract, and so on. The card is then passed on to someone who types in the data on the contract and forwards the contract to the customer.

Should the customers called not be in, the salespeople place the cards in a stack for follow up the next day or later that day. If the purpose of the call is to set up an appointment, then the card is forwarded to the field salesperson, with the appointment date, time, and other pertinent information indicated.

The procedure is similar with a computer terminal. Information received is entered directly into the computer. If a follow-up call is required, the account is placed in a follow-up file within the computer program. The computer can be programmed to sort follow-up calls in the order those calls are scheduled to be returned. When a field salesperson makes sales calls, the appointments can be routed to the sales department and printed on the field salesperson's terminal.

The customer account cards (or copies of the cards—you can use multipart forms) can be routed back to you for evaluation. Since the cards are coded, showing which telemarketing salesperson is assigned to each account, it is easy to analyze how many calls are made in a given day, how many contracts are sold or appointments made, and what the reasons are for lost sales. This information can help you determine if the telemarketing personnel need further training, if revised or additional contracts are required, if the prices are too high or too low, or if more salespeople are needed. Again, the computer can sort the data faster and more accurately than you can manually.

Remember that customer account cards or computers are tools, not substitutes for good management decisions. When putting together a marketing program, you should remember that the basic elements are the same, whether you're selling to a homeowner or a major corporation. You must consider the needs and benefits of the potential customers when developing the feature-benefit analysis and when assembling the competitive analysis. Writing the telemarketing script is the same situation. Many times managers believe that their industry is unique and they can't use the marketing concepts presented here. Reflect on it. You will find that, if not all, many of the concepts are applicable to your situation. You only have to adapt them to your industry.

Person-to-Person Sales

The techniques outlined for telemarketing are also applicable to person-to-person sales. Complex installations and large accounts may require calling at the customer's place of business. The telemarketing group can research the account—itemize the equipment it has, how it is presently serviced, and so on—and also set up an appointment for a salesperson to call.

To set up an appointment, telemarketing people follow the steps outlined earlier, with some revision. When telemarketing people tell the customers what the company has to offer, they simply outline the program to hold the customer's interest. They answer any questions, then use the trial close technique to set up an appointment: "Will Monday at 9 A.M. be okay, or Tuesday at 10 A.M. be better?" They confirm the appointment, then say good-bye.

When selling face to face, salespeople enjoy some advantages over those selling via the telephone, but they must also deal with some disadvantages. One advantage is that salespeople can read the customer's body language during the presentation. Body language involves facial expressions and body movements. For example, it is generally thought that a customer who leans back with arms crossed in front is taking a defensive position, and this position tells the salesperson that the prospect is not receptive to what is being said. Under these circumstances, a salesperson attempts to build trust, usually through questioning and with other body language. By asking exploratory questions, the salesperson can determine the interests and needs of that customer. Once those needs are determined, the problem can be addressed.

Other defensive signals of body language include the customer's turning away from the salesperson and leaning back with hands behind the head. If the customers clasp their hands or touch their faces, they are indicating uncertainty or nervousness. If salespeople recognize these signals, then they can act to reassure customers of sincerity and a desire to be of assistance. When customers lean forward, open their arms, turn and face the salesperson, and tilt their head to one side, they are displaying interest in what is being said and are receptive to the ideas being presented. The salespeople know they are getting their messages across.

Just as body language tells the salesperson how the customer feels, so the body language of the salesperson tells the customer about that salesperson. By developing a relaxed, open posture, the salesperson can encourage an attitude of trust and friendliness in the customer. Whether consciously or unconsciously, customers read a salesperson's body language. If salespeople grasp the chair firmly, clasp their hands, hunch their shoulders, look at the wall or floor when they speak or hold their attaché cases on their lap, they are signalling to the customer that they are nervous and uncertain of themselves. By the same token, a slouched or overly aggressive posture usually turns off the customer. Salespeople should be trained to sit erect, yet appear relaxed when speaking. Good body language develops the customer's confidence in the salesperson. A salesperson can't sell service contracts unless customers believe the contracts will be beneficial to them. Effective body language helps build that confidence.

The question that arises is how to go about building this confidence in your sales personnel. The answer is through training. People can be made aware of the importance of body language, effective questioning, and quality presentation skills. By teaching them these skills and how to use them, you can build an effective sales force. Develop confidence through role playing. Have sales personnel play the role of prospect as well as salesperson as each goes through a typical sales situation. If a video camera is available, tape the role playing so the participants can later observe their mannerisms and review their questioning and presentation skills.

Many companies retain a professional consultant and trainer to help develop these skills. Effective training is a good investment, since it quickly brings personnel up to a high level of proficiency. The sales force can be generating sales instead of spending time trying to learn such skills through trial and error, which results more often in poor selling habits.

In addition to the extra communication through body language, person-to-person sales offers the advantage to salespeople of being able to show customers the service contracts and point out their features. Also, testimonial letters can be shown and sales aids demonstrated. A disadvantage of person-to-person sales is that salespeople cannot use a script, as can the telemarketer. Customers inevitably go into a defensive posture if a salesperson sits in front of them and reads a script. Salespeople must prepare their presentations (script, if you will) and go through them from memory. It is difficult, but a professional, well-trained salesperson can do it and do it well.

Another disadvantage of person-to-person selling is the high cost of each sales call and the time wasted traveling from prospect to prospect. A telemarketing person has the advantage of speaking with prospects anywhere in the world at any time. If a prospect is not in or is busy, the telemarketer can immediately call another prospect and get back to the busy individual later. Salespeople who must visit customers' places of business do not have that kind of flexibility. To make the best use of time, they must set up and confirm appointments, as well as plan their appointment schedules to minimize the travel between places of business. This is called effective time and territory management.

To determine which method of sales approach is best, you must review the type and cost of the service contracts you are selling. If the cost of a contract is high and the provisions complex, customers may demand to see a salesperson. If a contract is straightforward and the cost low, then telemarketing, direct mail, or another form of direct marketing is the best way. Generally, you should determine if some form of direct marketing is possible before using a field sales force. Look at the cost of your desired marketing method to see if it can be justified. Presently, it costs over $100 to make a person-to-person call to a consumer and over $200 to make a similar call on a commercial or industrial customer. If a contract sells for $100 or $200, your organization will lose money before you even begin to fulfill the contract. Lastly, you should understand your customer base to determine which marketing methods these customers will respond to best, then select the most cost-effective alternative.

Organizing the Service Contract Marketing Function

The question that often arises within a company is whether the servicing group or the product sales function is best equipped to handle the service contracts sales or, for that matter, service sales in general.

There is no simple answer to this question. On the surface it may appear that since product sales personnel are trained in selling techniques, they can do a more effective job. However, they are trained in selling a tangible product, and service contracts are intangibles. Also, the relative cost of a service contract usually is small in comparison to the dollar value of the product. This may lead sales personnel to concentrate on product sales and ignore contract sales, especially if they are working on commission or have high quotas.

Establishing and training a separate service sales division can be time consuming and costly. To sell service contracts, the service sales personnel will be calling on the same customers as product sales people, thus duplicating effort and doubling travel costs. Also, customers may be put off by having to meet with different sales personnel from the same company.

How then does the servicing division decide how to market its contracts effectively? To begin, you must look at your total company and the products you service. If your firm's business is limited to service, that is, it is not engaged in product sales, then you don't have a product sales force and that option is eliminated. Let's consider this situation first.

The Service Firm

What are the options open to the manager of a servicing firm? The manager must first look at the nature of the product being serviced. Is it a consumer or an industrial product? Will the contract price be relatively high or low? Will the company be selling consumables that will be used by the customer in operating or maintaining the product? For example, if you are selling service contracts to homeowners with water softeners, will your firm be selling the salt that is consumed by this product? If your firm is selling service contracts on computer printers, will you also be selling computer paper, ribbons, and so on?

Once you assess the full scope of your selling activity and determine the approximate price of the contract, you can more intelligently evaluate your marketing options. If you are selling a low-cost contract and also selling consumables, then you may consider using telemarketing. Telemarketing sales personnel can establish a close rapport with customers and maintain an on-going relationship, not only to sell the contract and the renewals but also the consumables. You may also look at using direct mail, either alone or in conjunction with tele-marketing. If you are selling very low-priced service contracts and if few if any consumables are also sold, the cost of a telemarketing opera-tion may not be justified. In these instances, your only options may be direct mail or advertising.

If your service agreement sells for a relatively high price, then you should assess whether the agreement can be sold via telemarketing or direct mail, or if the only way the customer will make such an invest-ment is through person-to-person sales. If a salesperson must be used, then you have several options. Assuming for the moment that your firm is not affiliated with a product sales function, you can develop an in-house sales organization or can use an independent sales group. The independents (often called manufacturer's representatives) generally will handle products, services, or both. They are purely sales compa-nies and usually work on straight commission. The advantage of this type of firm is that you will only have to pay them when they sell a contract, thus the cost of selling the contract is variable. A problem that may arise when using independent sales firms is that they represent other companies at the same time, and your organization will be com-peting with these other companies for their selling time. However, the independents normally try to handle compatible products so that when they visit customers they can sell more than one product or service. It is important that you review the other products that they are selling as well as the commission rates they receive from those suppliers to en-sure that your service contract sales get the attention they require. If the other suppliers are also service companies, and they are paying a higher commission rate than you are, your contracts may not command the attention they deserve.

The Service Function in a Larger Organization

If your division is affiliated with a supplier of the product, then you have the option of using its product sales personnel to sell your contracts. Doing this will save you the fixed costs associated with es-tablishing a sales function, including office space, desks, chairs, tele-phones, file cabinets, automobiles, and so on. Additionally, the sup-plier will hire and train sales personnel. On the other hand, if you hired sales personnel, you would have the undivided attention of these people because their sole responsibility would be selling service.

If you decide to use product sales personnel to sell service, establish a basic understanding with the corresponding sales and marketing managers as to how the sales force will be deployed to sell contracts. Establish commission rates and other incentives. Assign quotas to ensure that contract sales goals are met, and establish a means by which they can report progress and problems to you. This reporting can take the form of weekly written sales reports, which include the number of each type of contract sold by territory and the dollar amounts of those sales. Use a data base program to track this information and sort it in a way that is useful to you.

Once you establish the method of going to market, you can turn your attention to developing a marketing management organizational structure. If the product sales force is to be used, then designate one person as the service marketing manager. This individual will act as liaison with the product sales function, develop sales aids, monitor the marketplace to ensure that current contract offerings are responsive to customer needs, keep track of sales to ensure goals are being met, and in general be responsible for the overall marketing of service contracts. In the small firm, this role may be filled by the service manager but if at all possible have someone who is marketing oriented to manage this important function. With an integral service sales organization, telemarketing, or extensive direct mail operation, you will need a larger marketing staff. At the minimum you should have a marketing manager and either a field sales manager for the field sales force or a telemarketing sales manager, either of whom will report to the service marketing manager. The service marketing manager should normally report to the service manager. Additionally, hire support personnel to assist these managers. A large sales force may require district managers; a sizable telemarketing operation may demand supervisors to assist the telemarketing sales manager.

View the total marketing operation, and structure your marketing organization in a manner that accomplishes your goals in the most efficient and economical way. It is important to explore all the alternatives and evaluate each carefully. Also look to the future and try to establish an organizational growth plan that easily and smoothly meets the demands placed on the marketing function as service contract sales grow.

An Overview of the Marketing Plan

For Seth, it was time to sit back and take a final review of his marketing plans. He would have to apply the various general marketing principles and techniques to his situation. In particular, he would have to consider first how his service function would sell the contracts and then how he would convince the distributors and dealers to take on the service contract program.

Selling a Servicing Organization's Capabilities

Seth knew that his firm had a sterling reputation for service. Unless your organization has a well-known reputation for fast, quality service, customers must be sold on its ability and willingness to provide prompt service. A service contract represents a promise to perform certain duties. The piece of paper stating that promise means nothing if the product isn't functioning and the customer can't get the needed service. A common question that a customer asks is, "How do I know you'll show up when I need you?"

When preparing to sell service contracts, you must develop a plan to sell your organization's capabilities and desires to satisfy the customer. First, you must show that the firm has the *means* to respond. Advise the targeted customer of the number of service vehicles and service centers, extent of your parts inventories, number of technicians, and extent and sophistication of your diagnostic equipment. Next, indicate your company's ability to respond *quickly* by pointing out that service vehicles are equipped with two-way radios, service technicians carry beepers, and there are a certain number of dispatchers to handle emergency calls. Third, indicate how many customers are actively being serviced. Emphasize the number who have been under contract with your organization for many years.

It's a good idea to provide sales personnel with a looseleaf book containing testimonial letters from satisfied customers. This is a strong motivator, since customers can read for themselves how others feel about your service company. The letters should be on customers' stationery. Also, it is a good idea to secure written authorization to use the letters in this manner from the persons who wrote them. You can obtain some letters simply by asking customers for them. A good time to do this is immediately after you receive a compliment. Customers are in a positive frame of mind, and will gladly put their thoughts into writing. If some customers don't get around to writing a letter shortly after you've asked them, offer to write it for them. If they agree, write the letters, have their secretaries type them on company letterhead, and then present them to the customers for their signatures. This gets you the testimonial letters with minimum effort on the customers' part.

For a telemarketing campaign, have the salespeople stress your organization's ability and willingness to provide service. Have them use the suggestions just mentioned and tell the customers about the testimonial letters. If customers want to see some of the letters, then forward copies either separately or preferably with service contracts ready for their signature.

Selling Contracts Through Distributors and Dealers

Companies like Seth's, that sell their products through distributors, dealers, or both ultimately are responsible for the servicing of those products, whether or not the distributor or dealer renders the service. The reason for this is that the manufacturer must ensure that its products are being serviced properly if it hopes to succeed in the marketplace. There is, therefore, a shared responsibility between the manufacturer and the distributor/dealer.

The manufacturer can fulfill its obligation by assisting distributors and dealers in establishing viable service programs. The manufacturer can develop standard suggested service contracts, marketing programs, and management techniques for successful implementation and administration of the service plans. If a service contract program is to be embraced by the distributors and dealers, they must be shown how they will benefit from such a program. For example, they must see how they can improve their profits through added service business, peripheral and add-on equipment sales, and so on. They must be shown how service contracts will solve their cash flow problems, improve their scheduling, and permit more efficient utilization of their service personnel.

Once you've presented the concept and shown the advantages, then introduce the tools and mechanics of establishing and administering the program. Include sample contracts, direct mail pieces and promotional items, and suggested direct sales and telemarketing programs. You may wish to conduct seminars on the implementation of the program, including record-keeping, maintenance, sales features and benefits, contract pricing, reserves, contract service scheduling, as well as advantages and implementation procedures of a contract insurance program.

In establishing a distributor/dealer service contract program, it is a good idea to develop a corporate title for the program. This helps provide a unified service image, even if service is rendered by independent outlets. On the surface such a program has its liabilities, since the manufacturer may receive complaints about poor service from a distributor or a dealer's failure to honor a contract. In reality these are not problems but strong points of the program because they help fulfill the manufacturer's goal of strengthening its position in the marketplace. By becoming aware of problems, the manufacturer can take corrective action to maintain a positive image.

Corporate contract support permits manufacturers to provide dealers and distributors with a standardized contract featuring the corporate name and logo, for example, *ACT No. 1 Service* or *ACT Preferred Service Agreement.* Nevertheless, make provisions within the contract to indicate that the agreement is between the customer and the dealer. You can further limit performance liability by taking service contract insurance or funding a policy for the distributors and dealers. This insurance provides customers with added protection, in that they know that either the insurance company or the manufacturer will back up the independent outlet. This helps enhance the product's value, especially at times when the dealer or distributor network is new and customers fear a possible shakeout. An example of this is the current proliferation of computer dealers. Often customers are concerned whether a dealer will be around in six months or a year. Contract insurance or a strong service contract program backed by the manufacturer helps allay these fears, and induces customers to buy a specific brand, even at a premium price.

When marketing service contracts, whether directly or through a distributor/dealer network, you have to plan your strategy. Utilize some or all of the techniques outlined here to formulate a marketing plan that meets your service contract sales goals.

8

Contract Administration

Seth was more confident than ever that the service contract program would succeed. With achievement on the horizon, he was not about to have all his work wasted because of poor execution or control. He understood that administering the contract program effectively was a key element in the long-term success of the project. Seth set out to establish the procedures for ensuring that systems would be in place to effectively monitor and control the service contract program.

One of the key elements of efficient administration is simplicity. This should be your byword in keeping records, scheduling service, and controlling the process as a whole. Using a computer not only improves accuracy, but eliminates most time-consuming routine labor associated with good record keeping and other administrative procedures.

The goal in selling a contract should be maximum standardization of the terms and conditions. Occasionally a customer will request special contract provisions; this is particularly true with industrial and commercial customers. Review such requests for special conditions carefully, since they can not only prove administratively expensive, but result in a record-keeping nightmare. Decide whether to accept or reject these special conditions based on your organization's ability to handle the request profitably. Consider also the impact that decision will have on future business with the customer. If you accept special conditions, add the cost of fulfilling those conditions onto the price of the contract.

An aspect of contract administration that easily can be simplified is the handling of payments. Payment in full, paid in advance, not only has cash flow advantages but cuts down on administrative expenses. Offer a discount to customers who pay in full, in advance. If the nature of the industry requires periodic invoicing, then the costs of multiple billings, as well as the loss of interest that would have been earned from a fully prepaid contract, should be reflected in the price. The computer can simplify a payment plan by generating invoices when they are due. Remember, however, to consider the extra cost of mailing multiple invoices, recording partial payments, and following up on delinquent accounts.

Special contract conditions and billing and collection are examples of two administrative concerns. There are many others, including how to generate useful reports and analyses and what forms are most effective for best record-keeping. Let's begin, however, with a primary concern—the efficient use of personnel—and eventually conclude with more information on billing and collection.

Efficient Use of Personnel

One of the major advantages of service contracts, as mentioned previously, is the more effective scheduling and utilization of service personnel. In scheduling personnel, consider the ratio of the time service technicians actually spend maintaining or servicing equipment to the time they are available to perform these duties:

$$\text{Utilization} = \frac{\text{Time spent servicing equipment}}{\text{Time available to service equipment}}$$

The ideal ratio is $1:1$. This means that service personnel are fully occupied during working hours.

Productivity, on the other hand, is a measure of how quickly service technicians complete assigned tasks. To measure productivity, compare the time it takes a service technician to complete a specific task to some norm—the norm being the established standard hours to perform a given task:

$$\text{Productivity} = \frac{\text{Standard hours}}{\text{Actual hours}}$$

How the norm (standard hours) is established will be discussed later in this chapter.

Anticipating Demand

The cyclical nature of service repair work necessitates having an adequate number of technicians to meet peak demand requirements while responding to calls within a reasonable amount of time. During peak demand periods, a servicing organization can experience high utilization of service personnel; conversely, during slack periods personnel utilization will be extremely poor. The service contract is the catalyst that allows the servicing firm to maintain a staff large enough to respond quickly to emergencies during peak periods, yet enjoy the economies of full personnel utilization during slack periods.

The maintenance portion of the service contract program provides the opportunity for service personnel to conduct routine, prescheduled preventive maintenance during low-demand periods. This uses their time and avoids idleness that might result with a high degree of unapplied labor. Offering preventive maintenance contracts is most important for companies servicing seasonal products, whose repair demands are high for only part of the year. The computer can schedule service personnel, balance work loads, record data, and produce reports.

For organizations that service products which do not require routine maintenance (for example, a television set), the service contract can still assist in full utilization of personnel. Refer back to Chapter 5, Pricing Service Contracts, to review how you can use statistical failure rates of products to develop your contract pricing. With the same data, you can estimate your work load based on the number of contracts sold (or to be sold). For example, if you calculate that the repair hours per contract, on average, are 15 per year and you have sold 500 contracts, then you can plan to occupy your technicians for 7,500 hours that year. Totaling all the hours planned for all the contracts sold for all the products gives you the total number of hours of service work for that year. Dividing this figure by the number of hours each technician is available to service equipment gives you the number of technicians that can be fully utilized. For example, if each technician produces

1,500 billable hours a year and the total projected contract repair hours for all products comes to 90,000 hours, then 90,000 hours divided by 1,500 hours gives you the planned full utilization of 60 technicians:

$$\frac{90{,}000}{1{,}500} = 60$$

Of course, the anticipated volume of time and material service calls must be added to these figures. Time and material service calls cannot be projected as accurately, and that is one of the advantages of selling service contracts.

Those organizations that service products which do not require preventive maintenance and are also seasonal in nature must balance their work loads by studying the marketplace and seeking out new products to service which are technically related and require service during another time of the year. For example, heating products are generally serviced in the fall and winter, while air-conditioning products are serviced in the spring and summer. If your servicing organization does not wish to compromise its image of specialization in a seasonal product, then it should consider forming a third-party servicing organization (see also Chapter 11). This organization could have a different name and address but would utilize the same technicians. In the winter, they would wear blue uniforms; in the summer, white ones. The key to success, of course, is to ensure that the technicians are well trained and competent in servicing both types of products. It is important that customers get the highest quality of service for which they are paying.

Scheduling the Calls

Computerized dispatch programs help prioritize and schedule service calls. The computer program permits you to establish priorities for service calls. For example, software can be set up to give first priority to service calls from contract customers; within that category, further priority can be given to calls from customers with special requirements in their contracts. In a similar fashion, the program can be designed to give regular time and material customers priority over occasional customers.

In addition to classifying calls, the computerized dispatch program can assign technicians to each call based on such factors as territory, product specializations, or previous experience with the account. The computerized dispatch program greatly assists the service dispatcher. In fact, it can issue a list of calls for each technician each day, without any involvement by service center personnel. Many firms feel that this system removes the human element, and opt to have a dispatcher review the computerized schedule to make adjustments necessary for good customer relations or for greater efficiency, should there be changes not yet programmed into the computer.

Your ability to meet your profit objectives depends on the skill and accuracy you employ in estimating and controlling costs. Scheduling costs can be controlled by ensuring that service personnel are properly trained to perform tasks quickly and accurately and by using cost-efficient technology (for example, by employing modern diagnostic equipment to troubleshoot a problem). One of the key elements in controlling costs is using effective scheduling procedures.

Setting Time Standards

Knowing how long it takes to perform service procedures is a key element in cost-effective scheduling. By establishing time standards for each task, you can estimate the total time to service a given product by adding up the times for individual tasks. This will be especially accurate for routine inspection and maintenance calls. If you've kept records on actual times to perform given tasks on particular products and this history can be sorted easily, then your work is greatly simplified.

Again, use the computer to simplify the job. For example, assume that you want to establish a time standard for replacement of the filter in Model AB123. Give the computer the command to sort all the occasions that this filter was replaced. (Obviously, the data had been entered into the data base from service records during a period of time— say, the last year.) See the following page for the computer display.

Obviously the average service firm would have replaced filters many more times during a given year than shown here. These 24 entries are sufficient to explain the concept, however.

Note that on two occasions it took the technicians 11 minutes to replace the filter, on two other occasions it took 12 minutes, on three occasions it took 13 minutes, and so on. The recorded times total 348

Time to Replace Filter Model AB123

Minutes

11
11
12
12
13
13
13
14
14
14
14
15
15
15
15
16
16
16
16
16
16
17
20

Total   348 minutes

---

minutes. With 24 times recorded, you can calculate the average (mean) time to perform this task:

$$\frac{348}{24} = 14.5 \text{ minutes}$$

Using 14.5 minutes as a time standard may be sufficient for many organizations, however you may wonder how the data were distributed. For example, you may be concerned that the time periods vary so much. If two technicians each took 14.5 minutes to perform the task, the average time would be:

$$14.5 + 14.5 = 29$$
$$\frac{29}{2} = 14.5 \text{ minutes}$$

On the other hand, if one technician took 15 minutes and the other took 14 minutes, the average time would also be 14.5 minutes. Now consider the situation in which one technician takes 4 minutes to change the filter and another, 25 minutes:

$$4 + 25 = 29 \text{ minutes}$$
$$\frac{29}{2} = 14.5 \text{ minutes}$$

You have the same average time as before, but there is a great difference in the technicians' performances. In the first two examples there is a notable uniformity; in the last example, there is a considerable difference. The technician who took 25 minutes would find a time standard of 14 or 15 minutes too stringent, and the one who took 4 minutes would find it too liberal. More important, this disparity should tell you that something is wrong. Lack of skill or training, sloppy workmanship, wasted time on the job, or such could be a cause of the wide spread in labor time. After investigating the cause, you could take corrective action. It should be your goal to minimize wide dissimilarities in the time, although this does not mean that if you achieve consistency you can be satisfied that you have a high level of productivity. They could all be performing the task consistently slow. It is, nevertheless, important to strive for similarity in performance, and your performance times should be the best achievable while maintaining quality workmanship.

How does a service manager determine that degree of consistency? And, based on this information, how can it be used to establish time standards? The answer is standard statistical analysis. You plot on a graph the various time periods that it took to replace a filter. The time period forms the X axis (or abscissa) and the frequency of occurrence is placed on the Y axis (or ordinate). Figure 8-1 shows that the plotted data will most likely fall into a bell-shaped pattern, commonly called a normal distribution curve, if all the like points are connected. The mean, or average, time period (that is, 14.5 minutes in this example) falls in the middle of the curve.

If you understand this concept of statistical analysis, you can find

Figure 8-1.   Distribution of times to replace filter.

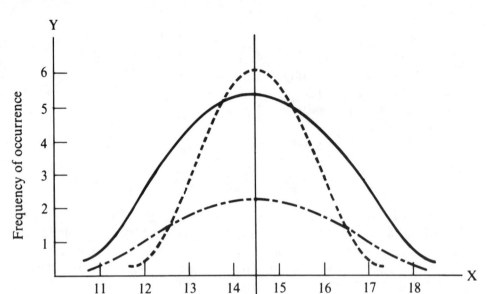

14.5

Time (minutes) required to replace filter

——————— normal time distribution

- - - - - - very consistent times

— — · — inconsistent times

out how consistent the time frames are, using the standard deviation from the mean. The standard deviation, symbolized by the lowercase Greek letter *sigma* (σ), tells you about the consistency of the time periods. If the time frames are extremely consistent, you will find that the bell curve will be tall and thin (represented in Figure 8-1 by a dotted line). On the other hand, if there is a lack of consistency, the bell curve will be short and wide (shown in Figure 8-1 by the dashed and dotted lines). The standard deviation, σ, permits you to assess that degree of consistency or disparity without having to plot the data to make the assessment. Figure 8-2 shows the key elements used in computing the standard deviation. The σ (*sigma*) is equal to the standard

Figure 8-2. Elements for calculating standard deviation.

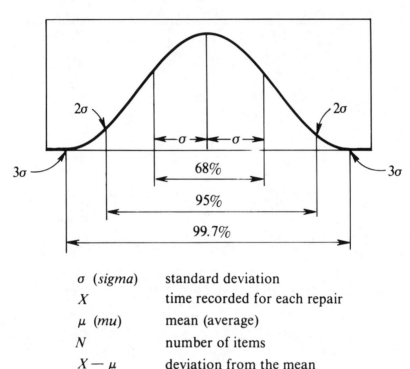

σ (*sigma*)	standard deviation
X	time recorded for each repair
μ (*mu*)	mean (average)
N	number of items
$X - \mu$	deviation from the mean

deviation; X equals the time periods (taken from service orders) for the replacement of each filter; μ (*mu*) represents the average (mean) of all the time periods; 68%, 95%, and 99.7% are the confidence intervals of combinations of standard deviations (this is discussed shortly); N equals the number of items recorded (in this example, 24 recordings were made); and $X - \mu$ is equal to the deviation from the mean, that is, how far from the mean each time period is.

Refer to Table 8-1 for a typical calculation of the standard deviation. The first column is a list of the time periods it took the technicians to replace the filter. The next column lists the deviation of each time period from the mean. For example, since the mean time was 14.5 minutes, and the first time was 11 minutes, the deviation from the mean is:

$$11 - 14.5 = -3.5 \text{ minutes}$$

Table 8-1. Calculating the Standard Deviation (Model AB123). Mean (μ) = 14.5 Minutes.

Replace Filter (X) Minutes	*Deviation from the Mean (X − μ)*	*Squared Deviation of the Mean (X − μ)²*
11	−3.5	12.25
11	−3.5	12.25
12	−2.5	6.25
12	−2.5	6.25
13	−1.5	2.25
13	−1.5	2.25
13	−1.5	2.25
14	−0.5	0.25
14	−0.5	0.25
14	−0.5	0.25
14	−0.5	0.25
14	−0.5	0.25
15	+0.5	0.25
15	+0.5	0.25
15	+0.5	0.25
15	+0.5	0.25
16	+1.5	2.25
16	+1.5	2.25
16	+1.5	2.25
16	+1.5	2.25
16	+1.5	2.25
16	+1.5	2.25
17	+2.5	6.25
20	+5.5	30.25
Totals 348	0.0	96.00

Time periods less than the mean are shown as a minus figure; those more than the mean are shown as a plus. For example:

$$16 - 14.5 = +1.5 \text{ minutes}$$

If you total all the deviations from the mean, you will always get 0, as the table shows. In order to eliminate the plus and minus signs, deviations from the mean are squared, as shown in the third column.

For example:

$$-3.5^2 = (-3.5)(-3.5) = 12.25$$

When the square of the deviation from the mean for each time listed is totaled, it comes to 96.0. Having arrived at this total, you can now calculate the standard deviation. The formula is:

$$\sigma = \sqrt{\frac{\Sigma(X - \mu)^2}{N}}$$

Therefore:

$$\sigma = \sqrt{\frac{96}{24}}$$

$$\sigma = \sqrt{4}$$
$$\sigma = 2 \text{ (standard deviation)}$$

It has been determined statistically that approximately 68 out of 100 recorded time periods fall within one standard deviation of the mean; 95 out of 100 fall within two standard deviations of the mean; and 99.7 out of 100, or virtually all, fall within three standard deviations of the mean. What does all this mean? Using this example, you can determine that 68 percent (68 out of 100) of the time periods fall in the range of 12.5 to 16.5 minutes:

$$14.5 - 2 = 12.5$$
$$14.5 + 2 = 16.5$$

Similarly:

$$14.5 - 2 - 2 = 10.5$$

and

$$14.5 + 2 + 2 = 18.5$$

This shows that at two standard deviations from the mean, 95 percent of the time readings should fall within 10.5 to 18.5 minutes. The 68, 95, and 99.7 percent ranges are called *confidence intervals*, that is, the degree of confidence you have that the time periods will fall within that range. Refer to Figure 8-2; the confidence intervals are shown on the bell curve.

You can now see that if the time periods are grouped closely around the mean or average time, a tall, narrow curve results, giving a small standard deviation. The standard deviation is a strong indicator of the consistency of performance. You can see this consistency, as mentioned previously, without having to plot a curve, just by determining the range of times at various confidence intervals.

Use statistical analysis to determine the consistency of performance without having to review every service order. If, for example, the data are not in a computer, you can select a random sample of service orders, calculate the mean and standard deviation from data in those service orders, and conclude statistically that the range of time periods at each confidence interval is consistent for all service orders. This is called *sampling,* and it is a common practice that saves time and money when compiling information. It is important to use a truly random sample to ensure accurate results. Use as large a sample as possible, and test your ability to random sample by taking several samples and comparing the results.

Once you've looked at the range of time it takes to replace a filter within each confidence interval, you can use this information to establish a time standard. You may decide, for example, that the filter should be replaced within the 68 percent confidence interval. The minimum time it should take is 12.5 minutes, and the maximum time would be 16.5 minutes. You would then select a time standard of, say, 14 minutes as reasonable. If the standard deviation had been very wide, so that the range at the 68 percent confidence interval was 4 minutes to 20 minutes, then you would look into the cause of such variance. On the other hand, should the standard deviation be 0.5, for example, then it would indicate that the service technicians are very consistent in their repair time periods and you can select the mean as the standard.

In setting time standards for routine maintenance procedures, generally you can select a standard that is lower or more conservative. By the same token, you might select a time standard that is more liberal for repairs. In this example, assume the time periods used for the filter replacement were the same for the replacement of a given component. Then you might decide to select the higher time period at the 68 percent confidence interval for your time standard: 16.5 minutes.

Don't look blindly at the numbers derived from statistical analysis, but rather use them as tools in conjunction with other knowledge about the technicians and the products. Once you've established the time standards, monitor them to see if they are being met. If not, investigate to determine the reason why and then take action to rectify the situation.

There are computer programs on the market that perform the statistical analysis described here. These programs not only access the data base to secure the needed information, but also calculate the standard deviation and plot the curve on the computer screen. Obviously these programs simplify the task; you must decide if their cost justifies the time saved.

In establishing time standards, also consider the morale factor. Standards that are extremely difficult or impossible to meet will have negative effects on personnel. If the standard times are reasonable, they will be accepted by the service technicians. Take care when establishing work standards for the first time because, if they are too liberal, it is difficult to cut time allocations without encountering personnel problems. New diagnostic equipment, more easily serviced products, improved training, and more efficient time and territory management all affect the amount of time required to perform service; these added factors can justify reductions in time standards.

You can establish narrower time ranges as more and more products employ either on-site or remote diagnostic equipment. Service dispatchers or representatives receiving emergency calls can question customers as to which indicators are illuminated on the control panel of their products or ask them to flip a switch that automatically connects a product's modem with your organization's computer. The computer can run through a series of diagnostic checks and state the nature of the problem as well as suggest corrective action. On many occasions customers can correct the problems themselves. If technicians are required, repairs can be made more quickly because the extent of the malfunction is known.

If a routine maintenance call is also due when an emergency call comes in, then you should advise the service technician to perform that service if possible. This saves the cost of additional travel, as well as the time to access the product. It also saves the expense of generating another service order for the needed maintenance.

At the conclusion of a service call, the service technician should inspect the product to ensure that all components, in addition to the repaired one, are functioning properly and another breakdown is not imminent. Remember, every service call that does not have to be made improves your gross margin.

Scheduling Work

When scheduling service personnel, take into account the travel time, products to be serviced, standard times for required service, geographical location of products, number of units in a given location, product mix, and anticipated level of emergency calls (peak or non-peak season for product usage). It is also essential that the sequence of service calls be set by the dispatcher (or scheduler), not the service technician. This guarantees that the dispatcher establishes the priority of calls, is aware of the location of the service personnel, and controls their travel times.

Travel time is nonproductive time. Service technicians are not providing a good return on the company's investment if they sit in a motor vehicle, even if customers are paying for travel time, and certainly not if they are making contract service calls. Through effective scheduling, you can cut travel time down to a bare minimum.

If you choose to have technicians schedule their own sequence of calls, then offer incentives for them to efficiently utilize their time. With incentives, they can see a direct benefit result from scheduling their calls in an efficient manner.

Train your dispatchers to improve productivity and maximize personnel utilization. Techniques that the dispatcher should use are:

1. Prioritize all calls for the service technicians.
2. As the number of service contracts grows and the customer base increases, you can schedule several days or weeks of work in a tight geographical area.
3. Assign a service technician to work full time in a single facility if it is a large commercial or industrial installation.
4. During the early part of a peak season, spread routine maintenance work over a period of time, permitting service personnel to respond quickly to emergency calls in their area, with minimum travel time. For example, one-half to three-quarters of a day could be scheduled for maintenance, with the remainder set aside for emergency calls. If emergency calls take up more than the allotted time, simply reschedule the uncompleted maintenance for another day.

Product mix also affects productivity and therefore influences scheduling. Certain technicians are more proficient in servicing particular products; direct service work to them in their areas of greatest competence. Similarly, you'll realize greater efficiency if one type of product that a technician is servicing is not mixed with another product on the same day or within a few days. By having a technician work on one type of product, you'll increase the level of proficiency servicing that product, thereby eliminating time referring to service manuals or diagnosing problems.

Response time and contract density are also important factors in scheduling. It can prove very expensive to maintain a 1- or 2-hour response time to emergency calls if you have only a few contracts spread over a wide geographical area. A high contract density permits you to locate technicians in these areas and facilitate faster responses to emergency calls. The response time you promise customers should be based on the level of noncontract service work your organization is doing, the product mix, and the nature of the product application (for example, what the customer's cost is if a product isn't functioning). Longer response times permit more efficient scheduling of calls in a given geographical area. Normally more calls will accumulate in a particular area during a 24-hour period than over the course of a 2-hour period.

You can also improve response time by providing service personnel with beepers or portable two-way radios. More sophisticated products display a message on a screen of the communications unit, saving a technician's time by not having to phone the dispatcher for instructions.

Computers in Contract Administration

It is possible to administer a successful contract program without a computer, however the costs saved and the speed and accuracy offered by a computer more than justifies the investment. With lower-cost personal computers now offering high RAM (Random Access Memory) and storage capacity in megabytes, a computer remains a possibility, even if access to a corporate mainframe or minicomputer is restricted. New software applicable to service administration continues to come on the market. Programs that may not appear readily applicable to your needs can, in fact, be appropriate once you understand their capabilities. Many other programs can be modified easily in order to meet your needs.

The data base program forms the heart of computerized service contract administration. With a good data base program, you can record and analyze product repair history; prepare contracts, invoices, and service orders; and schedule work. You can use it to balance work loads and overtime, schedule routine inspections and maintenance, analyze costs, prepare reports, and establish time standards. The computer's uses are as varied as your imagination permits.

In selecting a data base program, establish your corporate needs and convey them to the software supplier or programmer. Prior to purchase, have the program demonstrated in a manner that shows how it performs the desired functions. Also, see how easy it is to enter and manipulate data. Simplicity in accessing the program is important; simple access saves time and limits the level of training required for the operators who will enter, retrieve, and utilize the data. A good program should not only sort data, but also handle computations (for example, totaling labor and parts costs on a given contract) and interface with other programs. The ability to link with other programs permits you to use data that may be stored in another data base or enter data onto a spread sheet program for further analysis. Your data base program also should be able to create forms and enter desired information on those forms or to enter data in the proper location on preprinted forms. When purchasing a packaged program, check the RAM and storage capacity, as well as its compatibility with your hardware (computer).

Many new programs are available which perform multiple functions for the servicing organization. These combine computerized dispatch with scheduling, report generating, inventory control, billing, parts ordering, maintenance scheduling, and tracking of technicians. These service software programs range in price from as little as $3,000 to over $200,000. As the programs become more common, the prices should drop significantly. Most will operate on a personal computer. In the future, such programs will offer an even higher level of sophistication combined with yet more simplified operation. Many software companies will provide training in the use of their product; they also will offer service contracts on their products!

The computer will help you increase productivity, if properly employed. Whether your organization is large or small, there are computer programs that can prove cost effective for you. Do investigate them, and find out what they can do for your servicing firm.

Multipurpose Service Forms

When designing service forms, give considerable thought to the purpose each will serve, not only in facilitating certain actions or conveying information, but in converting that information into useful data for future analysis.

The service order is one of the key forms in the service operation. From the service order can be generated numerous reports and operational necessities, such as invoices. With the computerized contract program, a standardized format is especially important, not only in how the form is structured, but in the way information is placed on the form. A common method of easily entering information is to use codes. A numerical or alpha-numerical coding system provides a means of entering descriptive information on the service order with minimum effort. For example, the service technician follows a code list containing a number followed by a description. The codes describe an action (replaced, tightened, and so on), the parts used, and so forth. The technician spends time referring to a code list to complete the report, but the codes soon become familiar and the time it takes to fill in the service order decreases.

Another method of easing the entry of information is to list all the items on the service order itself, so the technician can check off the applicable information. This type of form is fine if the amount of data is limited. If not, you're left with a lengthy service order, with information spread over several pages, resulting in a great deal of paper.

Yet another method is to have the service technician provide a written description of the action taken, the parts used, and so forth. The difficulty with this method is that its success depends on the technician's ability to describe the action accurately and to write it clearly. In addition, the information must then be converted at the office to facilitate its entry into the computer—a time-consuming process subject to errors from the interpretation of what the technician wrote.

The computer has assumed its useful position in the service order area as well. There are a number of software companies that offer a computerized reporting system. Instead of providing technicians with a service order form, you furnish them with a hand-held unit about the size of a unitary telephone handset. This unit has a small display screen and a key pad with alpha-numeric buttons similar to those on a telephone. The questions normally asked on a service order have been programmed into the unit. Though systems and programs vary from manufacturer to manufacturer, they generally work something like this. Each morning the technicians telephone a number that connects them to the service department's computer. They then place the phone handset in the designated recess on the back of their unit. The computer enters into the unit the service calls to be made that day. When all the information is entered, the unit signals that fact. Technicians hit a designated key on the key pad, and the name and address are displayed for their first customer on the list; the unit also instructs as to services needed or nature of the complaint.

When technicians complete their first service visit, they strike another designated key, which starts the service order process in motion. Appropriate questions flash on the screen, and the technicians reply to each question, listing work done, parts used, and so on. After they enter all the required information, the unit displays the name, address, and description of the next service call. At the end of the day, the technicians go to a telephone, dial the number of the computer, and place the phone handset on the back of their unit. The data from the service orders are transmitted back to the central computer.

The advantages of this system are many. It eliminates a considerable amount of paper work. With service order information transmitted to and from the technicians electronically, much time is saved and errors are minimized. Technicians must answer the required questions as each appears independently; this eliminates the problem of their forgetting to answer a question or failing to enter pertinent data on the service order. The system is fast and efficient. You can determine the status of parts inventory or other service data instantly, without the normal time lag for handwritten service orders to be entered into the computer. The disadvantages, if you consider them as such, are that the cost is high (although prices are dropping) and that technicians do not have printed copies of their service orders to leave with customers. This latter problem can be solved by generating hard copies at the office and mailing them to customers. Again, with technological advances always on the horizon, it seems likely that a compact, portable printer could be made to work in conjunction with the technician's unit so as to print the service orders in the field, if needed.

Let's return to the problems of the service order form itself. When generating a service order, consider certain items for inclusion, such as the following:

1. Service company name, address, and phone number. Also the name of the technician assigned to the call. This information is needed to identify the form as your service company's service order.
2. Customer name, address, and phone number. This is to identify the customer.
3. Location of product to be repaired. This is to identify the actual location of the item to be serviced, since it may be different from the customer's office address.
4. To whom service is charged. This is to verify whether service is to be charged to a warranty reserve, a Full Repair and Maintenance contract, a Maintenance Only contract, a Repair Only contract, time and material, a call-back, or a new installation. In this manner, technicians and billing personnel will know the extent of services to be charged to the servicing organization and to what account they should be assigned. Similarly, they can determine what charges should be billed to the customer. This helps maintain proper cost controls. Additionally, technicians will be alerted when customers do not have repair coverage, for example, and will know that customer approval is required before making a repair.
5. Terms of sale, whether contract, charge, cash, or no-charge. This helps avoid errors, because technicians know exactly how the service call will be paid for. The no-charge category is for call-backs or free calls of any other nature.
6. Service contract number. This is for control purposes.
7. Customer restrictions, such as time or day service or if maintenance can or cannot be rendered.
8. Date and time service is scheduled.
9. Date and time work is started.
10. Date and time work is completed.
11. Time standards. Here the standard time is indicated for preventive maintenance or repair services performed. In this way technicians become aware of the time allocated for each service call.
12. Make, model, and serial number of product.
13. Reason for service, whether scheduled maintenance or an emergency call. The nature of the problem should be indicated, including a read-out of product's diagnostics if so equipped.

14. Action taken by service technician. Codes or a checklist can be used, but space should also be provided so technicians can write in any additional pertinent information.
15. Parts and materials used. Here the technicians list the part number, quantity, description, source (vehicle or stockroom), and price if technicians are to collect payment at the time service is rendered.
16. Labor hours and rate. This is calculated when service orders are returned to the office. The labor hours multiplied by the labor rate provides the total billable labor hours. This amount is then billed to the customer on time and material service calls or charged to the appropriate account (contract service, warranty, and so on). Computers can be programmed to make these calculations, or they can be done manually. If payment is to be collected at the time service is rendered (as is often the case in the repair of consumer products), then technicians make the calculations so that the full amount due can be collected at the completion of service calls.
17. Taxes. Any sales taxes due should be shown on the service order.
18. Total amount due. Include the sum of parts, materials, labor, and tax.
19. Recommended additional services or peripheral equipment. This serves as a reminder for follow-up sales action, or, if a copy of the service order is presented to the customer, it advises the customer of needed equipment or services.
20. Comments. Leave a place for technicians to comment on aspects of the service calls.
21. Customer acceptance statement. Include a statement indicating that the customer is satisfied with and has accepted the service performed.
22. Customer signature. This indicates acceptance of and satisfaction with the service rendered.
23. Payment received. This indicates that the customer has paid for the service (used if payment is collected when service is rendered). Technicians usually date and sign service orders and return a copy to the customers as a receipt. The customer's copy only has information of interest to the customer; internal data do not record.

Information for items 1–8, 11–13, 16 (rate only), and 21 can be printed by the computer before you give service orders to the technicians. Technicians should carry blank forms for emergency calls received in the field. When the emergency call is assigned, the dispatcher can provide technicians with the customer name, contract number, and so on. When the completed service order is returned to the service department, the data can be entered into the computer data base.

Administrative Reports

Service order data can be used to generate a wealth of reports. The reports can be designed to provide useful information, but if a report becomes outdated or is no longer needed, don't continue to have it generated. The computer creates reports on command, and there is a tendency to produce obsolete material. Be vigilant and only create reports that assist you in managing the service business. The following are some computer-generated reports that will help you properly control the service business.

Contract Cost and Profitability Analysis

This report helps ensure that profitability goals are met. It identifies problem areas in pricing and cost control or major trends in product failure. It also helps determine which contracts are profitable and which are not. This computer-generated report can also identify those products costing more to service than previous data had indicated.

Figure 8-3 is a blank Service Contract Cost and Profitability Analysis. With it, you can keep a record of the number of contracts you plan to sell each quarter (3 months) and the number sold to date. These sales and their resulting profits can be included in the cost and profit analysis to see what impact contract sales have on product sales and on overall corporate profits. But in developing the analysis remember to include the cost of materials such as lubricants, cleaning items, and small parts (screws, washers, and so on). The individual cost per service call for these materials may be small but they add up and impact on profitability. Include such costs as overhead or factor them into the selling price of the contracts.

Figure 8-3. Typical service contract cost and profitability analysis.

Service Contract Cost and Profitability Analysis

No. of Service Contracts Planned to be Sold	No. of Service Contracts Sold	Labor Hours Planned	Labor Hours Actual	Labor Cost Planned	Labor Cost Actual	Parts and Material Cost Planned	Parts and Material Cost Actual	Trans-portation Cost Planned	Trans-portation Cost Actual	Total Cost Planned	Total Cost Actual	Profit Planned	Profit Actual	Period
														1
														YTD
														2
														YTD
														3
														YTD
														4
														YTD
														Annual Totals

Review this analysis on a quarterly basis. For better control, review it monthly or even weekly. Frequent reviews are advisable when
you start the contract program and have little performance history. As
your confidence grows in the program, consider longer periods between reports.

Trend Reports

A trend report is used to monitor labor and material costs, and thus
to determine any movement away from planned costs. Prepare these
reports periodically, on a year-to-date basis. The layout for a Trend
Report by Product is shown in Figure 8-4.

In the first column is the name and model number of the product
being analyzed. Below that are the periods during which the product
has been serviced: for example, less than a year, one to two years, and
so on. Done this way, the analysis reflects the effect age has on the cost
of labor and parts and materials. Dividing the sum of the labor and
parts and material costs by the number of units from which the data are
gathered provides an average cost per unit serviced. The number of
units that make up the base is listed to ensure that decisions made from
this information are based on a significant number of units, not just one
or two. The percent change column allows you to compare last year's
experience with the present situation. For example, a unit currently
one to two years' old might be experiencing the same average cost as a
unit that was one to two years' old last year. This helps you determine
if costs for current units of similar age are increasing or decreasing.
Instead of breaking data down by years in service, you can design the
report to show number of cycles, number of copies (for copiers), hours
of operation, or another variable applicable to the products you service.

The Past History section of the report shows the average service
cost per unit for units of a similar age during previous years. From this
data you can see if costs are going up or down. If they are increasing
significantly after you've adjusted for inflation, it may indicate poorer
quality control or less efficient service procedures. A decrease in costs
may indicate better quality products, improved diagnostics, or another
reason. Using the data from this report, you can investigate and determine the cause of such trends.

The Trend Report is an important tool in contract pricing and
administration. It can be refined further to separate the cost of servic-

Figure 8-4. Typical trend report.

Trend Report by Product
Product AB123

Date:

	Current History				Past History	
Years in Service	Labor	Parts and Material	Total	Number of Units	Average Cost per Visit	% Change for Similar Age Unit Last Year	Average Labor and Material Costs per Unit Year 1　Year 2　Year 3
0–1							
0–2							
0–3							
0–4							
0–5							

ing products under contract from those not under contract. Of course, a favorable report indicating that servicing costs for products under contract are significantly lower than for those that are not may be used as a sales tool. Customers can be shown how scheduled maintenance reduces down time and overall expense. Lastly, Trend Reports can also be developed to compare actual labor hours to standard hours to see if such time standards are improving productivity.

Formats for Reports

In preparing reports, first decide what information you need, then see if that information is available or can be generated on the computer. Format the report in readable layout, and generate it. For example, if you need information on how actual costs and profits compare to anticipated costs, list the items that influence these two factors: labor cost, labor hours, parts and material costs, and so on. Having made your list, review it and add or delete items as required, then check if the data can be generated in the form you want. If not, what can you do to put it in the desired form? How is it structured now? Is this form useful? Can it be made useful? Decide how you would like the report to look, but remember that it must also make sense to the others reading it. Finally, have the report printed. Your results may look something like the Service Contract Cost and Profitability Analysis shown in Figure 8-3.

Again, when developing reports, remember that they are devices for managing your servicing operation. Arrange them so they achieve this goal. Once again, don't generate reports that you aren't going to use. The computer is a great tool, but don't let it bury you in paper.

Billing and Collection

Another important administrative function is billing and collection. An extended accounts receivable can affect the cash flow and profitability of a servicing firm. Service contracts solve the problems normally associated with collecting payments from accounts because payment is received in advance of rendering the service. This is one of the big pluses of service contracts. Of course, the form of billing used is to some extent influenced by the market, competitors' billing procedures, and type of product being serviced. Whether it is a consumer or a commercial and industrial contract, the price affects how a customer will pay for it.

Payment in Advance or at Time of Service

In general, service contracts for consumer products should be paid in full when the contract is signed because the cost is relatively low. Periodic billing adds unnecessary costs to the contract price and can introduce collection problems.

For convenience, it is usually a good idea to permit the customer to charge the contract amount to one of the national charge cards (MasterCard, Visa, and others). If a major store chain is selling the contract, use the store's charge account. Using charges not only eases payment for the customer but helps close the sale. Equip your service vehicles with charge forms so service technicians can collect payments (when services or goods are not covered by contract). It is obvious that collecting money in advance or immediately after service is rendered virtually eliminates collection problems.

Period Payments and Late Payments

You should make every reasonable effort to have all contracts paid in advance. However, the nature of the product, the cost of the contract, and the competitive situation may necessitate periodic payments. These factors also influence the frequency with which those payments can be collected.

A contract selling in the five- or six-figure range may demand monthly billing; others selling for less may involve quarterly or semiannual payments. Periodic billing adds to the administrative cost of the contract program. Sending out multiple invoices, recording payments, and pursuing slow-paying accounts add to costs. Likewise, delayed billing introduces the need to collect the monies due and the potential of pursuing delinquent accounts.

If payments are not received on the due date, send friendly reminders the following day. Do not indicate that they have 5, 10, or 15 days to make the payment; this can lead customers to believe that being a few days or weeks late is acceptable. Slow payments impede your cash flow while improving the customer's. If you do not receive payment within 5 to 10 days, call the customer asking why. The phone call should be friendly but businesslike. If the reason is acceptable, ascertain when payment will be coming. It is important that you establish a date before the call is concluded. Remind customers that failure to pay their bills in a timely manner can result in breach of contract and termination of service.

If the reason for nonpayment is unacceptable, then take a firm approach. Advise the customer that all amounts due must be paid on time, as agreed. Set a date for when the check should be received. If you have reason to believe that payment will not be made, then send a note confirming your phone conversation and the date the check is to arrive.

If the payment is not received on the date promised, send a letter by certified mail, return receipt requested, advising that payment has not been received. Inform the customer that he or she is in breach of contract and that further service will not be rendered. A certified letter protects your interests. If a customer claims he never received notification, there is the possibility that he might sue for breach of contract if you don't respond to a service call. If payment is still not received and the customer has not contacted you, turn the matter over to your collection department or attorney for further action as company policy may dictate.

The form letter has lost much of its power to collect bills past due. Companies (and individuals) view these letters as something a computer has generated, and attach little significance to them. The letter does serve as a reminder to those who forgot to pay or who misplaced an invoice, but will do nothing to move those who hope to stretch out their payments as long as possible. That is why the phone follow-up is recommended early in the collection process. It puts the customer on notice that a person—not a computer—is aware of the delinquency.

The phone call also serves another purpose. It makes you aware if customer dissatisfaction is the reason for nonpayment. The phone call permits correction of any lapses in quality service as well as resolves the payment situation.

It is important to develop a clear, easily understood billing and collection policy that everyone can follow without difficulty. Remember, the payments that remain in the customer's hands affect your working capital, your cash flow, and your profits.

Collection

Many companies use in-house collection personnel, outside collection agencies, or corporate or private attorneys to collect delinquent accounts. The service manager of a small organization may have to wear several hats, one of which is collector. The service manager of a large organization, on the other hand, may have an entire collection department. Whoever does the collecting should know the laws of the states in which the company is operating.

The opportunity to collect a delinquent account has many times been lost because proper action was not taken in a timely manner. For example, in some situations you can file a "mechanic's lien" against a debtor. If a company is in serious financial trouble, there may be other firms also filling mechanic's liens against that debtor. In most states these liens are settled in the order in which they are filed, thus the company that files late may find that the debtor does not have any funds left to pay its claim after the companies nearer the top of the list received what money was available.

The collection agency is an independent firm in business to collect past-due accounts for its clients. Generally, collection agencies do not charge for their services until payment is received from the delinquent account. If and when they are successful, a percentage of the amount received is deducted for the collection service and the remainder is forwarded to the client. When choosing a collection agency, review its track record on collections as well as its fee structure. Collection agencies vary in quality and aggressiveness. Choose carefully.

Attorneys also can be effective collection agents because people as a rule respond more quickly and positively to a collection letter from an attorney. However, most attorneys charge a fee for their time, irrespective of whether the bill is collected.

Which method you choose depends on your circumstances. For small amounts you are willing to write off as a loss, the collection agency is a good option. If it collects, fine; if not, you take the loss. If a large amount of money is due and there are complex legal ramifications, then the attorney may be the better choice. Many collection agencies do pursue large amounts of money, so it boils down to selecting the one that ultimately will prove most successful at the lowest cost. Don't discount your own ability to collect delinquent accounts; often this is the least expensive and most effective method.

Breach of Contract

If a customer breaches the contract and is notified of this breach and of the nullification of the contract, then you should determine how much, if any, service has been rendered under the contract. Prepare a bill for the service as if it were performed as time and material work. From the total bill deduct any contract payments that were made and claim the balance. The delinquent customer should pay for the services rendered, and it is important that you go on record for the full amount due. If a collection proceeding goes to court or if the customer sues your firm, it may harm your case if later on you suddenly decide to submit the higher bill.

In Summary

Effective administration is the key control function that determines whether the service contract program is successful. A servicing organization can develop excellent service contracts, price them profitably, and market them effectively yet still lose money. Failure of an organization that appears to be doing everything right can usually be tied to poor administration. Inevitably, the service manager of a troubled firm has no idea of what actual costs are or what the technicians are doing. It is easy to assume that everything will go well, especially if the marketing program has been successful. Don't make that assumption.

The words *control, control, control* rang through Seth's mind. He resolved that he would institute an effective administration program and implement it properly.

9

Service Business Ethics

A key to success in the marketplace is the establishment and maintenance of a reputation for honesty and fairness. Seth understood this; all the aspects he had been considering in the development of a service contract program were based on this premise.

Good business ethics make sound business sense. The company that believes it can take advantage of customers by not properly fulfilling their contracts or not providing quality service is ultimately the true loser. The company loses because its reputation becomes tarnished as customers realize they are getting less than they bargained for. Word spreads about the unscrupulous behavior of a servicing firm, with a snowball effect that eventually puts the company out of business. Ethical behavior not only is morally right but also is a prime element in continued business success.

Questionable Practices

Most servicing firms soon realize that they are operating in a highly competitive environment. Some firms mistakenly believe that if they use deceptive tactics to get business, the customer will be none the wiser. A typical scenario involves the servicing firm that realizes when customers call for time and material service, they normally ask what the technician's hourly rate is. To get the business, some firms quote a very low hourly rate, then make up the difference by charging exorbitant prices for parts and materials or, worse, by charging for parts not even replaced. The latter instance is theft, and the persons involved are subject to criminal penalties. By charging very high prices for parts the servicing firm is only fooling itself. At best, the customer pays the bill and the chances are they will never call again. At worst, the customer refuses to pay and the servicing organization has a collection problem.

Occasionally servicing firms unintentionally injure their reputation and develop a profile for unethical behavior. This often occurs when a firm decides to provide its service personnel with an incentive for parts that they install. It usually is a small commission, but the result is that technicians with low ethical profiles replace parts that are perfectly serviceable. Eventually the customer finds out, either through investigation or by accident, and the reputation of the firm is damaged. Never pay commissions on parts replaced because there is no plausible reason to do so. If a component requires replacement, it should be replaced; if it doesn't, the repair shouldn't be made. There is no selling effort on the part of the technician, so why pay a commission?

If the servicing organization chooses to have its technicians sell service contracts and peripheral or add-on equipment, a commission makes sense. In this situation, customers have a choice whether to purchase what is being offered. A caution is in order, however, if a service manager plans to pay technicians a commission on the sale of service contracts or equipment. Unless controls are established, it is possible that salaried technicians will see an opportunity to earn extra money selling these items and may forget that their primary responsibility is to service equipment. The result is that little service work gets done. You should set standards for the level of service performance, making the incentives for selling contracts or equipment of secondary importance.

Ethics also play a major role in selling the contract. Whether the servicing organization uses direct mail, telemarketing, a direct sales force, or other means it must be conscious of how the contract program is presented to the customer. There are federal and state laws that govern truth in advertising. False or misleading statements can lead to dealing with the Federal Trade Commission for violations of federal statutes. An all-too-common infraction is the "puffing" of the offer's value. For example, customers are told that they are getting two years of protection on a product for $100. In reality, customers get one year's protection for the $100 because the other year's coverage is provided by a one-year product warranty whose cost is included in the price of the product.

Telemarketing sales representatives or field salespersons are normally viewed as agents of a company, thus any promises or statements these people make can be binding on the company. This is true even if a service or marketing manager is unaware that those commitments were made. In fact, the courts have held that independent manufacturer's representatives are agents of their firm and their commitments are binding. Generally, if customers have reason to believe that someone representing your company has authority to make a commitment, they will usually win should a dispute be litigated.

Good Business Practices

The way to avoid trouble is to train your personnel to be ethical. Make sure they understand clearly that your company operates according to high ethical standards, and digression from those standards will not be tolerated. Most states have laws that permit consumers to cancel agreements within some specified period (usually three to five days) after they are signed. The law's purpose is to give consumers time to reflect on their purchases and determine if they were "fast talked" into the commitment. Usually sales personnel are required to advise customers of this provision in the law.

In reality, providing good service means serving customers beyond the norm. When customers buy service contracts they expect the servicing organization to respond promptly, provide quality parts and workmanship, and generally fulfill the terms of the contract. True service distinguishes a servicing firm that does things above and beyond what is expected. A genuine desire to help, friendly office personnel and service technicians, faster response than the contract specifies when there is a special need—all these are characteristics of a customer-oriented servicing organization. They are the characteristics that distinguish the firms which increase their market share and are able to command good profit margins. They are ethical organizations that are also good business people. Customers become aware of the extra value of this service and are willing to pay for it. In the final analysis, remember, it is the customer's perceived value that counts.

As service manager, Seth would establish the ethical tone of the business. He would do this, perhaps, by writing a slogan that reflected the moral objectives of his firm. He would train his staff to conduct business ethically, whether they were service technicians or salespeople. And he would encourage his entire staff to be courteous and helpful. After all, Seth realized that good ethics is good business.

10

Controlling Service Parts and Materials

Seth knew that, in a successful service contract program, service parts have to be available. Yet he also realized that a parts inventory can represent his single largest investment. If he is to build a reputation for quality service, not only will he have to respond to service calls quickly, but once the technician is on the repair site he will have to return the equipment promptly to full use. Seth also realized that having parts on back order both inconveniences the customer and proves costly to his own operation. An initial call to diagnose the problem, then a return call to replace the part add to his overall operational expenses and diminish his profits. Additionally, the time his customer service personnel and dispatcher take to respond to a customer's inquiries as to when the part will be replaced also contributes to higher costs. Seth would put together an inventory program that minimized the liabilities of a parts operation, thereby enhancing his profit potential and customer satisfaction.

The problem, then, is to determine which parts to inventory and how many of each item to stock. It is compounded further by having to determine the mix of parts to be maintained in the service vehicles.

Parts availability is important not only in fulfilling the contract obligations, but also in the future sales success of the product line. If customers perceive difficulty in getting components, they will be reluctant to purchase the product. As service manager, then, you have to stock the parts in sufficient quantities for the necessary length of time. Additionally, you must know the techniques to control parts usage to effectively prevent stockouts and shrinkage.

A responsive parts program begins with a corporate policy statement backed by an effective plan to carry out that policy. The policy statement outlines the corporate commitment to maintain an adequate parts inventory necessary to ensure customer goodwill. The plan outlines the procedures for determining which parts to stock and for how long. It delineates a method for maintaining adequate quantities in inventory and determining reorder points.

In drawing up the plan, consider procedures for handling warranty and nonwarranty components. Find out whether it is necessary to return defective items to the manufacturer or vendor or scrap them in the field. Spell out who (manufacturer, servicing organization, or dealer) has first priority on parts should there be shortages because of strikes, delivery problems, and so on. Similarly, provide procedures for handling parts replaced under a service contract. Develop the plan only after considerable thought and reflection. In the long run, the time you spend formulating a good plan will prove less costly than that wasted by office and field personnel trying to interpret a poorly conceived or written plan. Most important, a good plan helps ensure customer satisfaction and thereby perpetuates the service contract program.

Inventory Requirements for Existing Products

The computer can be of invaluable assistance in determining inventory requirements. If repair records have been kept, you can determine the number of times a component has failed in a particular model. The data can be refined further to account for such factors as age, cycles, hours of operation, and so on, as well as highlight the possible seasonality of such failures and the average number of failures per year for a given number of units. For example, suppose the data indicated that a certain model had ten failures per 1,000 units each year. By dividing 10 by 1,000, you'll get the number of failures per unit:

$$\frac{10}{1000} = 0.01, \text{ or } \tfrac{1}{100} \text{ of a failure per unit per year of Part A.}$$

If your organization has 10,000 units under contract, then you can calculate the number of part A components you need in stock to service those units. Multiply 10,000 by 0.01 to get the answer of 100 part A components needed for the year:

$$1000 \times 0.01 = 100$$

Therefore, you know that statistically you will consume 100 of those parts. You will have to calculate the number of failures per unit per year anyway in order to price the repair contract. Once you know the annual failure rate per unit, you can automatically calculate annual inventory requirements. The database program can make all these calculations for you.

Inventory Requirements for New Products

With new products, you have no history upon which to base your parts requirements. How then do you determine the quantity of each component to stock? Work closely with your research and development, engineering, manufacturing, marketing, and quality control departments to assess the potential life and subsequent failure rate for each part in each new product. The R&D and engineering departments can provide the results of field tests and give their estimates of the vulnerability of each component. A review of the manufacturing and quality control processes can provide insights into how close vendor items will be inspected, the quality control procedures employed in the plant, the handling and packaging of the product, as well as the component stock levels that will be maintained by manufacturing as a backup to service inventory. Marketing can provide projected sales, the markets that will be served, and the expected level of customer use of the product, including frequency and severity.

Having reviewed this information you can develop a feel for the anticipated failure rate and subsequent parts requirements. If your confidence level is high, fewer parts need be stocked; if low, more components should be stocked initially. An important hedge is the component inventory maintained by manufacturing and your ability to draw from it. The corporate policy and plan should include a provision to share these components when necessary to maintain the maximum level of customer satisfaction and confidence. You should review also how difficult it will be to service each component, so you can develop time standards to use in pricing service contracts and estimating personnel needs.

A manufacturer's servicing organization would use this knowledge to develop stock lists for its service facilities and service vehicles. If the product is sold through distributors or dealers, the manufacturer should provide them with recommended stock lists so that they can maintain adequate stock at their facilities. Distributors and dealers should always ask manufacturers to provide recommended stock lists, since the reputations of both manufacturer and dealer are at stake.

Once you've determined a stock level, monitor it constantly for changes in parts demand either for existing products or anticipated parts for new products. An increase in failure rate dictates an increase in parts inventory. Similarly, an increase in product sales necessitates an upward inventory adjustment to meet the anticipated parts usage increase. Conversely, a drop in failure rate and a decrease in product sales indicate that downward adjustment of parts stock is in order.

Economic Order Quantity and Inventory Costs

The question that a service manager must answer is, "Knowing the annual parts demand, how much or how many units should I order at one time to avoid stockouts yet keep costs as low as possible?" A popular device that helps you determine how many units to order at one time is the Economic Order Quantity (EOQ) formula. This formula takes into account critical factors that impact on costs, such as the annual parts usage, the cost to place an order (process an order through the purchasing department), the cost of the component itself, the costs incurred in the storage and handling of the part, and the cost of money tied up in inventory. (Money that has been spent on inventory does not generate revenue until the component is sold.) Here is the EOQ formula:

$$EOQ = \sqrt{\frac{2\,NC}{PI}}$$

N = Number of parts used per year
C = Cost in dollars to place each order
P = Part cost in dollars
I = Inventory carrying cost, expressed as a percent of inventory value (includes cost of storage space, insurance, labor, money, handling, and so on)

The following illustrates how the formula is used. Assume the following conditions exist for Part A: $N = 1{,}500$ units; $C = \$75$; $P = \$12$; and
$I = 30\%$:

$$EOQ = \sqrt{\frac{2\,NC}{PI}}$$
$$= \sqrt{\frac{2(1500)(75)}{12(.30)}}$$
$$= 250 \text{ units}$$

Therefore, the purchasing department will order 250 units at a time.
Should the result be a fraction (249.6), then normally the order will be
rounded out to the next higher quantity (250).

The next step is to calculate how often an order will be placed.
Use the following formula:

$$\text{Frequency} = \frac{\text{Annual usage}}{\text{Ordering quantity}}$$

Therefore, in the example just shown for Part A:

$$6 = \frac{1500}{250}$$

An order for 250 parts will be placed six times a year, or approximately
every 61 days:

$$\frac{365}{6} = 60.8, \text{ or 61 days}$$

Next, calculate the amount that must be paid to the vendor for each
order. Use the following formula:

$$\text{Cost of part} \times \text{order quantity} = \text{purchase order amount}$$

Therefore, in our example for Part A:

$$\$12 \times 250 = \$3{,}000 \text{ purchase order amount}$$

An important cost item to know is how much money it costs to keep the necessary quantity of this part in inventory for the year. Use the following formula:

Purchase amount × inventory carrying cost = cost to maintain inventory

Therefore, for Part A:

$$\$3,000 \times 0.30 = \$900 \text{ per year}$$

It costs $900 to keep this part in inventory for one year.

As the demand for parts increases or decreases and the parts, purchasing, and inventory costs go up or down, you should recalculate the EOQ. It is evident by looking at the formula that a change in any one of these factors will change the EOQ.

How is the cost of placing an order (item C in the EOQ formula) calculated? In lieu of a detailed cost analysis, you can arrive at a reasonably accurate value by taking the annual operating costs of the purchasing (or ordering) department—including telephone, rent and other overhead factors, and salaries—and dividing that figure by the number of orders placed in a year.

The computation for inventory carrying cost is a more complex calculation that is essentially the sum of all the expenses related to keeping the part in inventory. With an inventory of perhaps thousands of parts, the problem becomes compounded. The computer can assist in these calculations in sorting parts by high or low bulk, with special storage requirements, according to cost, and so on, so that various categories can be established for parts with relatively similar storage charges. Then you divide the total expenses to store and maintain the inventory by the value of the inventory to get the cost as a percent of inventory value expressed in decimal form. The financial department or an accountant can assist you in arriving at these cost figures.

Don't blindly follow the EOQ formula. Many other factors, such as quantity price breaks, may require you to purchase larger (or smaller) numbers of units. For example, if you find that the vendor charges $12 per unit for quantities of less than 255 units and $10 for quantities of 255 units or more, then you would most likely order 255 units and save over $500 ($12 − $10 = $2; $2 × 250 = $500). Similarly, if the vendor announces that prices are rising by 10 percent in 30 days, you may wish to order a greater quantity to take advantage of current lower prices. How much to buy depends on the cost of money and of storage. The corporate financial officer can assist you in making such financial decisions.

Another factor that influences the purchase quantities is an anticipated shortage of a component. You may be prompted to place a larger order as a hedge against the potentially more costly problem of running out of parts. Similarly, by looking at seasonal demand, you might increase your order for peak seasons and lower it for slow periods.

Safety Stock

Safety stock represents insurance against a stockout. Safety stock is the number of parts carried above the normal amount needed to meet demand. Its purpose is to ensure that parts will be available should demand be higher than anticipated or if a delivery is late.

How large should a safety stock be to prevent a stockout without incurring the expense of an extremely high inventory? Complex mathematical formulas and statistical analyses have been developed to determine safety stock levels. They involve looking at the past fluctuations in demand, the ability of manufacturers or vendors to deliver on time, and the critical nature of the part. There is always a risk of a stockout, no matter how large the safety stock. A 100 percent guarantee against a stockout requires having an infinite number of units—an impractical solution. Experience and logic should help you determine a reasonable safety stock level. You may wish to carry a large safety stock for critical parts and no safety stock at all for nonoperational items (such as cosmetic trims).

Using the Computer for Parts Management

There are many software programs on the market that take much of the burden off of inventory management. They also ensure that parts are reordered in a timely fashion. The programs list thousands of items in hundreds of categories; they also maintain records of where the parts are stored, with a cross reference between your organization's part number and the vendor's ordering number. These programs keep records of the cost of components and can even handle parts billing with any applicable discounts. They can trigger a purchase order or notify the parts manager when designated reorder levels are reached. The programs can match ordered quantities with those received, as well as compare the price on the purchase order with that on the invoice. They provide status reports on any given day, including a list of items out of stock. Reports can be generated showing gross margins earned by part or a gross margin for all parts sold. The number inventory turns can also be reported. The computer can be programmed to develop just about any inventory report in any form desired. Of course, as emphasized throughout this book, use the computer only to develop reports that are meaningful and useful.

Stocking the Service Vehicle

The adage "time is money" is most true in the servicing business. In many cases, labor represents the most costly part of fulfilling a service contract obligation. If a service technician must return constantly to the warehouse for parts, considerable productive time is lost. This, in turn, increases the cost of the service contract program, thereby reducing profits. The key to higher profits is in minimizing the service technician's returns to the warehouse. Maintaining an adequate parts inventory in the service vehicle saves labor and helps ensure customer satisfaction.

Determining which parts to stock in the service vehicle is as important as choosing the items to stock in the warehouse. In reality the service vehicle is an extension of the warehouse, with a portion of the warehouse stock stored in the vehicle. Make a study of the products serviced by each technician, especially if service specialization is employed. It is useless to have an individual who is trained only in routine maintenance carry spare parts for complex repairs. Once you have a profile of the repairs and their anticipated frequency, then stock sufficiently varied items in quantities large enough to meet the needs of the technicians.

Organize the vehicle in an orderly, logical fashion. If the vehicle does not have a well-planned, properly marked and filled bin system, technicians will waste considerable time looking for parts. Additionally, they will make many extra trips to the warehouse for parts that are on the vehicle but cannot be located. Maintaining a neat, well-ordered vehicle is synonymous with proper repair procedures.

A good way to ensure that service personnel are aware of inventory located in the service vehicles is to provide them with a list of all parts carried, their quantities, and their location in the vehicle. In this way, service technicians can quickly check if they have a needed part. Keep in the computer a consolidated inventory of the stock in each vehicle so you have quick reference to the location of all parts. A stockout in one vehicle can be resolved on short notice by parts from another vehicle in the same vicinity.

When a completed service order is returned to the office, the parts usage indicated on the order is entered into the computer which, in turn, will generate a replenishment order to bring the service vehicle stock back up to the prescribed level. Properly stocking the service vehicle means having the right parts in quantity all the time. In contrast, having a vehicle actively involved in service calls without an adequate parts stock is playing Russian roulette with profits and customer satisfaction.

Assign technicians a day and time to report to the parts warehouse to have their vehicles' parts stock replenished. How often they return depends on their normal parts usage and the quantity of parts stored in their vehicles. They may have to return weekly, every two weeks, or only once a month.

You'll save time by having both the parts manager and the technicians know when their vehicle stocks will be replenished. Each day the parts manager can review which technicians are coming in for parts the next day. The manager can then check the computer to see how many parts were used of each type by each technician. The computer then prints the replenishment list. A parts clerk can make up orders of replacement parts for the technicians. When the technicians arrive, they are given a carton with their parts and their lists. They check each item and its quantity. Then they sign one copy of the list indicating it is correct and then return the list to the parts manager, keeping a copy for their own records.

If, when checking the computer, the parts manager notes that a particular technician's usage of a given part or parts has increased over the last few replenishment periods, then the manager may decide to increase the quantity stocked in the vehicle. In preparing the next order, the manager would add the number of units necessary to prevent a stockout of the vehicle's supply. Technicians are advised as to why the quantity is increased. By monitoring usage in this way, stockouts are avoided, thereby saving technicians' travel time in returning for needed components.

Preparing the replenishment stock in advance saves time and money. Technicians are paid to service equipment, not spend hours picking up parts. Additionally, the system places accountability for all service items on both the technicians and the parts manager. This is a key element in reducing shortages and controlling shrinkage.

Controlling Parts Usage and Reducing Shrinkage

Proper control mechanisms can ensure adequate inventories and reduce shrinkage. Shrinkage is the shortfall in inventory resulting from breakage, loss, or theft. The open stockroom where service technicians wander in and help themselves to what they need is nothing short of disastrous. You have no control over inventory levels and shrinkage is inevitably high. The stockroom or warehouse must be controlled by a parts manager with the responsibility of maintaining its integrity. Records must show the disbursement of parts, to whom, and why. Reconciliations between parts usage and disbursements should be made regularly. Service technicians should understand that they are accountable for the parts stored in their vehicles.

Here again the computer lends support by maintaining the required data and assembling it in the form required to reconcile inventory accounts. If the same concepts outlined for vehicle parts storage are adhered to in the warehouse or stockroom (neatly labeled bins, inventory lists, and so on) shrinkage is virtually eliminated. Even shrinkage from damaged or broken parts can be accounted for readily.

Seth realized that good control of parts usage and disbursement is synonymous with maintaining planned inventory levels and minimizing shrinkage. He would begin at once to review his present systems for ways to integrate these new ideas.

11

Third-Party Service

Having assembled a successful servicing organization and with an effective service contract program underway, Seth wondered if his knowledge and the strength of his servicing firm could be directed toward further growth and profitability. Seth felt that the first step was to make a list of his company's assets in the technological area. He listed such things as knowledge of computers and electronics, ability to employ sophisticated diagnostic equipment, capability of repairing precision mechanical equipment, and so on. Next, he evaluated his human resources. He listed items such as the number of technicians and the high level of technical training they possessed for a variety of products. His people had a firm grasp of company philosophy, and therefore understood and exercised good customer relations. The organization had strengths in data analysis, financial knowledge, administration, scheduling, organization, good employee relations, and so on. Seth put every conceivable asset down on paper, even if it didn't seem important or applicable. He then examined the list for areas of weakness—liabilities—and indicated those, too.

For days, Seth kept looking at his list, adding new items as they came to mind. Then he showed the list to others in the company and asked them to expand on it. When he felt confident that there was nothing more to add, Seth began to underline in red ink those assets which were the firm's greatest strengths. How could he profitably employ these areas of competence? The idea then came to him. Why not use these assets to service products in areas we're not currently involved in? His mind raced with ideas. He could service competitive products, repair and maintain other products that contain electronics, or perhaps handle precision components . . . . The opportunities seemed unlimited. But what about the image of expert and specialist in the products the firm manufactures? Seth thought, "Will we be diluting our impact in the marketplace? Will we be perceived as a jack-of-all-trades? How can I preserve our current image, yet build on it as I enter new markets?" Seth was reeling from the excitement and challenge. It then hit him. Why not form a separate organization that would service products in the targeted markets? A separate company would leave his present company image intact, yet permit him to use the knowledge and strength from years of hard work to enter a new area of profit opportunity. The answer, then, was to form a third-party servicing organization.

Opportunities Abound

Third-party servicing organizations probably have been around since the beginning of time. On television we often see Westerns in which the residents of the town bring their horses to the blacksmith to have shoes put on. The blacksmith is not affiliated with the person who raises and sells the horse; he puts a shoe on any horse regardless of breed or brand. The blacksmith is a third-party service person.

The Industrial Revolution created a need for people to repair machines and the products those machines produced. The corner washing machine repair shop and the local garage are other examples of third-party servicing firms.

With the proliferation of new, more sophisticated products, demand for service is greater than ever. Whereas the corner washing machine repairer of the past did not need to know sophisticated marketing, administrative, and financial procedures, such service people must know them now if they are to survive in our highly mobile society characterized by greater options. In early years, customers had little choice but to call the local service company. Today they look in the Yellow Pages and select from many competing firms.

Because many segments of the business world are going through rapid technological advances, firms use their financial resources in research and development to keep their products positioned on the leading edge of technology. When coupled with the need to invest in manufacturing facilities and machinery to make the new products, there is little money left to invest in personnel and equipment to service the merchandise they produce. Thus many firms depend on distributors and dealers to fulfill the service role, leading to independent (nonaffiliated) third-party servicing organizations.

Types of Third-Party Businesses

The means to enter the third-party service market are many. A company can furnish time and material service or offer any of the types of service contracts outlined earlier in this book. Additionally, opportunities exist to administer third-party contract programs or to insure them.

In deciding which form of third-party enterprise is best, follow Seth's method of assessing your company's strengths and weaknesses. Look carefully at your capabilities and see how they can be employed creatively in the marketplace. Having done that, look about to see how service is rendered by competitors within your industry. Then look at other industries, other types of products, and other markets to see if your firm's expertise—its strength, if you will—can be used successfully to render service in these other areas. If you run a national servicing organization with parts depots, service centers, and service personnel spread out across the country, consider signing up small dealers or distributors to purchase service from you or to sell your service contracts. The small dealer will, in effect, become part of a national servicing organization. It will not have to employ technicians nor stock parts, and it can make a profit on the service or service contracts it sells for you. Dealers and distributors can do the thing they probably do best: sell. They can sell the product and the service. Your third-party servicing organization fulfills the service obligation profitably—for both parties.

National accounts also offer great opportunities. Many products must be purchased through local dealers; it is the only way the manufacturers will sell them. If you are such a manufacturer, have you considered how you will provide a national account with national service contracts? If not, here is an opportunity. Form a third-party servicing organization with a national service force to approach the national account and offer a service contract that covers the customers' units no matter where they are located. A third-party servicing organization that can offer such a program may capture a sizable amount of business at the expense of independent local servicing facilities.

The small third-party dealer or distributor may ask, "Where does this leave me?" In many cases, in a very good position. Though the national organization may be able to deal efficiently with a national account, it may be at a disadvantage selling service on a local basis. The organizational and communications network necessary to service a national account can be expensive, thus necessitating higher prices. Local organizations can be more competitive because of lower overhead costs. Also, locally owned and operated servicing firms can develop close relationships with the principals of customers' firms. When service is needed, they know the owner of the servicing firm on a personal basis—a comforting feeling. As mentioned before, look at your strengths and go after the market that plays to those strengths.

Another option available to companies that sell through distributors or dealers is to either create a national account department or a separate third-party organization to sell service contracts. A manufacturer could negotiate the service contract and then offer it to its affiliated dealers for fulfillment. The dealers garner additional business by servicing equipment located at the national account's local facility.

Similar to a national organization selling service contracts, there are companies that issue and administer service contracts without rendering repair service themselves. In this situation, the national organization (it can be regional, for that matter) selects the given products, assembles a service contract or contracts for those products, and offers these contracts through independent dealers. Dealers have packaged contract programs with contracts backed by either the issuing firm, the manufacturer, or an insurance company. The dealers are reimbursed for any expenses incurred in fulfilling the service contract in a manner similar to insured service contracts. Customers receive national coverage because the issuer of the contract (not the dealer) can arrange to have any dealer make the necessary repairs.

Another form of third-party organization taking hold in the servicing industry is the franchised firm. This type of company offers individuals an opportunity to enter the profitable servicing business knowing that they will receive assistance and guidance in the operation of that business. In return for a franchise fee and usually a percentage of gross revenues (every franchisor has a different formula), the franchisee receives assistance in such areas as site selection, training in the products being serviced, management, marketing, finance, and operations. Additionally, the franchisee may receive counseling in the day-to-day running of the business and in personnel relations. The franchisor generally either provides or assists the franchisee in securing tools, diagnostic equipment, vehicles, uniforms, stationery, and so on. The advantage of the third-party franchise is in the assistance that the individual receives. Being part of a national franchise organization also means being part of a national advertising program, having national identification, and offering a national service contract program. There is, of course, a price that the franchisee must pay for these benefits: the lump sum, the percentage franchise fee, or both. The price may be well worth the benefits, however. From the franchisor's standpoint, the high quality of the individual selected to operate a franchise is essential to its success. Mutual success of such a program rests on the premise that the franchisee selects a franchisor that offers a profitable program and that will be in business for a long time.

Benefits to the Customer

In an effort to position themselves as experts in servicing the products they make, many manufacturers only service their own products. This policy works well if the products are unitary in nature, that is, self-contained.

When a product is part of a system, and the owners of that system choose to purchase components from different manufacturers, a situation develops that presents an opportunity for the third-party servicing organization. These owners of such systems might have purchased components from different manufacturers because they perceived a difference in quality, features, benefits, or value. But when faced with a problem, these owners of what they consider their ideal systems may have to call different service firms to repair or maintain each component. This could mean multiple service contracts.

To further compound the problem, these owners can find themselves with an inoperable system no one is willing to fix. If various servicing firms each determine that the cause of failure is not in their component but in the unit furnished by another manufacturer, this can lead to complete frustration. The owner is left with an inoperable system and no one willing to repair it.

The third-party maintenance organization, however, can offer these customers a service contract that covers all the components in the system, regardless of brand. Owners now have a single source for service. They know that no matter what the failure or from which component, the third-party servicing firm has contracted to locate the problem and correct it.

In a similar fashion, third-party organizations can offer customers a single source of service (and a single service contract) for a wide array of unitary products at a single location. For example, they can sell a service contract that covers all the copying machines, typewriters, and word processors for the same company. These products may each be from a different manufacturer. Either way, the customer has one service contract from one servicing organization.

Other Considerations

When developing a third-party servicing company, give careful attention to the selection of products. Determine if you can secure service manuals and possibly training from the manufacturers. Will the manufacturers send you all the service bulletins as they are issued? How available will parts be and what price must you pay for them? Is there a secondary parts market so that your organization can still get necessary components should they not be available from the manufacturer? If service contracts are to be offered, determine if the manufacturer will furnish data on failure rates and repair times. If the data are considered proprietary, then you must decide whether you can reasonably project the failure rate. (Your projection would have to be based on an investigation of the product and also through testing; this was discussed in Chapter 5, Pricing Service Contracts.) You must also evaluate how the manufacturer will fulfill its warranty obligation. Find out, for example, if the servicing firm can be authorized to handle warranty claims. Performing warranty service encourages the purchase of service contracts. If, on the other hand, the manufacturer performs the warranty service, then a third-party servicing organization has a more difficult task in establishing itself with the customer.

Another opportunity available to a firm interested in entering the third-party servicing market is with carry-in or, as it is sometimes called, depot maintenance. For a servicing firm without mobile service technicians, depot maintenance offers a viable option to get into the third-party servicing field. Carry-in service requires customers to carry their products into the repair facility or to ship them there. Repair is made immediately or else the customers are advised when their items will be ready for pickup or shipped back. In considering this option, determine whether the product is easily transportable and if customers are willing to make the effort to get it to you. As with any service operation, the operating cost must be considered. In this instance, compare the cost of depot maintenance to that of service at a customer's home or place of business. Also, consider if the savings associated with depot maintenance (if there are any savings) are a sufficient incentive for customers to carry the product into the facility.

Third-party maintenance offers another source of profit for a service manager. Seth realized that the service contract base can be large because of the potential variety of products that can be serviced. Seth would have to be creative in assessing the various marketing opportunities and in applying his servicing firm's assets to a new servicing situation.

PART II
Corporate Profiles

A. *Xerox Americare*

History

In 1982, the Xerox Corporation's service arm, the Xerox Service Business, began to look for opportunities to expand its service business beyond its current product lines. It conducted a study to determine what segments of the service industry were growing the fastest. An assessment was made as to how Xerox's service capabilities matched the service needs of each market. Next, an evaluation of its capabilities to penetrate the market was made. It considered the extent and sophistication of competition and balanced this against market potential. In short, Xerox was looking for a situation that offered a substantial opportunity for the profitable employment of their technical, service, and marketing resources.

The research pointed clearly to one market that offered not only great current opportunity, but future opportunities as well. The area that showed the greatest growth and overall potential was the servicing of personal computers (PCs).

In evaluating this market, Xerox discovered that the sophistication of the PC was increasing with each new model introduced. This broadened the customer base, which would result in greater and greater growth each year. Xerox looked at who was providing service for this exploding market. The industry was dominated by companies started by entrepreneurs who were primarily design and manufacturing oriented. For the most part, the PC companies were not large corporations with unique service organizations in place, but rather initially were small organizations with limited resources. Thus, the entrepreneurs for the most part concentrated their efforts in product development and distribution of those products. From the standpoint of distribution, they chose not to develop extensive direct sales and service networks but to rely on independent dealers and retailers. As such, they did not have a nationwide service capability. They depended on this loose federation of dealers and retailers to render service. Xerox saw this combination of a growing market and an absence of a national service organization to support this market as offering it a great opportunity.

Xerox then took a closer look at who was buying these personal computers. It was found that though the home user was indeed purchasing the products, the market was transcending into business and school markets. The increased sophistication and capabilities of the personal computer almost made the term *Personal Computer* a misnomer. Xerox found that the local dealer in most instances would have great difficulty supporting a company that purchased computers for use on a regional or national basis. What was needed to support the business community was a national service organization that could render service wherever it was needed. There was a void to be filled that offered an opportunity for the right service company.

Xerox took a good look at itself to see if it could profitably fill this void. Xerox had 82 service centers spread across the United States which had been established to service its Memorywriter electronic typewriters and Telecopier Facsimile Transceivers. This organization was separate from the division used to service its copying products. In addition to the 82 service centers, Xerox also had in existence 45 retail stores which had been established in another marketing move to sell non-Xerox products. The service centers were charged with supporting the service needs of these retail establishments. With all these service centers and several hundred technicians staffing them, Xerox felt that it was in good shape to handle the anticipated needs of its potential customer base. Xerox next assessed its technical competence to ensure it could handle the required repairs. Its knowledge of microprocessors—the heart of the computer—was extensive. Microprocessors were not only used in Xerox's own computer line but also in its copying machines and typewriters. To round out its evaluation, Xerox knew it had a highly recognizable name, a positively perceived reputation for service, and a parts distribution network that could support any number of service locations. Xerox felt it had the service competence to impact on the PC market as well as a good knowledge of the business as a whole. The management of the Xerox Service Business felt it measured up pretty well. The market played to its strengths. The proposal to senior management outlined these positive attributes. It concluded that Xerox would be a premier third-party service organization as the market matured and a short-term investment would pay handsome dividends in the future.

In May of 1983, Xerox introduced its entry into the third-party service business at the COMDEX Show in Atlanta, Georgia. COMDEX is a major computer conference and exhibition. In its initial introduction, Xerox made it clear that its business was going to be devoted solely to the servicing of personal computers, microprocessors, and associated peripherals. It also made it clear that Xerox Americare would not sell equipment nor service copiers, minicomputers, or mainframe computers. Its goal at the show was to attract independent dealers that would be interested in affiliating themselves with a national third-party service organization with a name that would be easily recognized by virtually any customer.

When establishing Xerox Americare, Xerox realized that it would have to develop access to service information and parts from the manufacturers of the products it would service. Xerox contacted the manufacturers of personal computers, printers, disk drives, and other peripherals. Its primary goal was to establish a working relationship with these manufacturers whereby Xerox Americare would be authorized to handle warranty work on the personal computer products sold by those manufacturers. Once authorized, Xerox Americare would receive reimbursements for any warranty service rendered. In those instances in which warranty service authorization could not be acquired, Xerox Americare would then attempt to establish a working arrangement with the manufacturers. A working arrangement would mean that though it would not be an official warranty service facility, and therefore would not be reimbursed for warranty service work, it still would have access to the manufacturers' parts and service manuals. In addition, its agreement would permit Xerox's technicians to attend any training schools and seminars offered by the companies producing the personal computer items. Xerox Americare was successful in signing up approximately 30 manufacturers during its first year of operation.

Contract Options

When purchasing Xerox Americare contracts, customers are given several options on how they can go about getting required service.

1. The customer can bring the computer and/or peripheral covered by the contract to the local dealer where the equipment was purchased or to any authorized Americare dealer or Americare Service Center in the United States. The dealer then calls the closest Americare Service Center, and Xerox has the component picked up and brought to the service center for repair. When the repairs are completed the equipment is returned to the dealer. The dealer then notifies the customer to pick up the repaired unit. The total repair process normally takes no more than 48 hours. This type of contract has the lowest cost of the three offered.

2. In the next, more expensive, option, the customer can have the product requiring repair picked up and returned to the place of business or home. It saves the customer the time involved in bringing the unit to and picking it up from the dealer.

3. The third, and most expensive, contract option involves having service rendered on site, that is, at the customer's home or place of business. This option offers the advantage of saving down time, since it is not necessary for the equipment to be transported back and forth from a service center.

The customer actually has another option available: time and material repairs. Xerox Americare performs time and material service work under any of the two methods used for service contracts. The customer can bring the computer to the dealer or Xerox Service Center or have it picked up at the home or place of business. The cost similarly increases with the degree of convenience offered to the customer. In this last option, the customer, of course, pays for the services rendered and parts used.

Xerox authorizes dealers to sell a contract for any product that Xerox has a working arrangement with or authorization to service. The products that can be serviced are outlined in a list and on price sheets published by Xerox. If the product is still under warranty, the dealer can enter into the contract without prior approval from Xerox. If, however, the manufacturer's warranty has expired, then the unit must be inspected by Xerox and any needed repairs authorized and paid for by the customer before a service contract is issued. There is a nominal charge for the inspection. Upon completion of the inspection the customer can have any needed repairs performed or just pay the inspection fee and not enter into a service contract.

Pricing the Xerox Americare Service Contract

To ensure accurate, profitable contract selling prices, the Xerox Service Business (XSB)—which is responsible for the success of the Americare program—devised a series of steps that it believes provide accurate repair cost data. When an agreement is reached with a manufacturer, the first thing the XSB does is gather all available product and service information on the products to be serviced. This includes catalogs, service manuals, and failure rate data. Xerox then sends engineers to the fabricator's place of business to review the material received and get clarification on any questionable areas. If the manufacturer will not or cannot provide needed data such as the life expectancy of components or the labor hours needed to effect a given repair, the XSB attempts to arrive at the answers itself through a Maintenance Task Analysis (MTA).

Production models of each product they plan to service are sent to Xerox's research laboratories in Dallas, Texas. Here skilled technicians completely disassemble a unit following the manufacturer's approved procedures. The technicians simulate the repair process by actually removing and replacing components. The amount of time and degree of difficulty to effect a repair are recorded. Additionally, the tools and diagnostic equipment needed to complete the repair are noted. If the manufacturer does not provide service procedures, then the technicians develop and document the optimal procedures for each step of a repair or maintenance process. As part of the Maintenance Task Analysis, an assessment is made of which parts can fail or break in the operation of each product. An analysis is made not only of the probability of failure, but of the frequency of failure based on a given amount of product usage. Critical components are put through extensive tests to determine their failure rate. The information gathered is used to verify the manufacturer's data, when provided, or to establish an anticipated frequency of repair profile when the manufacturer does not supply the facts.

Having gathered all the possible knowledge on a product, the next step is to price the contract. Knowing the anticipated or actual frequency of repair for each component, the amount of time to effect each repair, and the cost of required parts permits the XSB to cost the contract. Overhead burden and profit are then added to these costs. The result is the wholesale price given to the dealer. A reasonable profit for the dealer is added to the wholesale price to arrive at the suggested retail price.

Service contracts are sold by the Xerox service centers, at the suggested retail prices, for customers wishing to purchase them directly from Xerox. The dealer can sell the contract at, above, or below the suggested retail price. Additional discounts are available to dealers that sell contracts in volume.

How Xerox Sells Americare

The Xerox Service Business sells the Americare service contracts through two primary means. A national sales force sells contracts to large organizations that own many personal computers. The size and complexity of this type of sale is usually beyond the capabilities of the average dealer. The second method (as mentioned earlier) is through dealers.

To assist those dealers that are interested in actively pursuing major accounts, the Xerox Service Business has developed an extension to the Americare program called the Major Account Support Team (MAST). MAST has the responsibility of supporting active Americare dealers and the Xerox direct sales force to secure service contract business from major accounts.

If a dealer makes contact with a major account and needs the help of MAST, it can secure assistance by calling the Americare Hotline, an 800 number Xerox has established for its Americare dealers. MAST assists by meeting with the dealer or Xerox sales representative (if a dealer is not involved) and the customer to assess the customer's needs. It assists the dealer or Xerox sales representative in preparing a proposal for the customer and helping close the sale. Xerox then fulfills the contract as it would any other Americare agreement.

Should a conflict arise between competing dealers or between a dealer and the Xerox sales force—for example, if both called on the same customer—a call to the MAST Hotline initiates a process to equitably resolve any conflict.

Sales goals are established for the dealer. To be considered an active Americare dealer these contract sales goals must be met. To assist the dealer in meeting these sales goals Xerox has put together a wide array of support materials and programs. The dealer is provided with training programs and merchandising support as well as standard-ized contracts.

The training program consists of six diskettes that are used with and available for a variety of personal computers. The diskettes cover such subjects as to how to sell contracts, how to handle objections, how to merchandise the contracts, how to complete the contracts, and how to fill out a service order as well as provide important information on contract administration. In addition to the diskettes, the dealer is sent monthly and quarterly newsletters that provide additional sales ideas and keep the dealer updated on the Americare program.

Sales aids are provided in the form of brochures, suggested retail price lists, sample direct mail letters, telemarketing scripts, and win-dow signs. Periodically, optional new promotional programs are intro-duced to the dealer.

Parts Inventories

All Xerox service centers are stocked with an inventory of parts to service all the different brands that are normally brought to the service center. The volume of service business is constantly monitored, and stock levels at each service center are adjusted to meet demand re-quirements. A central parts distribution facility is maintained with an on-line computer connected to each service center. Should a stockout occur, the service center enters the need in its terminal, has the part sent on its way, and receives it normally within 48 hours.

The distribution center keeps a running record of the stock levels of each service center. Reorder points for each part are maintained. When a reorder level is reached at any service center, the distribution center automatically ships the necessary components to bring the ser-vice center's inventory up to the desired level. In this manner the service center is assured that necessary stock levels are maintained.

Contract Administration Procedure

When customers need service, all they have to do is show a service center attendant their contracts and the computers or peripherals are repaired. Depending on the type of contract, customers either bring their units to a service center or dealer, have the units picked up at their home or place of business, or arrange with the service center for on-site service. Copies of the contract are maintained at each service center for those units which are located in the service center's area of coverage. Copies of all contracts are kept at Americare headquarters in Rochester, New York. With this system, verification on coverage, if required, can be accomplished with little difficulty.

Data are gathered on labor hours used on contract fulfillment and parts consumption. These cost figures, coupled with overhead costs, are sent to Xerox's financial and administrative group for analysis. The information is interpreted and monitored to ensure the continued profitability and success of the program. Parts consumption data are also used not only to resupply the service centers but to initiate orders to manufacturers to resupply the distribution center. Xerox does not use parts not produced or authorized by the computer or peripheral manufacturer.

Benefits of the Americare Program

Xerox believes that the Americare program offers customers benefits that are not or cannot be provided completely either by the manufacturer or the dealer. The reasons it believes that customers choose to purchase an Americare contract are:

1. Xerox Americare service is as good as, if not better than any other source.
2. Xerox has well-trained people with a high level of technical competence.
3. Xerox's goal is to price its service below that offered by the manufacturer (in those cases in which the manufacturer has a service organization).
4. Xerox services mixed systems. For example, the computer can be of one manufacturer, the printer of another, and the disk drives of a third. Manufacturers that offer factory service often only service their own products, forcing owners to seek separate sources to service each component. Xerox Americare is a "one-stop shop."
5. With Xerox you can get service practically anywhere in the

United States. Local dealers can only offer service in their areas of operation.
6. Because Xerox is a major corporation, customers are confident that the company will be around to fulfill the contract. When Osborne Computer ran into difficulty, Xerox immediately purchased Osborne's entire parts inventory to ensure it would have the necessary parts to satisfy its customers' service needs. In fact, Xerox is confident that it has enough parts in stock to satisfy the needs of Osborne's entire computer population.

As Xerox sees it, the benefits to dealers in joining the Americare program as authorized dealers are:

1. This presents a retail profit opportunity for dealers. Dealers purchase the contract from Xerox at a wholesale price and sell it at a profit.
2. Dealers can offer the customers nationwide service because they are part of a national organization.
3. The Xerox name builds confidence and helps sell the contract.
4. The dealers do not have to maintain a parts inventory.
5. Xerox does the physical repair, saving dealers the costs of technicians, tools and equipment, and overhead.
6. When customers bring units into the dealership for service, it helps build traffic.

Xerox looks, from its viewpoint, to greater profits for its corporation and better utilization of its service centers. The Xerox Service Business believes that, in the long term, the channels for selling personal computer hardware are not going to be able to service it. With less than 5 percent of the personal computers under service contracts today and with the number of PCs presently being sold numbering in the hundreds of thousands (if not millions, with sizable growth projected into the future), Xerox sees great opportunity for third-party maintenance organizations. It sees itself as one of the largest and premier servicing organizations in the microprocessor business today, with great opportunity for continued profitable growth in the future.

B. Marsh & McLennan Group Associates

History

Marsh & McLennan, founded in 1870, is the world's largest insurance brokerage firm. It entered into the business of product warranties in the late 1940s, when a home freezer manufacturer approached it for ideas on how to increase freezer sales. Marsh & McLennan came up with the Food Spoilage Warranty. This warranty, which has become a virtual industry standard today, offers to reimburse the purchaser of the freezer for any food spoilage loss incurred (usually up to some stated dollar limit) should the freezer fail to function owing to a mechanical defect. From this beginning, Marsh & McLennan went on to insuring the compressors in freezers and refrigerators, and this led to insuring air-conditioning equipment.

Today the Marsh and McLennan Group Associates division entertains virtually any basic warranty, extended warranty, or service contract program that an organization wants insured. It will insure both new and older products that meet certain standards. These standards include knowledge of the products' failure experience and maintenance history. Marsh & McLennan is involved in insured service contract programs that extend from air-conditioning, heating, and solar energy equipment to automobiles, artificial turf, and windmills.

Organization

The Product Warranty Department is the section of Marsh & McLennan Group Associates that is responsible for assisting manufacturers, distributors, contractors, or retailers in developing insured service contract programs.

Headquartered in Chicago, Illinois, the Product Warranty Department has a staff trained in assembling programs designed to meet the objectives of its clients. Depending on the goals established, the department works with the clients' marketing functions, service departments, or both. For example, it assists marketing personnel in developing an insured warranty program that is designed to increase product sales. Conversely, it aids the service department or independent service company to generate an insured service contract plan designed to meet certain income objectives.

Insured Service Contract Procedure

Marsh & McLennan Group Associates has developed a Product Warranty Insurance application form that asks the general questions which need to be answered when an insured service contract program is established. Or, as Marsh & McLennan Group Associates prefers to call the insured service contracts, product warranty insurance. Because the application is general in nature, a representative of Marsh & McLennan Group Associates generally has an initial conversation with a client to explore the type of program desired. Then, after conducting some research into the industry, the type of product involved, and so on, it develops the questions that are applicable to the particular program or product. What type of warranty is to be insured? How long is the warranty being proposed? How many individual units will be insured? What are the types and extent of costs to be incurred? Who will be rendering the service? Does the client have any data on actual failure experience?

Since Marsh & McLennan Group Associates is a broker, it must determine each client's needs and then convey those needs to an insurance company, often called an underwriter. Depending on the nature of the program, Marsh & McLennan Group Associates may require a great deal of detailed information to satisfy the requirements of the underwriter. The role the insurance broker plays is that of consultant and intermediary between the client and the underwriter. He uses his knowledge and expertise to guide the client and bring him together with an appropriate insurance company.

After interviewing the client, the broker drafts a policy that is appropriate to the client's needs. This insurance policy is then presented to an insurance company. After the insurance company reviews, negotiates any modifications, and accepts it, the policy becomes effective.

Pricing the Insured Service Contract

For products that have been in existence for some time, the pricing of the insured contract is easy. This is especially true when good repair records have been kept. For a new service contract program or a new product, the pricing of the initial offering becomes more difficult. Marsh & McLennan Group Associates works with the client to establish some reasonable basis for a fair price to pay to the insurance company so as to sell the contract competitively. Many times it becomes a cooperative effort among the client, Marsh & McLennan Group Associates, and the underwriter. In some instances, Marsh & McLennan Group Associates works with the client to draw up a service contract containing the desired level of coverage and then puts the proposed contract out to several insurance companies for bids. In this way it can attempt to get the best price for the client.

Benefits of the Insured Program

Marsh & McLennan Group Associates sees its role as that of being behind the scenes, helping insure a contractual liability of a warrantor.

A warrantor is the person or company issuing the contract or warranty. Depending on the desires of the client, the insured service contract can be written in a manner that clearly indicates the contract is insured or, on the other hand, conceals that fact entirely. In cases in which the contract insurance is publicized, Marsh & McLennan Group Associates feels the insurance factor adds to the credibility of the contract program. An additional benefit to the warrantor on an insured service contract or product warranty (remember, a company can insure its initial new product warranty) is that the cost is guaranteed. In the case of the product warranty, the guaranteed cost to offer the warranty should be built into the price. Similarly, in the case of the insurance contract, the cost of offering the contract is known. If the client chooses, Marsh & McLennan Group Associates handles the administration of any claims, thus acting as a buffer between those placing claims against the warranty or service contract and the seller of the contract. This option also saves the client the cost of having to establish its own claim-handling facility.

From the customer's viewpoint, a service contract that is insured and advertised as such provides added protection in that the customer can get claims settled by the insurance company directly, should the company that issued the contract go out of business. It may also help the issuer to stay in business, since it is not subject to any catastrophic losses on the contracts or warranties issued. Marsh & McLennan Group Associates makes it clear that its role is not to provide legal advice, and it always suggests that any legal questions concerning a program be referred to the client's attorney. It also makes clear that its and the underwriter's prime function is to provide reimbursement to the client for that client's liability under the warranty or service contract. It is still up to the manufacturer, distributor, retailer, or whoever else is responsible for the service program to provide quality service and parts.

Basic Insured Contract Administration Procedure

The administration of each program is different, but the outline below is a sample of a particular plan:

1. An enrollment application is processed.
2. The insurance policy is issued to the warrantor, along with application forms for those issuing the service contracts. For example, if a manufacturer establishes an insured service contract program for its dealers, the policy is issued to the manufacturer and the application forms are passed on through the manufacturer to the dealers to apply for insurance coverage under the terms of the program.
3. The application (or dealer applications) is processed, and the

contracts are sent to the issuers of the service contracts (that is, dealers).
4. When a claim occurs, a claim form is completed (for example, by a dealer) and submitted to Marsh & McLennan Group Associates for reimbursement.
5. The claim is processed, and payment is sent to the warrantor (for example, the manufacturer or dealer, depending on the terms of the policy).

Support Programs

To assist the client in advertising and promoting an insured service contract program, Marsh & McLennan Group Associates maintains a full-fledged advertising department at its Chicago offices. This department has the facility to design and produce full marketing programs that can include direct mail pieces, brochures, signs, and so forth.

Marsh & McLennan Group Associates uses data processing extensively to compute product failure experience and performance of insured contract programs. Additionally, it uses the computer to issue policies and claim drafts.

Marsh & McLennan Group Associates provides an alternative to the organization issuing or planning to issue service contracts. The choice is between self-insuring the risk or passing it on to an insurance company. Marsh & McLennan feels that insurance is an option the issuer of the contract should evaluate.

C. NCR Corporation

History

The NCR Corporation was founded in 1884 as the National Cash Register Company. With its expansion into areas beyond the basic cash register, it changed its corporate name to NCR. NCR is involved in a wide array of markets supported by an equally wide spectrum of products. In retailing, it provides products for the small corner grocery to the large department store chain. In the financial market, it provides for the product needs of banks to brokerage houses. NCR products are available to meet the management requirements of supermarkets, hotels, hospitals, the federal government, and manufacturing plants. The demands of these markets have brought the company from the hand-cranked cash register to state-of-the-art computers and electronics.

For the small retail store, NCR can furnish an electronic cash register (ECR, as it's called in the industry). The large department store chain, on the other hand, will likely require NCR's complete telecommunications network to keep track of cash receipts and inventory. A typical system for a department store chain begins with point-of-sale terminals (what looks like cash registers to the novice). These point-of-sale terminals feed data (cash received, items sold, and so on) to a unit located in a back office. This unit is called a concentrator, and it consolidates all the data into categories prescribed by the managers of the department store chain. The concentrator can send, on command, the consolidated data through phone lines to a larger system that gathers the data from all stores. Depending on the type of system and its programming, the data can be used for such purposes as inventory analysis and control, sales evaluations, employee worktimes and locations, cash income, number and extent of voids and returns—virtually any information that the store chain management needs to manage the business effectively.

Similar systems can be set up for supermarkets, including scanners to read the bar codes so common on products today. Once the scanner reads the bar code, the price is recorded as well as the reduction of that item from inventory. The various analyses previously outlined in the department store example apply here, too.

In the financial markets, NCR furnishes products that range from tellers' terminals to computers used for the control and maintenance of individual accounts, loans, and so on. The degree of sophistication needed by the financial institution is conveyed to NCR, and the most effective system is furnished.

In industry, NCR products are used in process control, inventory control, and time management. The system can be programmed to track an item through various processes or operations in manufacturing. Based on information in the programming of the system, a completion time estimate can be determined at any point. This helps improve the flow through the plant by flagging bottlenecks or problem areas. It also helps improve customer relations by assisting the manufacturer in providing accurate delivery dates.

Organization

There are three areas of specialization in the NCR Corporation that relate to direct service to the customer. The first is sales, which makes customer contacts and sells the system hardware. The second is system support, which specializes in developing and supporting the customers' programming (software) requirements. The third and final area of specialization is the corporate service function, which is responsible for maintaining and repairing the hardware, that is, terminals.

To provide service support for the products NCR sells, it has established its own large servicing organization. The present national servicing organization consists of 15 regions. Within these regions are 111 districts. Each district is composed of anywhere from one to five service centers staffed by approximately 6,500 field service engineers. The field service engineers are supported by dispatchers, parts personnel, and administrators.

The field organization is backed up by service facilities maintained at the plant manufacturing the equipment. These plants are located around the world. The facilities are staffed with service specialists who assist the field service organization in solving problems, making modifications to products to meet customer needs, and helping determine if a product is still serviceable or requires replacement.

NCR also maintains a Central Technical Education Center in Dayton, Ohio, to train its service technicians in the repair and maintenance of particular products so that they are fully qualified to service the hardware. The field organization is also supported by a Business Planning Group that provides the field service organization with financial services. These include such items as parts pricing and the establishment of selling prices for service contracts. Service is such an important function at NCR that it has created a separate division called the Customer Services Division to incorporate all the service and service support functions just described.

The NCR Service Agreement

NCR calls its service contract an MAB Maintenance Agreement. The letters *MAB* stand for Maintenance Automated Billing. The agreement is usually sold by the sales force when the product is purchased. Most agreements are sold in this manner because the customer usually is concerned with how much the product will cost over a period of time. By including the cost of the agreement in the analysis, the salesperson can give the customer a very accurate "cost of ownership" because not only is the product cost included but also the cost of maintenance and repairs.

MAB Maintenance Agreements are written on an annual basis. Agreements are billed annually in advance. Customers can cancel an agreement at any time and receive a refund for the service period not used, provided they give NCR 30 days' notice of intent to cancel. NCR can also cancel the contract on 30 days' notice prior to the annual renewal date or if the customer has added peripherals or modifications that would, in NCR's opinion, affect the proper functioning of the product. The agreement is automatically renewable on its anniversary unless cancelled by either party. NCR will normally send customers a bill for the next year's payment 30 days before the current agreement term expires.

The basic MAB Maintenance Agreement is broken down into various service categories by product. Electronic Cash Registers (ECR),

point-of-sale registers, and concentrators are normally covered to provide service Monday through Saturday, 8 A.M. to 5 P.M. Similarly, large
systems and banking systems normally used only in weekday business
applications are covered to have service rendered Monday through
Friday, 8 A.M. to 5 P.M. Travel and labor time for service requested by
the customer for time periods not covered in the agreement is billed
separately. Parts covered by the agreement are provided at no additional charge, no matter when the service is rendered. On those products in which the number of hours the product is used is a key factor in
maintenance and repair requirements, the agreement stipulates that
the basic contract price covers service for a specified number of hours
of operation. Any usage in excess of this amount in a given month is
billed at some specified rate.

    NCR will tailor an agreement to meet a particular customer's
needs. For example, if a department store wants coverage seven days a
week, including holidays, and longer hours, say from 8 A.M. to mid-
night every day, then NCR will apply a surcharge to the basic agreement price and render service during the requested time periods and
days with no additional service charges for calls made during those
periods. The surcharges to be added to the basic agreement price are
provided to the sales and servicing organization for commonly requested variations by the Business Planning Group. They are in the
form of percent price increases to the basic agreement price. In this
way the local organization can price most requests without having to
contact NCR headquarters for special pricing. This not only saves time
and expense but permits the salesperson to close an order without the
undue delay that might be encountered in getting special pricing.

    For a customer's existing equipment that has not been covered by
a maintenance agreement, NCR first inspects the equipment, brings it
up to standard, and then issues an MAB Maintenance Agreement. The
customer is charged for the inspection and any work performed to
bring the apparatus up to standard; this charge is in addition to the cost
of the MAB Maintenance Agreement.

    In order to price its contracts accurately, NCR gathers data on
labor and parts costs to maintain and repair each product it manufactures. This information is gathered at headquarters for analysis. All
pricing of the contracts, amounts and types of surcharges, and approv-
als for nonstandard variations that have not been published originate
with the Business Planning Group at NCR headquarters.

Parts Handling

NCR has developed a parts handling system that it calls the Field Engineering Inventory Management System. Expendable items such as small parts are stocked outside the stockroom security area. When field service engineers need some of these expendable parts, they remove the parts needed from the storage racks, complete a form listing the type and quantity of items taken, and give this list to the parts clerk. For large and expensive items, field service engineers must request the items from the parts clerk (or parts manager), since these items are stored in a secured area. Field service engineers sign for the parts issued. Defective parts, which new parts are replacing, must be returned to the parts area upon completion of the service call. The parts clerk then issues signed receipts to the field service engineers as their evidence that the defective parts have been returned. This procedure ensures the control of critical parts and helps maintain the integrity of the parts room.

NCR has instituted a computerized tracking system to assist in the location of needed parts. All the components in stock in each service facility throughout the United States are kept on file in the computer. If for some reason a service facility is out of stock on a given part, it can call up the item on its computer terminal and the terminal will display every location that has the needed item, as well as the quantities in stock in those respective stockrooms. Then it is simply a matter for the parts clerk or manager to contact the nearest facility with adequate quantities and arrange to have the needed items shipped from there. Upon shipment, the computer automatically reflects the transfer of the item from one facility to the other.

Fulfilling the Agreement

Each service district is managed by a district manager. Reporting to the district manager are zone managers. The zone manager is responsible for managing a given service territory within the district, and is assigned a number of field service engineers. In addition to supervising their activities, the zone manager also must interface with sales and other districts as needed to fulfill NCR's obligation to its customers. Another responsibility of the zone manager is to sell service agreements to customers who do not purchase one at the time the equipment is purchased. Reporting to the zone manager are group leaders who are highly experienced, technically proficient field service engineers. Each group leader is responsible for anywhere from six to eight field service engineers. Their role is that of problem solver and customer relations representative. Should one of their assigned field service engineers have a technically complex problem, the group leader is called in for assistance.

In order to ensure customer satisfaction, NCR provides each customer with what it calls an "escalation procedure." Customers are advised how to go about getting service and the procedures to follow if they are not getting the response or satisfaction they desire. Essentially, the escalation procedure is that if they have a problem, they should advise the dispatcher. If the dispatcher does not solve the problem, they can call the zone manager. If still not satisfied, they can contact the district manager. If still not satisfied, they are advised to call the regional manager, and so on. This procedure gives customers the tools necessary to get results without having to go hunting for people in the chain of command. The subtle implication of the procedure is that it keeps everyone in the NCR organization conscious of customer satisfaction because each knows that the customer is aware of whom to call if an individual does not provide the best possible service.

The field service engineer is also given an escalation procedure to solve difficult problems. As mentioned previously, the field service engineer calls the zone manager; if the zone manager can't solve it, the field service engineer goes to a factory support group, which will find a solution if one is possible.

The district manager, through the company notification network, receives a weekly report listing all the products sold and to be installed in the district. For example, the report going to the Boston district manager may show that 30 units of a given product were sold in Los Angeles, California, for installation in Boston, Massachusetts. The district manager reviews the report with the zone managers to see what additional training, field service engineers, or parts are going to be required to support these additional products to be installed in the district. To assist them in this planning, the company furnishes parts lists and estimated work loads needed to support the additional service requirement. By using the notification network, the district manager has time to prepare for the arrival of the items sold and can therefore render proper service with ultimate customer satisfaction.

National Accounts

Since national accounts play a major role in NCR's success, the company has developed a program called Matrix Management to effectively meet its service goals with this type of customer. A national account is a large purchaser of products or services with the decision and/or installation sites located in several areas across the United States. For example, a customer with stores in New York, Chicago, Atlanta, and San Francisco would be treated as a national account.

Under the Matrix Management system, the district service manager where the customer's headquarters is located becomes the customer's key contact for service. This district manager has the authority to call any zone manager in the United States and ask for a response to the needs of a national account in that zone manager's zone of responsibility. The zone manager, under the directives of the Matrix Management system, must give this request priority. When calling a zone, the district manager informs the zone manager of the nature of the problem and by what date the problem must be resolved. If it must be resolved that day, then the zone manager must use the resources necessary to resolve it that day. NCR feels that the Matrix Management system is the strength of its organization. Under the system, the customer has to deal with only one person to solve a problem anywhere in the country.

Miscellany

Most of NCR's products are sold and serviced by NCR employees, but NCR does sell some products through dealers. The dealers are broken down into two categories: servicing and nonservicing. The nonservicing dealer just sells the product and refers customers to NCR for service. The servicing dealer normally services the products it sells and may offer its own service contracts. Customers have the option of purchasing a maintenance agreement from NCR, even if the product was purchased through a dealer. Similarly, customers can call NCR for time and material service. This provides assurance to customers that NCR service is available on all NCR products, no matter where they were purchased—either direct or through a dealer.

It is NCR's policy to not have the field service engineer sell peripherals. The reason for this is that the solution to a customer's needs can result in a combination of hardware and software products. It is felt that the customer's best interests can be served by an individual knowledgeable in the account's history and requirements. In such instances, the field service engineer is instructed to forward the perceived need on to the account manager assigned to that particular customer.

As mentioned previously, bills for renewal of agreements are sent out 30 days in advance of the renewal date. If customers do not pay on time (prior to the effective renewal or new agreement date), they are contacted by phone to find out why. If payment is not received within 30 days after the effective date of the agreement, then the agreement is cancelled. Any service that was rendered during the grace period is then billed to the customers on a time and material basis. Though collection is not a major problem, NCR feels it is important to have a collection policy for those instances when it does arise.

NCR believes that its direct service organization and the control and organizational systems it has instituted result in the desired degree of customer satisfaction. The MAB Maintenance Agreement forms the basis for effective cost control and clearly defined value from the customer's viewpoint and an effective sales and profit instrument from NCR's perspective.

D.   *Adesco, Inc.*

History

Adesco, Inc., is the largest administrator of automobile service contracts in the United States. It has 11 regional offices that serve as sales offices as well as service centers to handle service contract claims. Adesco is owned by the Minnehoma Insurance Company.

The Minnehoma Insurance Company established the predecessor of Adesco, Inc., to market and administer the automobile service contract programs that are developed and insured by them. With company-paid account executives spread across the United States, whose role it is to market the various service contract programs, Adesco has been able to develop its strong position in the marketplace.

In the early 1970s, Minnehoma started to enter the mechanical breakdown insurance market by offering insurance policies to cover mechanical repairs on automobiles. From this beginning, it has expanded into Extended Service Contracts, with Adesco, Inc. as the administrator. Today Adesco has contracts that cover virtually any domestic or foreign car sold in the United States and Canada. Neither Minnehoma nor Adesco perform any repair work on a vehicle. It is the auto dealer or independent service repair facility that actually performs the service. A bill for the authorized repair (repairs must be authorized by a Minnehoma Insurance Company claims representative before work is started on the vehicle) is sent to Minnehoma Insurance Company, which holds the funds and pays the claims. Adesco is the organization that handles the sales, dealer development, service contract processing, and other administrative functions.

From the legal standpoint the contract in most cases is an agreement between the dealer, distributor, or manufacturer and the customer. The customer is protected in the arrangement by the backing of the contract by Minnehoma. Therefore, if the dealer should go out of business Minnehoma, through its administrator Adesco, will help the customer arrange for service elsewhere. Similarly, if the customer happens to require a covered repair and is at a location distant from the selling dealer, Adesco will arrange for the repair at another dealership or other repair facility. In fact, Adesco/Minnehoma has agreements with large national repair organizations (AAMCO Transmissions, for example) to facilitate the repair of a contract holder's automobile anywhere in the United States or Canada. From the dealer's standpoint, its liability under the terms of its agreement with Adesco is limited to the cost of the contract. The insurance company (Minnehoma) issues a policy to the dealer, assuring this protection.

Marketing the Service Contract

Adesco has developed four basic marketing strategies in its service contract business. These strategies are:

1. To develop, insure, and administer service contract programs for manufacturers of automobiles.
2. To provide service contracts to national accounts such as car rental companies.
3. To develop private-label programs for independent organizations.
4. To promote and sell its own contracts directly to dealers.

Many manufacturers do not offer their own corporate contract programs. Adesco sees these companies as potential customers. It could take a manufacturer several years to develop a contract program, establish the claims administration network, and sell the program to its dealers. Since Adesco has the mechanism and personnel in place to sell and administer the program, the manufacturer can get into the market with a minimum of difficulty. To this is added the bonus of minimizing risk by having the Minnehoma Insurance Company insure the contract.

Nissan is one such company that has Adesco administering its contract program. Nissan and Adesco designed the program to meet Nissan's requirements. Some of the provisions of the plan include a zero deductible, a wide variety of month and mileage combinations of coverage, and the agreement written between Nissan and the customer (as opposed to it's being written between the dealer and the customer). By paying claims on first dollar of covered repairs, making Nissan a party to the contract, and offering coverages for as long as 60 months and 100,000 miles with transfer provisions to subsequent owners, the program helps perpetuate Nissan's quality image. One of the advantages in using Adesco is that Nissan saves a fair amount of time in establishing a program and considerable money in start-up costs. Nissan is able to offer its customers the type of service contract they desire while having an experienced administrator process its business and an insurer pay the claims: a win-win situation.

Adesco identified another growing market for its services in national accounts. In particular, it saw the major automobile rental companies as potential customers for service contracts. The car rental companies realized that a service contract could enhance the resale value of their used cars by minimizing any concerns customers would have about potential major repair expenses that might be incurred. Because the automobile rental companies sold their used cars through company-owned outlets as well as through franchises, they were faced with the problem of how to offer customers protection yet do it effectively through both types of outlets. National Car Rental, for example, developed a warranty program with Adesco to apply to every used car National sells through its corporate outlets. National offers its customers a 24-month, 24,000-mile limited warranty with every used vehicle sold. This same warranty is offered to its franchises at a corporate rate that is included, at the franchisee's option, in the selling price of the automobile.

Other car rental companies have chosen a wide variety of approaches to provide their customers with mechanical protection on used cars. Some self-insure and administer their programs. Others, such as Thrifty Rent-A-Car, Budget Rent-A-Car, and Dollar Rent-A-Car, have arranged with Adesco to develop service contract programs for their franchisees. These programs insured by Minnehoma permit independent car rental dealers to offer mechanical breakdown service contracts to their customers with Adesco handling repair claims. The service contract program assists the franchisee in alleviating any customer apprehension in purchasing the used automobile and helps the franchisee realize added profits through the sale of the contract.

Adesco's third strategy is to offer private-label contracts to companies. It does this by developing several contract programs under various titles. These programs are developed and sold to organizations that wish to market service contracts to some dealer or customer base. The selling organization may simply be looking for an easy, risk-free way to get into the service contract sales business, or it may be interested in marketing the service contract as part of the franchise arrangement to a group of dealers. Adesco formulates and administers the desired program with Minnehoma Insurance insuring it. Adesco has put together a number of these programs for such marketing groups.

Lastly, Adesco markets a number of its own programs directly to dealers. Many dealers do not have or wish to participate in manufacturers' programs, or they may wish to supplement a manufacturer's offering. Adesco sees this as an attractive market and, as such, has developed programs for new and used vehicles. Minnehoma has formulated the contracts and rates for virtually all new and used cars sold in the United States. These programs are sold to dealers through Adesco's own sales force.

In order to develop strong ties to dealers and assist them in selling the service contracts offered by Adesco, a Dealer Development Program was created. With this program, Adesco provides dealers with a wide array of services. These include assistance in recruiting personnel, from interviewing to testing candidates. They also help with financial analysis and the training of service contract sales personnel. Dealer development specialists visit the dealers monthly and review service contract sales progress and profitability. These specialists are trained to assist the dealers in financial planning and control as well as in achieving customer satisfaction. In addition, the dealers have access to personal computers and software to help them manage their businesses. Dealers can also purchase credit life and disability insurance from Adesco's Credit Life carrier to sell to those customers financing their vehicles through them.

Adesco does not charge dealers for the services of the dealer development specialist. The only things dealers must pay for are the computer and software (if they choose to buy them) and a nominal charge to send their personnel to Adesco's training school. From Adesco's viewpoint, the Dealer Development Program provides dealers with good returns on their investments by increasing their proficiency in the sale of service contracts and credit life and disability insurance.

Though a dealer does not have to participate in the Dealer Development Program to be authorized to sell service contracts, Adesco has been successful in signing them up by showing how other dealers have profited from active participation in the program. It is the responsibility of the account executive to present the program to the dealers and sign them up. Once this is done, a dealer development specialist is assigned to each dealer. This specialist visits the dealer at least once a month to review progress, make suggestions for improvement, and render needed assistance.

Pricing the Contract

To price a contract accurately, Minnehoma gathers data on every type and model of car it insures. Each model car is given a four-digit number. All repairs, including type and cost, are entered in the computer for each model car, using this control number. Additionally, the dealer making the repair is noted as well as the section of the country in which the car is repaired. Using this extensive data base, Minnehoma monitors each insured component of each model vehicle. Loss ratio reports are reviewed regularly. A loss ratio report is simply money out versus money in. For example, if an insurance company receives $100 for a service contract and pays out $100 in claims, it has a 100 percent loss ratio. Similarly, if the insurance company takes in $100 and pays out $50, then it experiences a 50 percent loss ratio. If the loss ratio goes above acceptable levels, then a review is made as to the cause of the problem and adjustments are forthcoming. The causes may include pricing that is too low, a failure rate in excess of the plan, or poor dealer performance. Corrective action may take the form of increased pricing or cancellation of dealers with excessively high loss ratios.

When a new model of a previously insured vehicle comes on the market, Minnehoma will review its mechanical components to determine which are the same or similar to components on previous models. Then it looks at new features and tries to determine their failure rates and how difficult they are to repair. Minnehoma then gathers the repair history, including the loss ratios, on those components that have been used in previous model years. The data, coupled with the anticipated failure rate on newly designed components, are used to determine an anticipated cost to repair the vehicle for a given number of miles of use. In pricing the contract, mileage plays a key role. The more miles a contract is written for, the greater the cost. The length of the contract in time is also considered, but not to the degree of the mileage factor. Minnehoma has programs in its computer to analyze the effect of time and mileage combinations and component loss ratios.

Once a price for a given specific model and year of a brand of vehicle is determined, Minnehoma adds its profit and passes this cost on to Adesco. To this cost, Adesco adds an administration fee to cover the costs to sell the contracts and administer claims. A profit margin is added to this figure, and the result is given to the dealers in the form of a rate card. The dealers then know their cost for a specific contract (months and miles) for a given vehicle. They normally add their profits to establish a selling price. When the customer buys a five-year, 60,000-mile service contract, the manufacturer of the new vehicle covers defects for some period of time and mileage. Since the term of the service contract begins on the day the vehicle is acquired, the exposure for Minnehoma as insurer of the service contract is limited during this period. Most service contracts include a towing reimbursement and a car rental allowance, which are not normally covered by the manufacturer's warranty. Minnehoma must cover these costs, but they are relatively small in comparison to the cost of repairs. Of course the degree of coverage offered by the manufacturer in its warranty is considered by Minnehoma in developing its service contract prices. This system of first-day coverage provides the customer with uninterrupted continuity of coverage because the selling dealer most often performs the warranty work as well as fulfills the terms of the service contract. Many dealers also arrange for needed towing and car rental.

Used vehicles present a different set of challenges when pricing is considered. Minnehoma has the history on a particular model car but does not know if the individual automobile being insured has been properly maintained and is in good mechanical condition at the time of sale. To help protect itself, Minnehoma stipulates in its dealer agreement that dealers make sure the automobile is in good condition prior to issuing a contract.

Service contracts for used cars are generally sold for only two periods: a 12-month, 12,000-mile contract, and a 24-month, 24,000-mile contract. The 12-month, 12,000-mile contract is sold on vehicles that have less than 100,000 miles. The 24-months, 24,000-mile contract is sold on vehicles with less than 50,000 miles on them. The basic contract is priced at the same rate for a given model less than six years old; a surcharge is applied for older vehicles. Rates are established for a particular model vehicle based on the number of miles accumulated on the odometer. Since all the factors of age, mileage, and length of contract are considered in pricing the service agreement, the levels of profitability for new and used contracts are comparable.

Deductibles are often applied in the service contract. A deductible of $25 or $50 is sufficient to prevent the customers from returning to the dealer with minor or frivolous claims. This keeps the administrative costs to manageable levels while providing the coverage for which the contract was intended, that is, major component failure. As mentioned previously, Nissan offers a zero deductible service agreement. From the customer's viewpoint, it's attractive; from Nissan's viewpoint, it enhances the value of the contract. As this indicates, Adesco and Minnehoma can design a wide range of contracts with provisions to meet the needs of a manufacturer and the demands of the marketplace.

Benefits of Adesco's Programs

Adesco cites several reasons for its success in the automotive service contract market:

1. The Minnehoma Insurance Company claim system. With 11 regional offices plus headquarters spread across the United States to handle claims and two claims offices in Canada, they can give the customer regionalized service. The advantage of regional service is that the Minnehoma Insurance Company personnel in a particular region get to know the dealers and other repair facilities in their area of responsibility and thus can respond to a customer's needs more quickly and effectively.
2. Adesco's 800 number system. Customers are given a list of 800 telephone numbers for each regional office. This permits them to call Adesco toll free for assistance, no matter where they are in the United States or Canada.
3. Seventy-two-hour turnaround in claims. It is Minnehoma Insurance Company's goal to send a reimbursement check to the dealer within 72 hours of receipt of the dealer's invoice for a covered repair. This helps dealers with their cash flow because they do not have to wait a long period of time for the money.
4. The dealer has a wide range of service contracts from which to choose. Thus, dealers can select agreements that meet their and their customers' needs.

5. Minnehoma's issuance of the mechanical reimbursement policy to the dealer. Dealers have written, legal evidence that all agreements issued by them under Adesco's program are fully insured by the Minnehoma Insurance Company.
6. Adesco has over 4,000 dealers involved in their programs in the United States. This is advantageous, because it permits Adesco to be able to refer a customer to a known dealer no matter where or when service is needed.
7. Their service contracts are generally priced lower than most contracts issued by manufacturers. This is an advantage to both the dealer and the customer. The dealer finds the contract easier to sell at a higher margin, thus earning better profits. The customer in turn can receive good coverage at a lower price.
8. Adesco's Dealer Development Program. This program, as mentioned previously, assists the dealer in improving service contract sales, profitability, and customer satisfaction.

Service contracts form the basis of Minnehoma's and Adesco's business. Together they are committed to the creative development of service contract programs that meet the needs of the marketplace, thus remaining a leader in the industry.

E.   A-Copy, Inc.

History

A-Copy, Inc., under the logo A-Copy America, is one of the largest independent dealers of copiers in the United States. The business was started in 1965 with a $1,000-investment and has grown into a multi-million dollar organization. With multiple sales and service locations throughout the Northeast, A-Copy, Inc. now handles several lines of copiers, as well as word processors and typewriters.

Service has been a key element in the organization's success. Today the service contract represents some 85 percent of all its service business, with the remaining 15 percent generated by time and material sales. A-Copy sells and leases copiers as well as sells the customer needed supplies.

Organization

The service function is headed by the general service manager. Reporting to the general service manager are regional managers. Regional managers have a number of field service managers reporting to them. Each field service manager supervises approximately 15 technicians. This organization provides the general service manager with an effective span of control. (A span of control is the number of people an individual supervises.)

The entire service organization is comprised of some 300 service technicians and 150 managers and support people.

Marketing the Service Contract

From the general service manager's viewpoint there is no one in the company who isn't a maintenance agreement salesperson. The salesperson selling an item of equipment will try to sell the service agreement to the customer. It is estimated that 10 to 15 percent of the contracts are sold this way.

For customers who do not purchase agreements, A-Copy will send follow-up mailings. These mailings describe the value of the maintenance agreement, inform the customer that the warranty is expiring, and explain how the maintenance agreement extends the warranty coverage. A-Copy finds this direct mail program to be effective in bringing in an additional 50 percent more of the products sold under contract.

The service technicians are also trained to sell the agreements. They are instructed to inform customers of the cost of any warranty repairs performed, so that the customers are aware that the warranty may have, for example, saved them $300. Customers are advised that, if it is purchased, the service contract will give them equal protection beyond the warranty period. This generally results in additional contract sales.

Maintenance agreements (A-Copy calls its service contracts maintenance agreements) not sold at this point are referred to the telemarketing group. The telemarketing group is responsible for selling maintenance agreements and supplies. Each individual in the telemarketing group is assigned a territory. Territories are assigned based on potential dollar sales volume. Each telemarketing person is also assigned a sales quota.

When a copier is sold, a copy of the sales order is forwarded to a telemarketing person. This individual immediately starts a card file on the customer. A review is made of the sales order to see if the salesperson who sold the product also sold the customer an initial amount of supplies as well as a service contract. If supplies were sold, for example, but not the maintenance agreement, the telemarketing person calls the customer and tries to sell an agreement. After 30 days, another call is placed to the customer asking the status of supplies. At that time the telemarketing person asks the customer for a meter reading on the copier. Using parameters furnished by the copier manufacturer, a determination can be made of the rate of supply usage. From this it is relatively easy to estimate when the supplies will need replenishment. A notation is made on the customer's card, and it is placed for follow up on the anticipated reorder date. The telemarketing people have been trained to explore the customer's needs for peripherals or additional copiers whenever they make a call.

The telemarketing people also call other companies to determine if they have copiers. If not, they try to sell one; if not successful, they pass the lead on to a salesperson. If the customer has a brand of copier that A-Copy services, then an attempt is made to sell a maintenance agreement. To assist customers in making the decision to enter a service agreement with A-Copy, the telemarketing person offers them a free service call provided they agree to purchase a contract. All required labor to inspect and repair the unit is provided at no charge. Customers must only pay for any parts used, and these are provided at cost.

A-Copy actively pursues the maintenance agreement business to increase its service density, which results in less travel time and greater profits. The more service contracts it has per square mile, the less travel time and expense is incurred between calls. Additionally, a company that purchases a maintenance agreement from A-Copy is more likely to purchase supplies from it.

If a prospect does not have a type of copier that is serviced by A-Copy, then the telemarketing person attempts only to sell supplies. Supplies consist of such items as paper, toner, drums, and so on— products that are consumable.

Pricing the Contract

In pricing its maintenance agreement, A-Copy reviews the manufacturer's recommended retail price for each type of contract proposed by the manufacturer. It then reviews its personal experience with the particular copier and the market conditions. From this information a selling price is established. A-Copy has found that using the input from manufacturers has simplified the mechanics of pricing the contracts. It comes down to simply verifying the manufacturer's data, including labor rates, parts pricing, and travel allowances and then adjusting the data for its market.

The Seven Promises for Office Productivity

A-Copy has developed a successful strategy that sells copiers and maintenance agreements. This strategy is expressed as the Seven Promises for Office Productivity:

Promise One. A-Copy guarantees the purchaser of a new copier that the unit will perform satisfactorily for 1 million copies or five years, whichever comes first, provided the customer continuously covers the copier with an A-Copy maintenance agreement and the customer purchases its supplies from A-Copy. If A-Copy can't repair the copier any time during this period, it will replace the copier at no charge.

Promise Two. A-Copy promises to respond to emergency calls within eight working hours for all holders of maintenance agreements. If it fails to do so, it will give the customer 1,000 sheets of copy paper free.

Promise Three. A-Copy promises to give maintenance agreement customers credit for their old copier as a trade-in toward a new one. Customers receive a 100 percent credit toward the purchase of a new copier if the present copier does not prove adequate within three months of purchase.

Promise Four. A-Copy will develop a lease-purchase, outright sale, or lease program to meet the customer's needs.

Promise Five. A-Copy promises to provide customers with top-quality supplies. Customers are given the option of prepaying for their anticipated annual supply needs, thereby guaranteeing the price of all supplies for the year.

Promise Six. A-Copy promises the holder of a maintenance agreement that the annual cost of each subsequent agreement will not increase in price more than the increase in the Consumer Price Index (CPI) in the customer's area. This protects the customer from a price increase that is in excess of the average increase in prices in that area.

Promise Seven. A-Copy promises the customer no aggravation. Should customers have problems, all they have to do is call one of A-Copy's special representatives. This individual is trained to solve problems and help ensure customer satisfaction.

Ensuring Top-Quality Service

To maintain its position as the largest independent copier dealer in America, and to ensure it will be able to honor its promises to the customers, A-Copy invests considerable effort in maintaining and motivating service personnel. To ensure that service technicians are well trained in the products they service, A-Copy maintains a staff of five full-time trainers. These trainers put new service personnel through a rigorous course in the maintenance and repair of the products A-Copy sells. It is estimated that because of this course, A-Copy can, within six months, have a new technician reach the level of service proficiency equal to that of a three-year veteran. All service personnel must attend technical training sessions every two weeks. During these sessions the service technicians are trained on new products or in product modifications. In addition they are given refreshers on the maintenance and repair of existing products. A-Copy cannot overestimate the value of its training programs and what they have meant to the success of the company.

To ensure customer satisfaction and maintain its profitability, technicians are trained to make each service call count. Technicians are instructed to perform preventive maintenance during every service call. A-Copy has found that this policy has doubled the number of copies made by customers between service visits. This, therefore, has cut the number of service calls in half. This program has also improved customer satisfaction, because customers perceive the presence of a service technician as a hindrance to office operation. By cutting the number of calls in half, customers have a better perception of the reliability of a product. For the most part, customers do not differentiate between a preventive maintenance call and a repair call; both disrupt the office. By combining both, A-Copy improves its service perception.

To further improve customer relations, each service technician is given proficiency goals and is rewarded for any increase in proficiency above those goals. The goals stipulate that a serviced unit must run for a specified number of copies between service calls, that there should not be a call-back within a specified number of days, and that the technician averages a minimum number of calls per day. A bonus is paid on each month's performance. For example, a goal may be established for a technician to achieve a 90 percent proficiency level, average a minimum of five calls per day, and go 15 days between call-backs. Let's assume that a given technician makes 100 calls in a 20-day work period, and receives four call-backs by customers in less than 15 days. First, the average calls per day would be checked. 100 divided by 20 days gives an average of five calls per day:

$$\frac{100}{20} = 5$$

The first requirement is met. Then the percentage of call-backs is calculated. This is done by dividing the number of call-backs by the number of calls; 4 divided by 100 gives a 4 percent call-back rate:

$$\frac{4}{100} = .04$$

Since the proficiency requirement is 90 percent, the call-back allowance is 100 percent minus 90 percent, or 10 percent:

$$100\% - 90\% = 10\%$$

To measure the degree to which the service technician exceeded the proficiency level, subtract the 4 percent from the 10 percent, giving a 6 percent improvement over standard:

$$10 - 4 = 6$$

The bonus is $25 per proficiency point above standard. The technician receives a bonus of $150 that month: 6 × $25 = $150. Table E-1 shows this:

Table E-1. Efficiency report for service technicians.

Technician's Name	Total Calls	Number of Days	Average Calls per Day	Number Call-backs	Percent Call-backs
J.C.	100	20	5	4	4

The proficiency allowance is as follows:

$$100\% - 90\% = 10\%$$
$$10\% - 4\% = 6\%$$
$$6 \times \$25 = \$150 \text{ bonus for month}$$

A-Copy found that this program has reduced the cost per call significantly because technicians are motivated to do quality work to reduce call-backs while realizing they must maintain a minimum average number of calls per day.

The service technicians are informed, as part of their initial training and orientation, of the importance of quality performance. To ensure that A-Copy's standards of quality service are maintained, periodic unannounced inspections are made of recent service calls.

A service manager reviews the calls an individual technician is scheduled to make on a given day. This is done on the evening before the technician will make those calls. The service manager arrives at the first scheduled call site before 8 A.M. This is to ensure that the technician arrives at the first call on time. One standard set for all service technicians is that they start work at 8 A.M. The inspector (service manager) asks the technician to select two of the previous day's service orders. The technician, of course, selects two that he or she believes are particularly good jobs in servicing. Then the inspector selects two more at random. With copies of the four service orders in hand, the inspector visits the customers, advises them that he or she is there for a quality inspection, and proceeds to inspect the copier. Using a quality control checklist, the inspector ensures that the unit was properly serviced and that parts indicated on the service order as having been replaced were indeed replaced.

The service technician is critiqued as to performance, with recommendations made as to how future performance can be improved. Or the technician is complimented on a job well done. From the customer's perception, the quality inspections give further assurance of A-Copy's interest and commitment to customer satisfaction.

Service technicians are trained to be conscious of customer needs beyond the servicing of the basic copier. Technicians are given a price list of peripheral equipment, and if they see a need for a given peripheral, they can sell it to customers on the spot. The service technicians are paid a small commission on peripheral and new maintenance agreement sales. However, since their primary job is service, they are not measured in any way on sales performance.

Inventory Control

Inventory is maintained in service center stockrooms under controlled conditions. The parts manager at each location is responsible for the integrity of the stockroom. Base inventory levels are monitored so that an average three-month supply of parts is maintained at all times. When a new product arrives, A-Copy reviews the manufacturer's recommended stock levels. Generally, A-Copy increases the number of parts indicated to maintain at least a seven-month inventory. This level of inventory is maintained until A-Copy has sufficient history on the product to be comfortable with lower stock levels. This is all done to help ensure customer satisfaction by having the needed parts in stock.

Technicians are given a two-week parts inventory to carry in their service vehicles. Based on the data received from service invoices turned in by the technicians, the computer monitors each technician's consumption of parts. The computer analyzes if the consumption rate is increasing or decreasing and will adjust the technician's base inventory levels accordingly.

Every two weeks, the service technicians come to the parts stockroom on a designated day. The parts clerk has, prior to the technicians' arrivals, checked the computer printout and determined what parts they used in the past two-week period and any needed adjustments in stock levels for the service vehicles. The clerk then gathers the parts and puts them in boxes. When the technicians arrive, they check the type and quantities of parts being given to them and sign for them.

To control shrinkage of parts in the service vehicles, two scheduled and at least two unscheduled inventories are made each year. The scheduled inventories are made at the close of the fiscal year and at midyear. These are complete inventories of every part in the vehicles' stocks. The nonscheduled inventories are surprise inventories conducted at random times between scheduled inventories.

To conduct a nonscheduled inventory, a service manager appears unannounced at a job site. He or she has a computer printout of the assigned stock of the vehicle, less any items shown as used since the last time the vehicle stock was replenished. The service technician is asked to provide copies of any invoices that have not been turned in, showing parts consumed since the date of the computer printout. The service manager deducts these from the net totals shown on the printout. The service manager then selects at random 20 low-priced items and 20 high-priced items and physically counts them. The number of each item counted should match the quantities calculated. Standards have been set as to acceptable shrinkage levels owing to loss or breakage. Also, the type of item short is considered. The manager would question seriously the loss, for example, of an expensive photo-receptor drum.

Reports and Forms

Service technicians carry four basic forms with them in their service vehicles: (1) a warranty claim form to be completed on products still under the manufacturer's warranty, (2) a service invoice to be completed on all time and material and maintenance agreement service calls, (3) blank copies of maintenance agreements (should the technician sell one, he or she can provide the customer with a copy on the spot), and (4) an expense report to secure reimbursement for incurred expenses (fuel for the service vehicle, tolls, and so on).

The service invoice is the form most predominantly used. The invoice is a three-part form with carbons provided to make copies of each entry. The first level is the customer original, which is left with the customer at the completion of the call. The second copy goes to the computer entry area for entry of all data including parts used, labor hours, type of call (maintenance, retrofit, call-back, and so on), primary cause of failure, customer name, machine ID number, and so forth. The third copy is a file copy used for future reference. To enter the type of call and primary cause of failure, a numerical coding system is used. If the copier is under a maintenance agreement or under warranty, the service technician still extends all labor and parts costs so that the customer is aware of the dollar value of the service. The technician will write on the invoice "no charge" in large letters. The value of these no-charge service calls is used as a marketing tool when the contract comes up for renewal.

The Service Tech Call Report is published monthly. This is a report of the proficiency levels achieved by service technicians. It mentions those individuals who exceeded goals and earned a bonus for the month. The report also shows the cumulative level of proficiency achieved by each individual during the previous six-month period. The report is further broken down by field service manager team. The performance of each technician in a particular service manager's team is listed below the manager's name. This report is distributed to the general service manager, the regional managers, and the field service managers.

The field service manager's performance is measured on the cumulative productivity and proficiency of the technicians on the manager's team. Items that are looked at are the number of service calls made per day, the cost per call, the response time, and the number of technicians that meet or exceed proficiency targets.

A Stack Ranking Report is generated to rank the technicians in order of proficiency. The data generated by the Service Tech Call Report are used to develop this listing. Top performers are given an assortment of incentives. Technicians earn points based on their ranking, which can be converted to prizes. To further motivate employees to strive for excellence, reports are sent each month to the technicians' spouses, indicating the technicians' ranking and point status. If individuals do not earn an award in one month, they still have an opportunity to accumulate points and earn a quarterly award. The program has proved extremely successful, in that spouses have helped motivate the technicians to win the monthly or quarterly prizes.

The Inventory Regional Summary shows the number of months' supply of parts in vehicles and in the parts rooms of each region. Since A-Copy's goal is to achieve four turns of inventory per year, it looks to have one month's supply of parts in the vehicle and two months' supply in the regional parts facilities. This report is supplemented by the Inventory Analysis Report, which shows dollars of inventory for each product line serviced. The report also gives the annual trend of inventory levels for each product line. In this way the general service manager can see if inventory dollar amounts for any given manufacturer are going up or down, and if this trend is consistent with increases or decreases in the number of units of that product line being serviced.

The Inventory Turn Summary simply shows the dollar amount of inventory on hand, the total dollar usage in the month, and the number of months' parts supply on hand in each region. It then summarizes all this information into corporate totals.

The most comprehensive report is the President's Report, designed to give the company president the status of critical corporate functions. This report, broken down by region, informs the president of such items as total sales, total expenses, operating expenses, service expense, and sales expense. It also includes a sales and gross profit analysis by product. Another category shows receipts from programs such as its participation in manufacturers' national account programs.

Using the Computer

A-Copy uses a mainframe computer to generate parts reports and service billing. It has purchased software from Modern Business Systems of St. Louis, Missouri. This software is designed for all kinds of dealerships and is not restricted to the copier industry. The program is customer-based in that any data entered on a customer is shared by all data base files automatically, that is, accounts receivable, parts, and so on. The system is capable of handling a computer dispatch program. It is utilized in the development of the data used in the reports outlined previously.

The A-Copy Advantages

A-copy sees the following advantages for the company in its service contract program:

1. The service contract provides a predictable, profitable source of revenue. This it feels is the prime advantage of the service contract.
2. The contract helps the company keep track of machines in order to assess their reliability.
3. The contract precludes competition. It eliminates shopping for service by the customer.
4. There are fewer collection problems.
5. Contracts help get repeat copier purchase business.

A-Copy's studies show that a new copier purchase decision is made every three years. Having previous maintenance agreements with the customers and the trade-in promise facilitate a sale. Similarly, at the expiration of the five-year, 1 million-copy promise, customers are in a good position for a sale.

The advantages of the service contract to the customer are seen as follows:

1. The customer has a fixed annual service cost.
2. A-Copy provides the customer with a guarantee of reliability.

3. The customer receives a guaranteed fast response to service calls.
4. A-Copy guarantees the authenticity of all replacement parts. It is in A-Copy's interest as well as the customer's to provide quality parts. Repeat calls owing to parts failure are costly to both parties.
5. The customer knows the machine is being serviced by qualified technicians. A-Copy won't service a copier it doesn't sell.

Credit and Collection

With a very high percentage of its customers under maintenance agreements, which are paid for in advance, A-Copy's collection of money due is not a major problem. The only area of concern is with time and material sales, and on these the technicians try to collect payment when the service is rendered.

Since the technicians price the invoices at the completion of their service calls, billing problems are virtually eliminated. The only billing usually necessary are the annual bills that are sent out for contract renewals.

A-Copy is very pleased with its Maintenance Agreement Program. It feels it has contributed significantly to the success and profitability of the company.

F.　*Canon U.S.A., Inc.*

Canon U.S.A., Inc., markets its copier products and renders service through authorized dealers. The profile begins with a description of how this company effectively markets its products and service through its dealer organization and concludes by describing how it uses these same dealers to implement a flourishing national account program.

Background of Canon's Dealer Organization

All Canon products, from cameras to copiers, are marketed and distributed in the United States by Canon U.S.A., Inc., a subsidiary of Canon, Inc., in Japan. The Copier Division is responsible for marketing Canon's NP and PC line of photocopiers. The NP line consists of midsize copiers designed for those customers requiring a unit to make 500 or more copies per month. The PC cartridge copiers are designed for those applications where the monthly demand is for fewer than 500 copies. Each line is marketed and serviced in a different way.

The NP copier is sold exclusively through combination sales and service dealerships. In order for a dealer to buy the NP line of copiers from Canon U.S.A., Inc., it must qualify as an Authorized Sales and Service Organization. The agreement signed by the NP dealer is a combination sales and service agreement. This simply means that the dealer not only assumes an obligation to sell the product, but also to properly service it. Each NP authorized dealer must send a technician to one of Canon's five service training locations in the United States for each NP product which is listed in the dealer agreement. The dealership designation is granted when the technician successfully completes the NP service course.

The PC line of copiers is sold and serviced in a manner different from the NP line. As previously indicated, the NP copier is designed for low- to relatively high-volume use and, as such, requires a large number of features in order to fill the potential customer's needs. The copier is not portable in nature, thus requires on-site service. Most often the dealer selling the product is called in to service the machine. This is the reason Canon requires NP dealerships to have both sales and service capabilities.

When the PC line was introduced, it was geared to the low-volume user: consumers, home office customers, and small offices. Canon reasoned that this type of copier would be sold through NP dealers as well as retailers of varying sizes. In establishing its sales and service organizations for this product line, Canon felt that a number of the retailers would not have service capabilities. Consequently, Canon established two separate agreements for the sale and service of the PC. This permitted a retailer to be an authorized sales outlet without having the responsibility or authority to service the product.

Canon developed an arrangement similar to that enjoyed by an appliance retailer or department store. A customer purchases the product at one of these outlets but brings it elsewhere for service. In order to market the PC in this manner, Canon had to establish independent service facilities. More than 500 Authorized Service Facilities (ASF) were established for the PC line of copiers. These are made up of retailers that both service and sell the PC, independent third-party servicing organizations, and NP dealerships that have signed separate PC Sales and PC Service agreements.

To be qualified to become an Authorized Service Facility for the PC copier, an organization (retailer, third-party service facility, or NP dealer) must have at least two technicians complete a course in servicing the PC copier. Since many of the smaller retailers opted to offer service, Canon devised a home study course for their technicians. The reason for this is that the small retailer normally cannot afford to send the two technicians to a Canon training center nor lose the services of these technicians for any period of time. Upon completion of the course of study, the technicians take an examination, which is sent to Canon and graded. If they pass the exam, they become certified. The ASF then must complete a service agreement, and the organization's name is added to the list of Authorized Service Facilities (after it is checked for a good credit rating).

This list of Authorized Service Facilities is given to each customer with the PC purchase. A PC customer can bring the PC to any Authorized Service Facility for warranty repairs. In the case of the NP, the selling dealer renders the warranty service.

Types of Contracts

NP Copier Line

Canon does not write service contracts on any of the copiers it sells. However, it assists its dealerships in suggesting prices for service contracts and in administering suggested contract programs. For the NP line of copiers Canon has developed three basic types of contracts that each dealer can use as is or modify to meet market conditions: (1) full coverage, (2) practical coverage, and (3) minimum coverage.

The full coverage service contract covers all components including consumable items such as the photo-receptor drum, webs, and so on, which deteriorate with age and usage in a copier. This contract is all inclusive and is the most comprehensive (and most expensive) offered.

The practical coverage contract offers all the services provided by the full service agreement but eliminates coverage on the consumables. The cost of this contract is less than that of the full service contract. This is the most popular type of contract sold, because it achieves a practical balance between the cost of the contract and the degree of service rendered. Most customers know that the consumable replacement requirements are dependent on usage and, in some cases, it is less expensive to purchase them when necessary, depending upon the user's needs.

The minimum coverage service contract covers only preventive maintenance service. Any necessary repair costs are paid for when needed by the customer. This is the least popular of the three service contracts offered.

PC Copier Line

Since the PC copier is a portable, consumer-type item, the servicing of this product is handled differently from that of the NP line. In the NP line of copiers, Canon U.S.A. covers the cost of warranty labor by offsetting it with the low wholesale selling price of the product and also covers the cost of replacement parts on an exchange basis. By an exchange basis, Canon means that it sends the dealer a replacement part for every defective part returned under warranty. In the PC line, Canon assumes the cost of both warranty parts and labor. Should a PC copier require service during the warranty period, the customer can return it to any PC Authorized Service Facility and have it repaired. The ASF then forwards a copy of the customer's original bill of sale, a completed warranty repair form, and any defective part to Canon U.S.A. The copy of the original bill of sale establishes the date the warranty period begins. Canon then pays the ASF a pre-established flat rate to cover labor costs and replaces any defective parts on an exchange basis.

There is one flat rate amount allocated per copier repair, irrespective of the amount of time spent working on the unit. It is expected that the ASF will be adequately reimbursed, since labor time spent on product repairs average out to an equitable payment for the services rendered. Once the warranty expires, the ASF can sell the customer a service contract.

The PC service contract is a carry-in agreement. There is only one type of PC contract offered, and it is sold by the Authorized Service Facilities. The contracts are written for a one-year period and entitle the purchaser to two free service visits plus any required parts at no charge. From the third service visit on, the customer pays a minimum charge for each visit. There is no additional cost for labor or parts beyond this minimum (or deductible, if you prefer).

The PC Authorized Service Facility actually prices and fulfills the service contract just as the NP dealer does. The customer's agreement is with the ASF, so when the customer purchases a service contract from a particular ASF, he or she must return to that ASF for service under the contract.

Pricing the Contract

Most of the products sold in the United States are first introduced in Europe and the Far East. The experience gained from the operation of a given product overseas helps to determine suggested service contract pricing. Canon, Inc., gathers data on the longevity of copier components and forwards this information to Canon U.S.A., Inc. Its experience with the product also provides information on the needed frequency and type of preventive maintenance services to ensure maximum product life. When a new product is going to be introduced in the United States, it is first checked in Canon U.S.A.'s North America test facilities to verify data received from Canon, Inc., which establishes a level of confidence in the product and its service requirements.

To price the service contract, Canon U.S.A., Inc., establishes the maintenance requirements and projected number and types of repairs that will be required for a certain number of copies made on a given model. The number of copies on which a contract is based is the anticipated number of copies the average customer normally makes in a year. This figure permits Canon to analyze the failure rate that normally should be experienced per year. Similarly, knowing the service requirements of a particular copier model for a set number of copies permits Canon to determine how many service calls will be needed per year. For example, assume a given copier is known to be used to make an average of 10,000 copies per month in the average office; that translates to 120,000 copies a year. Also assume that it is known from test and field data that a certain component of that copier will last an average of 100,000 copies before needing replacement. In pricing the annual contract, the replacement cost of one such component will be included. Similarly, if it is determined that the unit requires maintenance a given number of times a year, then the cost of rendering that maintenance can be calculated.

Having determined the number and extent of repair calls that must be made, coupled with the number and type of maintenance calls that are necessary, Canon has the basis for pricing the contract.

Knowing the total number of hours needed on average to repair and maintain a given product model permits Canon to price the labor cost. To accomplish this, it is simply a matter of multiplying the sum of the hourly labor cost for the average technician, including benefits and overhead attributable to the technician, times the total number of hours previously generated. To this figure is added the cost of parts and materials that will be required to service the unit for the term of the contract. The mileage rate is established for a typical service vehicle, and categories of various distances from the service facility to the customer (for example, 0–25 miles, 26–50 miles, and so on) are established. The cost of time, fuel, vehicle depreciation, insurance, and so forth are added to the cost of the contract for each category. All the costs are added up; to this, a profit margin is added to arrive at a contract price.

Before the suggested prices are passed on to a dealer, a review is made of competitive pricing and market conditions to ensure that the suggested prices are viable in the marketplace. The suggested service contract prices for each product and for each category of travel distances are sent to each authorized dealer.

Since each contract is priced based on a given number of copies made per year, the dealer potentially can experience a loss if a particular customer exceeds that norm. To protect the dealer and to price the contract fairly, Canon gives the dealer a per-copy dollar amount to be added to the contract cost for those customers exceeding the average number of copies on which the contract is based. Most dealers then state in the contract that this agreement is based on a given number of copies and the customer must pay a certain amount for each copy made in excess of this stated number.

Look back at the previous example. It could be stated that the contract price is valid for the first 120,000 copies and that the customer will be billed, say, one cent, for each copy made during the contract period in excess of the 120,000 copies. It is relatively easy for the dealer to monitor the number of copies being made on a given copier since each NP unit is equipped with a meter that counts the number of copies.

Canon further assists dealers in pricing the contract by producing a suggested payment schedule for those customers who will be paying for the contract on a monthly basis. The annual cost of a contract paid on a monthly basis is higher than those paid entirely in advance. The reason is that when a contract is paid in installments, the dealer does not have use of the full contract amount as would be the case if the entire contract price were paid in advance. Plus, additional costs are incurred in recording monthly payments and in pursuing delinquent accounts.

In pricing the PC contract, a similar procedure is followed. Since the product is carried into the service center, travel expense is not a factor to be included. Also, since the cost of a PC contract is relatively low, Canon recommends that the contract may be paid in full, in advance.

The dealer or Authorized Service Facility ultimately establishes its own pricing, so Canon only provides recommended selling prices for the particular contracts to assist those dealers in establishing their prices. For those organizations that wish to develop their own prices, their own contracts, or both, Canon provides assistance by issuing data on the anticipated service lives of all consumable components. In this way, dealers or ASFs can use the data not only in pricing their own contracts, but in anticipating when a component needs replacement. The data are supplemented with an extensive service manual that provides suggested service intervals and also furnishes detailed information on how to effect that service. Canon's broad assistance is designed to help the dealers look at service as a profitable part of their business, not as a function in which they hope to just break even.

Using this information, the dealers (or ASFs) can modify the suggested price schedules as well as contract verbiage to meet their needs. Dealers may vary the number of copies covered by the basic contract. For example, a customer may only run 5,000 copies a month or 60,000 a year. A dealer might tailor the pricing to reflect this customer's lower usage with a commensurately lower price on the base contract. The result is that the customer receives a price and a contract that meet his or her needs.

Parts Support

Canon maintains parts stock in its central warehouse to support all the models of products that have been sold in the United States. The company maintains a seven-month inventory to ensure adequate supplies of parts, helping secure dealer and customer satisfaction.

Each dealer and ASF is provided with a recommended spare parts list for each copier product manufactured by Canon. The dealers or ASFs can alter the recommended parts to be stocked, depending on their particular needs. They can also designate any mode of transportation, since dealers pay for freight when they have parts shipped to them. The dealers or ASFs are also provided with repair facilities for printed circuit boards. Since this item is commonly repaired, dealers can send defective boards to Canon. In turn, Canon sends the dealers repaired boards on an exchange basis. This exchange keeps the costs of printed circuit board repairs at relatively low levels.

Replenishment orders for parts are sent by Canon U.S.A. to Canon, Inc., via satellite. When an order is ready to be shipped to Canon U.S.A., Canon, Inc., again sends Canon U.S.A., via satellite, a complete listing of all the parts being shipped. When the information is received, it is entered into the computer. This system facilitates getting large quantities and varieties of parts into the system rapidly. When the parts arrive, it is a simple matter of changing the "in-process" notation (designation that the parts are in transit) to an "available" notation (indication that the parts are in stock).

With its completely computerized inventory and order processing system, Canon U.S.A. easily facilitates the entry, shipment, and control of inventory. When a dealer orders a part, an inventory operator checks inventory on a computer terminal. The terminal shows the number of units in stock as well as the price of the component. The operator passes the order along to an order entry clerk, who enters it into the computer for shipment. The computer prints a hard copy of the order, and this hard copy goes to the parts picking area. The parts are picked and sent to the shipping area for packaging and shipment.

To avoid erroneous inventory information from being given to a dealer or ASF when a call is received for a part, the computer automatically reduces the available inventory by the number of units ordered as soon as the order is entered. In this way the operator has a current status of all items in inventory. When an order is shipped, an invoice is generated and sent to the dealer.

To ensure continued customer confidence in the purchase of a Canon copier, it is Canon's policy not only to maintain adequate stock levels of currently sold products, but to maintain parts for any discontinued product or model for at least seven years.

Benefits of the Service Contract

From Canon's viewpoint, the service contract is a highly beneficial investment for the customer. It provides the customer with needed service at a discounted rate when compared to the cost of having a comparable amount of service rendered on a time and material basis. Canon feels that a customer who does not have a service contract will tend to neglect the needed maintenance and required service. This neglect tends to shorten the life of the product, thereby denying the customer the full use and satisfaction that can be derived from the copier.

Canon is interested in maintaining a quality image in the market-place, and the service agreement helps it achieve that goal by ensuring the longevity of its products.

From the dealer's standpoint, the service contract provides numerous benefits in added profits through the sale of the service contracts, consumable items, and additional copiers.

The Future

Canon sees the future of the copier business as highly competitive. To ensure a strong position in this market it feels it must differentiate itself from the competition. Canon sees customer relations and technical competence as two key areas that must be in the forefront to achieve success. Training programs in customer relations are being developed for the technicians. These, coupled with improved built-in diagnostics in the products and supported by troubleshooting guides provided to the technicians, result in less down time for the copier and greater customer satisfaction.

Through the service contract and the resulting interdependence with the dealers, Canon sees its position as a strong one in the marketplace. It is convinced that service contracts play an important role in protecting Canon's good name.

Canon's National Account Program

Canon U.S.A., Inc., established a national account program to help authorized dealers expand their business. The program is designed to assist dealers in securing product and service contract sales that would be difficult, if not impossible, for them to acquire on their own. The reason these contracts would be difficult to sell is that many potential accounts have the need for a large number of copiers, necessitating a sizable cash outlay by the dealers to purchase the products from Canon and resell or lease them to the customers. Many dealers do not have the financial resources to handle such an arrangement. Additionally, most large accounts have requirements that are national in scope. A sale to this type of account presents logistic and administrative problems for local dealers in arranging for the shipment and service of units that would be dispersed around the country. Remember, Canon U.S.A., Inc., sells its products and renders service exclusively through its dealer organization. A dealer that enters into an agreement for the sale or lease of copier products to be used by the customer in distant locations would have to contact dealers in each locale and arrange for local service—a formidable task.

In many instances the national account is reluctant to buy from a local dealer, since it is concerned that the dealer may not be able financially to handle the transaction, arrange for national service, or provide competitive pricing. There is also concern on the part of the customer that if the dealer should go out of business or sell the firm to someone else, it may have difficulty getting the terms of the agreement fulfilled.

Canon U.S.A., Inc., understood these customers' concerns and its dealers' needs. Thus it developed its national account program. A national account is defined as an organization that has business which is national in scope and that is willing to commit to the purchase or lease of at least six copiers. Since the goal of the national account program is to support the dealer organization, it is the dealer that identifies the sales potential and requests assistance from Canon. Canon U.S.A., Inc., does not solicit business directly; those few potential accounts that call Canon directly are sold products in conjunction with a dealer.

Once a potential national account has been identified, the dealer's sales representative and Canon U.S.A.'s area manager call on the account. From this point on, the area manager and the dealer work together closely to identify the customer's needs and establish the pricing. When the sale or lease is consummated, the agreement is written between Canon and the national account. This assures the customer that the terms of the sale, service contract, or lease will be fulfilled.

Canon has established a dealer compensation plan for both the sale and lease national account programs. When the customer purchases the equipment, the dealer receives the entire margin between the selling price of the copier to the customer and the lowest wholesale price, less an additional 6 percent cash discount. From this margin the dealer covers the warranty labor costs and profit. Remember, Canon provides replacement parts at no charge during the warranty period. If warranty service is to be provided by a dealer other than the selling dealer, then the margin is split, with 50 percent going to the selling dealer and 50 percent going to the dealer responsible for the installation and service of the unit. Because the selling dealer is intimately involved in the sales negotiations with the national account, it is cognizant of the margins available and may choose to deviate from the formula when required to effect a sale. A situation can arise, for example, in which the selling dealer may accept 20 percent of the margin and provide the installing dealer with 80 percent in order to adequately compensate the installing dealer for the installation and warranty labor costs when the margins are narrowed owing to competitive pressures. Should a national account have its purchasing decision decentralized, and selling effort is required by several different dealers located in various parts of the country, the dealer that identified the national account and calls on the account's headquarters receives 25 percent of the margin, no matter where the sale or installation is made. The dealer making the actual sale receives another 25 percent of the margin, and the installing dealer gets the remaining 50 percent of the margin. For example, if a dealer in New York City identifies a national account and calls on it with Canon's area manager, then determines that some copiers will be purchased and installed in Los Angeles and others in Atlanta as well as New York, then Canon contacts an authorized full-line dealer in Los Angeles and another in Atlanta. Through its area managers in each locale, Canon coordinates the sales efforts of all three dealers and assists them in closing the sale. In this situation the dealer in New York receives 100 percent of the margin earned on the sale and installation of units located in New York and 25 percent of the margins earned in the sale of any units effected in Los Angeles and Atlanta. The dealers in Los Angeles and Atlanta each receive 75 percent of the margins earned on the copiers sold and installed in their respective areas. To further extend this scenario, assume the dealer in Atlanta sells some copiers in Atlanta to be installed in Birmingham; the Atlanta dealer gets 25 percent of the margin. The New York dealer gets another 25 percent (because it established the national account), and the Birmingham dealer gets the remaining 50 percent of the margin for its role in installing the equipment and fulfilling the warranty obligation. In all instances, Canon contracts with the customer for the delivery and service of the equipment. Canon then sends credits to each dealer reflecting its share of the margins. These credits are sent out when the equipment is shipped. Canon then bills the customer and is responsible for collecting the invoice amount from the customer. The product is shipped directly to the installing dealer. The dealer checks it out (pre-installs) to ensure it is functioning properly and that there was no shipping damage. Once this is done it is brought to the customer and installed. As part of the sales negotiations, the dealer and Canon also try to negotiate a service contract. The price of the contract is then given to the dealer that will fulfill the service contract obligation. Again, the service contract is written between the national account and Canon, with the dealer fulfilling the service obligation.

The majority of the national accounts prefer to rent their copiers as opposed to purchasing them outright. If the customer chooses to rent (lease) the equipment, as in the case of a sale, the agreement is written between the customer and Canon.

The compensation program for the dealer in a rental situation is different from the one employed for the equipment purchased by the customer. This program has two basic elements: an origination fee and a servicing commission. The origination fee is paid to the dealer that identifies the customer and sells the lease to the national account. It consists of a flat dollar amount paid on each copier leased. Should more than one dealer be involved in the lease, then this origination fee is split, with half of it going to the dealer that established the national account and the other half going to the dealer or dealers that close each lease with the national account's various branches. Each time the lease is renewed, the dealers split an amount equal to half the original origination fee to compensate them for their efforts in securing the renewal.

The servicing fee is an amount established to reimburse dealers profitably for servicing each unit leased under the agreement. It is paid in addition to the amount paid in the origination fee. Approximately 60 to 70 percent of the total revenue derived from a lease goes back to the dealers involved with a particular national account. In its dealer agreement, Canon stipulates that regular maintenance is to be performed at predetermined intervals on all Canon equipment leased by a customer under the national account program. The dealer is required to record the meter readings (which indicate the number of copies made on the machine) each time the unit is serviced. In this way Canon can determine if the maintenance is being rendered on a timely basis. The meter log is also helpful in ascertaining whether the up time (time the copier is available for use) is in keeping with Canon's standards as well as in assuring that the copier meets any performance standards that Canon has stipulated in its agreement with the customer. In addition to recording the meter readings, the dealer records the date and time

an emergency call is received and the date and time the copier is
returned to service.

The national account program has provided dealers with an opportunity to secure business that most likely would not have been available to them. Canon looks to the national account market as the premier source of business for larger, more sophisticated products it has
recently introduced. The program provides the dealers with revenue
not only from the sale or lease of the copiers, but also from the additional service business that the service contract or lease (which incorporates a service contract) brings to the dealerships.

Appendix One
Worksheets

Worksheet 1.

Pricing Repair Contracts
Parts and Materials

Date _____

Product model number _____

Product age _____

Length of contract _____ Years or months

Average use per owner per year _____(A)

B	C	D	E	F
Part Number	Mean Time between Failures	Number of Failures During Contract Period	Part Cost	Total Cost
		$\frac{A}{C}$		$D \times E$

Total cost of parts _____

Worksheet 2.

Pricing Repair Contracts
Labor

Date _____

Product model number _____

Product age _____

Length of contract _____

Hourly labor rate (Salary plus benefits) _____

A	B	C	D	E
	Repairs Per Year	Hours Per Repair	Hourly Labor Rate	Repair Labor Cost
Part Number				
	B ×	C ×	D =	E

Total Repair Labor Cost _____

Worksheet 3.

Pricing Repair Contracts
Travel Labor Cost

Date _____

Product model number _____

Product age _____

Length of contract _____

Hourly labor rate (Salary plus benefits) _____

Radius from service center _____

Average travel time within radius _____

Number of Repairs × Average Travel Time × Hourly Labor Rate

= Travel Labor Cost

_____ × _____ × _____

= _____

Worksheet 4.

Pricing Repair Contracts
Summary

Product model number _____

Product age _____

Length of contract _____

Total parts and material cost   _____

Total repair labor cost   _____

Total travel labor cost   _____

Total cost   _____

Worksheet 5.

Alternative Pricing Technique

STEP 1 *Establish goals*. (Sales dollar volume, a given number of technicians, a given percentage of customers and/or
products under a service contract, profit, etc.)

_____

_____

_____

_____

_____

STEP 2 *Outline known factors*. (Labor rates, vacation, sick leave allocations, holidays, unapplied labor, etc.)

_____

_____

_____

_____

_____

STEP 3 *Calculate labor cost*.

A. Gross hours = 52 weeks × _____ = _____
 Hours Gross
 worked/week hours/technician

B. Determine nonbillable hours.

		Number	Labor Cost/ Day		
Vacation days		_____	× _____	=	_____
Holidays		_____	× _____	=	_____
Sick Days		_____	× _____	=	_____

Unapplied labor 52
    weeks   × _ Hrs./Week = _____

Total nonbillable hours per technician   = _____

Total Gross Hours Per Technician   = _____

− Total Nonbillable Hours Per Technician   − _____

Total Productive Hours Per Technician   = _____

× Number of Technicians   × _____

Total Productive Hours   = _____

Total Labor Cost = $\dfrac{\text{Productive Hours}}{} \times \dfrac{\text{Average Wage}}{}$ = _____

STEP 4 *Calculate labor-to-parts-and-materials ratio.*

$$\frac{\text{Labor cost}}{\text{Parts and material cost}} = \text{_____}$$

STEP 5 *Calculate labor, parts and materials, and general and administrative overhead costs.*

Labor overhead   _____

Parts and materials overhead   _____

General and administrative overhead   _____

Total overhead   _____

STEP 6 *Calculate total costs.*

$$\overline{\text{Total cost}} = \overline{\text{Labor cost}} + \overline{\text{Parts and material overhead}} + \overline{\text{Total overhead}}$$

STEP 7 *Calculate contract sales or profit objective.*

$$\text{Total Sales} = \frac{\text{Total Cost}}{1 - \dfrac{\text{\% Profit Before Taxes}}{100}}$$

STEP 8 *Determine labor rate.*

A. Calculate labor burden

Labor cost   _____

Labor overhead   _____

General and administrative overhead
to be assigned to labor   _____

Profit to be generated by labor   _____

Total labor burden   _____

B. Calculate labor multiplier

$$\text{Labor multiplier} = \frac{\text{Total labor burden}}{\text{Labor cost}}$$

C. Calculate billable labor rate

$$\overline{\text{Billable labor rate}} = \overline{\text{Hourly labor rate}} \times \overline{\text{Labor multiplier}}$$

A second method to determine labor rate:

$$\text{Billable labor rate} = \frac{\text{Total labor burden}}{\text{Total productive hours}}$$

STEP 9 *Determine parts and materials (P and M) rate to be charged.*

A. Calculate parts and material burden

Parts and material cost   _____

Parts and material overhead   _____

General and administrative overhead
to be assigned to parts and materials   _____

Profit assignable to parts and materials_____

Total parts and material burden   _____

B. Calculate parts and materials multiplier

$$\frac{\text{Total P and M burden}}{\text{P and M cost}} = \underline{\hspace{3cm}} \text{ Multiplier}$$

STEP 10 *Check calculations.*

Billable hours _____ × Labor rate _____ = _____

P and M cost _____ × Multiplier _____ = _____

Sales total   _____

Total service contract sales goal   _____

Appendix Two

Sample Contracts and Brochures

AMERICARE...It's the Answer to Your Biggest Question — "What Do I Do When My Computer Breaks?"

The day you bought your personal computer, you solved most of your information handling problems. Suddenly, your office, maybe even your home, was freed from the drudgery of manually processing the increasing words and numbers so essential to our lives.

But your personal computer also brings new concerns:

What do you do when your computer needs repair?
Where do you go?
How long will it take?
How much will it cost?

Now, you can take care of your personal computer as easily as it takes care of you.

With AMERICARE from Xerox...where more than 3000 dealers coast to coast are ready for your call.

AMERICARE answers all your questions about personal computer service!

Q. How does an AMERICARE Maintenance Agreement work?

A. Simple. You and your dealer will have an agreement that says for a period of 12 months, your personal computer will be fully covered for all repairs. This means no matter what needs fixing, all parts charges and all labor charges are eliminated. The only price you pay is the initial contract fee when you make the agreement.

Q. What kind of Maintenance Agreements do you offer?

A. Three...one just right for you:
1. You can bring your personal computer in to any authorized AMERICARE dealer for service. (Call 1-800-238-2300 for the AMERICARE dealer nearest you.)
2. You can have your personal computer picked up and delivered.
3. AMERICARE will provide on-site repair either at your place of business or at your home.

Q. When is the best time to buy an AMERICARE Maintenance Agreement?

A. To avoid a gap in protection, you should purchase an AMERICARE Maintenance Agreement while your personal computer and peripherals are still under the manufacturer's warranty.

Q. What if my personal computer is out of warranty?

A. It will be inspected for an initial fee, brought up to original specifications at a time & materials cost, and then your dealer can provide the maintenance agreement you need.

Q. Is a Maintenance Agreement the only way I can get AMERICARE service?

A. No, you can also get service on a time & materials basis. For those systems used infrequently, this may be the lowest cost service option. However, if your machine is used on a regular basis, the parts for some repairs may cost as much as 30 or 40% of the cost of your equipment. An AMERICARE Maintenance Agreement can remove the risk of these high costs.

Q. Is the AMERICARE Maintenance Agreement renewable?

A. Yes! Once you're covered, you can continue service protection without additional inspections.

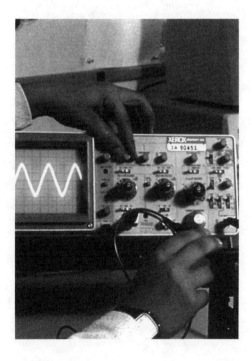

Q. Let's say I need repairs…how long do I need to wait?

A. We know how important it is to have your system up and running at all times. Being without it can create a real work pile-up…even business losses! AMERICARE service can repair your computer usually within 48 hours…sometimes faster! Endless downtime is a thing of the past.

Q. Suppose I move. Can I find AMERICARE service in other cities?

A. That's why it's called AMERICARE. Throughout the country, there are over 90 Xerox Service Centers supporting more than 3000 authorized AMERICARE dealers.

Q. What about the cost of AMERICARE service?

A. For every brand of personal computer and peripheral covered by AMERICARE, you'll find a reasonable service price. Your computer system investment is a substantial one, so you deserve the best value. With AMERICARE, you get that value.

Q. Why have so many dealers become AMERICARE dealers?

A. Because it benefits *you*. The personal computer business has been exploding in the past few years, creating the need for the most expert service this country can provide. AMERICARE helps your dealer give you the best and fastest service possible…ensuring the dealer's #1 objective – your satisfaction. And a satisfied customer keeps coming back!

Q. Now, what brands of personal computers and peripherals are covered by AMERICARE?

A. Presently, AMERICARE services this list:

Personal Computers

CompuPro	IBM Compatible	Morrow
Corona	Boards	NEC
Direct	• AST	Olivetti
Epson	• Persyst	Osborne
IBM	• Quadram	STM
	Kaypro	Xerox

Printers

ACS	Epson	Okidata
Datasouth	Mannesmann Tally	Silver Reed
Diablo	NEC	Xerox
Enter		

Terminals

Direct	Liberty

Monitors

Amdek	NEC

Rigid Drives

Shugart	Tallgrass

Local Area Network

3Com

Floppy Disk Drives

Exclusive alignment/repair capability

And we're adding new products all the time!

XEROX

12 Month
Xerox Maintenance Agreement

Customer/Company Name

Maintenance Agreement Type

☐ Customer Carry-In to
   Xerox Service Center

☐ Xerox provided Shipment Services
   to/from Xerox Service Center

Street Address

City   State   Zip Code

Attn:

XMA Price   _____
*Sales Tax   _____
Total   _____

Telephone No:

(_____) _____ - _____
Area Code

Method of Payment (Check One):
☐ Cash   ☐ Credit Card   ☐ Billed
☐ Check   Customer Number _____

Credit Card Data (When Applicable):
(Check One)   ☐ American Express
             ☐ Master Charge
             ☐ VISA

Card No.:   Expiration Date:

XMA Contract No.:   Dealer Number:

Equipment Information

Manufacturer & Model: Serial No.(s) of unit and accessories to be included in Service Contract:

Original Purchase:

☐ New   ☐ Used

Manufacturer Warranty/Contract in Effect:

☐ Yes (Exp. Date ___/___/___)   ☐ No

Commencement Date of Contract:

___/___/___

Service Center Inspection (If required)

Inspector's Name _____ Inspection Date _____ Center Number _____

Customer agrees to purchase, and Xerox agrees to provide, the Full Service Maintenance (FSM) in accordance with the terms and conditions set forth herein and, for the Initial Term hereof, at the prices set forth by Xerox Corporation in the Price List in effect on the Commencement Date of this Agreement.

Customer   **Xerox Corporation**

_____   _____
Name (Please Print)   Name (Please Print)

_____   _____
Signature   Signature

_____   _____
Date   Date
     If your firm is tax exempt, you must attach
     a copy of your certificate to this Agreement.

_____
Service Center Location

Form 60970 (5/84)   **ORIGINAL**

XEROX

12 Month Customer Site
Xerox Maintenance Agreement

	Customer/Company Name

Customer Location from Xerox Service Center

	Surcharge	
0-25 miles	0%	☐
26-50 miles	10%	☐

Street Address

City   State   Zip Code

Attn:

XMA Price _____

*Sales Tax _____

Total _____

Telephone No:

(_____) _____ - _____
Area Code

Method of Payment (Check One):
☐ Cash   ☐ Credit Card   ☐ Billed
☐ Check   Customer Number _____

Credit Card Data (When Applicable):
(Check One)   ☐ American Express
☐ Carte Blanche   ☐ Master Charge
☐ Diners Club   ☐ VISA

Card No.:

Expiration Date:

XMA Contract No.:   Dealer Number:

Equipment Information

Manufacturer & Model:

Serial No.(s) of unit and accessories to be included in Service Contract:

Original Purchase:

☐ New   ☐ Used

Manufacturer Warranty/Contract in Effect:

☐ Yes (Exp. Date ___/___/___)   ☐ No

Commencement Date of Contract:

___/___/___

Service Center Inspection (If required)

Inspector's Name _____ Inspection Date _____ Center Number _____

Customer agrees to purchase, and Xerox agrees to provide, the Full Service Maintenance (FSM) in accordance with the terms and conditions set forth herein and, for the Initial Term hereof, at the prices set forth by Xerox Corporation in the Price List in effect on the Commencement Date of this Agreement.

Customer   **Xerox Corporation**

Name (Please Print)   Name (Please Print)

Signature   Signature

Date   Date

*If your firm is tax exempt, you must attach
a copy of your certificate to this Agreement.

Service Center Location

Form 60971 (9/84)   **ORIGINAL**

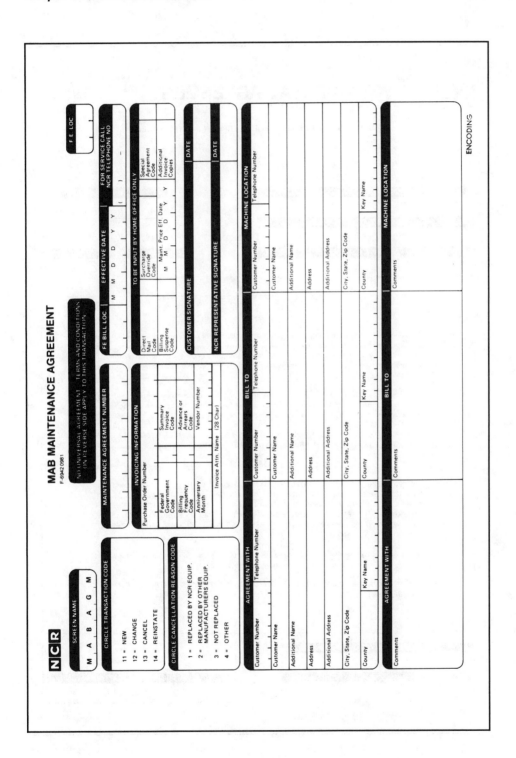

NCR Corporation

UNIVERSAL AGREEMENT
F-8231 1/80

CONTINUING AGREEMENT FOR EQUIPMENT AND SERVICES

CUSTOMER NAME	CUSTOMER NUMBER

| STREET ADDRESS | |

| CITY | STATE | ZIP CODE | D.A.O. CODE | DATE |

NCR Corporation (NCR) and Customer agree that all equipment, programs, and services hereafter obtained from NCR, either directly or indirectly through the use of a leasing company, other financing institution or purchasing agency, shall be furnished only under the terms and conditions of this agreement. Unless the context otherwise requires, the term "Customer" shall mean the Customer listed above.

The terms and conditions of this agreement shall prevail in spite of any contrary printed provision of any purchase order utilized by Customer in effecting the furnishing of any equipment, programs or services and any such form, letter or order must state on the face of it:

FURNISHING OF THE EQUIPMENT, PROGRAMS AND/OR SERVICES IS DONE ONLY IN ACCORDANCE WITH AND PURSUANT TO OUR AGREEMENT DATED_____ .

IMPORTANT

THESE PROVISIONS ARE INTENDED TO STATE ALL OF THE RIGHTS AND RESPONSIBILI-TIES BETWEEN NCR AND CUSTOMER. THEY TAKE THE PLACE OF AND SUPERSEDE ALL WARRANTIES, EXPRESS OR IMPLIED AND WHETHER OF MERCHANTABILITY, FITNESS OR OTHERWISE. THE REMEDIES PROVIDED FOR OR REFERENCED HEREIN ARE EXCLUSIVE. CUSTOMER AND NCR WAIVE ALL OTHER REMEDIES INCLUDING BUT NOT LIMITED TO, CONSEQUENTIAL DAMAGES.

This agreement shall be effective only when executed by both parties. Notice of acceptance is waived although Customer will be furnished a copy showing acceptance by NCR.

THE TERMS AND CONDITIONS ON THE SUBSEQUENT PAGES ARE PART OF THIS AGREEMENT.

EXECUTED BY (TYPE OR PRINT)	NCR CORPORATION
SIGNATURE TITLE	AUTHORIZED SIGNATURE

1.   GENERAL — Customer may order equipment, programs and services by submitting an order setting forth 1) the description, 2) whether to be purchased, rented or licensed, 3) any cash with order amount and if purchased, whether the remainder is to be in installments or if rented or licensed, the term, 4) the charge and 5) any other appropriate circumstance or condition. NCR reserves the right to reject any order if in its opinion it cannot comply with the description or requirements of the order. Neither Customer nor NCR shall be bound by any order until it is accepted by NCR and at such time both shall be bound and a contract shall exist in accordance with the terms of this agreement and the order. The contract, comprised of this agreement and the order shall constitute the entire agreement of the parties relating to the products or services ordered and shall supersede all prior agreements and understandings whether oral or written and all negotiations, letters, other papers and proposals except as attached to the order or specifically incorporated by reference. Any applicable NCR furnished form signed by Customer shall be a part of the contract.

This agreement may not be changed or modified in any way subsequent to the date of execution except by an instrument in writing signed by the Customer and accepted by NCR. No contract or amendment entered into after this agreement shall amend by implication any provision of this agreement. Any notices required or authorized to be given shall be deemed to be given when mailed by certified or registered mail, postage prepaid, as follows: if to the Customer, to the Customer's address as shown on the face of this agreement; if to NCR, to its local District Office. This agreement shall remain in effect until terminated by either party on 30 days prior written notice. Termination shall not operate to terminate any contract then outstanding.

If any provision of this agreement, or any contract, is illegal, invalid or void under any applicable state law it shall be considered severable, remaining provisions shall not be impaired and the agreement or contract shall be interpreted as far as possible so as to give effect to its stated purpose.

2.   DELIVERY — NCR will use its best efforts to accomplish delivery by any indicated delivery date. However, unless otherwise specifically provided, NCR will not be liable for any expenses or damages incurred as a result of actual delivery or certification after such indicated date, if any. Customer agrees to pay the appropriate NCR distribution charge, and in the case of rented equipment back to the distribution point and due to any change of location of the equipment. Such charges shall be added to the first invoice and paid by Customer. Customer agrees to pay any applicable installation and de-installation charge. Title to (and possession of unless otherwise stated on the order) traded-in equipment will pass to NCR on delivery of the ordered equipment.

3.   RENTAL AND LICENSE TERM AND CHARGES — Each contract for rental equipment or a licensed program shall become effective on the date of its acceptance by NCR and shall remain in force, except as otherwise provided, for the period of the term and thereafter until terminated as provided in section 18. The term of equipment rental shall begin on the first day of the month for which the full rental is paid. The rental charge shall begin immediately upon certification or delivery of the equipment by NCR or on the expiration of the previous term as the case may be. The term of a program license shall be monthly if not otherwise stated. The term shall begin on delivery, or when a test period is provided, the term shall begin on expiration of the test period or when put in productive use, whichever is earlier. Basic monthly rent, license fees and other scheduled charges shall be billed in advance, and other charges shall be payable as accrued. Charges for a fractional part of a month shall be computed at the rate of 1/30th of the monthly charge.

Rates may be changed after the expiration of the term or period for which paid on 30 days prior written notice. Rates may be increased during or before the initial term on 90 days prior written notice provided that (a) if an equipment rental increase exceeds the increase in NCR's maintenance charges or (b) if the license fee is increased, Customer may terminate the contract by notice given within 30 days after receipt of notification from NCR.

Payment of the rent or license fee entitles Customer to the applicable use of the equipment or program.

4.   PURCHASE TERMS — NCR shall invoice the Customer for the purchase price balance or, if applicable, the first installment of it upon certification or delivery of the equipment by NCR. The entire unpaid purchase price balance shall, at NCR's option, become due and payable upon refusal to accept delivery when tendered, to make any payment when due or if Customer sells, conceals, removes, damages or destroys the equipment or attempts to do so prior to final payment of the entire price. Customer may prepay the time payment balance in advance and shall in such event be entitled to a credit against the finance charge determined in accordance with the rule of "78's".

5.   BILLING AND PAYMENT — All invoices shall be due and payable in accordance with their terms. Failure to pay any amount when due shall entitle NCR to collect the

2

late charge or interest stated on the invoice. If it is necessary to refer any claim to an attorney not an employee of NCR, Customer agrees to pay reasonable attorney's fees if Customer is found to be in default and such is allowed under applicable state law. If customer requests a postponement in delivery, the price may be subject to any increase.

6. **TAXES** — The stated rental charges, purchase price, maintenance fees or charges, program license fees, system service and programming charges or other amounts to be paid pursuant to any contract do not include any Federal, State, County or local sales, use or other excise tax however designated, whether levied on seller or buyer and whether based on such price, charge, the equipment, part, product or service or their use or the contract. Any such taxes and interest on them (if not due to NCR's delay) required to be paid by NCR shall be added to the invoices. Customer shall pay all personal property taxes assessed after delivery of any equipment, part, product, program, or service except if equipment is rented NCR will pay personal property tax. Any taxes to be paid by Customer but in fact paid by NCR shall be reimbursed to NCR. In the event any taxes to be paid by Customer but levied on NCR are not paid until audit, NCR may then invoice Customer.

7. **ADVANCE PAYMENT** — The advance payment plus any interest credited to the Customer shall be applied against the purchase price or the first and subsequent rental or license fee payments until the total amount has been exhausted.

8. **SUPPLIES** — The price, monthly rental charges, the warranty, maintenance, programs or other services does not include furnishing of supplies or other expendable items unless otherwise indicated. NCR agrees to sell to the Customer, at NCR's then established prices and upon NCR's regular invoice terms, supplies or other expendable items so long as NCR has them available for sale. Damage to equipment or other loss sustained due to use of supplies not meeting NCR specifications shall be the sole responsibility of Customer.

9. **PATENT, COPYRIGHT AND TRADE SECRET INDEMNITY** — NCR will defend, at its expense, and will pay the cost and damages made in settlement or awarded as a result of any action brought against Customer based on an allegation that the equipment or any unit or part of it or any program furnished by NCR infringes a United States patent, copyright, or trade secret, if NCR is notified promptly by the Customer in writing of any such action or allegation of infringement, and if NCR shall have had sole control of the defense of any such action and all negotiations for its settlement or compromise. If a final

injunction shall be obtained against Customer's use of the equipment or any unit or part of it or program by reason of such infringement, or if in NCR's opinion the equipment or any unit or part of it or any program is likely to become the subject of a claim of such infringement, NCR will, at its option and at its expense, 1) procure for the Customer the right to continue using the equipment, unit or part, or program, 2) replace or modify the same so that it becomes noninfringing, or 3) if 1) and 2) are not feasible, terminate the rental or license or if purchased, repurchase the equipment on a depreciated (5-year straight line) basis. NCR shall not have any liability to Customer under any provision of this clause if any infringement or allegation thereof is based upon the use of any program or the equipment or any unit or part of it in combination with any program or equipment or any unit or parts of it not furnished by NCR or if the equipment is used in a manner for which the equipment or units or parts of it were not designed. The above states the entire liability of NCR with respect to infringement of patents, copyrights, or trade secrets by any program or by the equipment or units or parts of it, or by their operation.

10. **NCR INTELLECTUAL PROPERTY** —
a. Definitions — "Program" shall mean instructions designed to achieve a certain result, whether denominated software or firmware, wherever resident and on whatever media and all related documentation furnished to Customer. "Programming Services" is creating a program or modifying an existing program to perform particular functions or to function in a particular manner for Customer. "NCR Intellectual Property" shall include 1) all Programs furnished by NCR whether specifically licensed or furnished as part of equipment rented or purchased and software services for them, except Programming Services, and 2) all other material furnished by NCR and any copies of it relating to the use and service of equipment, including the information contained therein.

b. This subsection applies to NCR Intellecutal Property. NCR Intellectual Property shall remain confidential and the proprietary property of NCR and is furnished to customer only on a license basis. Customer agrees to continue to treat it as such, except such as may be established to be in the general public domain or which Customer may be required to disclose pursuant to judicial or governmental action. Customer shall acquire no rights in NCR Intellectual Property except to use it solely for the purpose of use with, and only during the time Customer uses designated equipment or for any period covered by a license fee in accordance with NCR's software license policies in effect at the time of the contract. Customer shall not use or cause to be used any NCR Intellectual Property for the benefit of any other party whether or not for a

3

consideration unless otherwise agreed. Customer shall not sublicense, sell, rent, loan, disclose or otherwise communicate, make available or assist any unauthorized third party to use, NCR Intellectual Property or any part or modification thereof or make it available to any person not in the employment of Customer. Customer shall use it only in connection with the designated equipment unless on backup equipment during the time required, and shall make no copies without the prior consent of NCR. Customer shall take all reasonable precautions to maintain the confidentiality of NCR Intellectual Property, but not less than that employed to protect its own proprietary information unless otherwise agreed to by NCR in writing. As to copies made by Customer with the consent of NCR, Customer agrees to duplicate and include NCR's copyright notice and any NCR proprietary notice on all copies, including copies in machine readable form, and to maintain records of the location of copies of programs.

If the equipment is rented and rental is terminated (except by purchase), or if the equipment is purchased and Customer ceases to use it, Customer shall thereafter cease to use any NCR Intellectual Property or any facsimile thereof, delete it from its library, return to NCR or destroy all NCR Intellectual Property, except for a copy retained for archival purposes, and notify NCR in writing.

If Customer desires to sell purchased equipment to a third party, Customer shall notify NCR in writing and may not transfer or provide NCR Intellectual Property to the purchaser from Customer without the prior agreement of NCR which shall be granted only if the purchaser shall have agreed in writing: (1) to the provisions of this section 10 and (2) to the continued payment of periodic license fees and/or the payment of any relicense fee in effect at the time of transfer.

NCR shall have and may cumulatively exercise all rights as it might have at law or in equity for the protection of NCR Intellectual Property, including an injunction enjoining the breach or treatened breach of this section.

c. This subsection applies to Programming Services furnished by NCR. Customer shall be the owner of the product of Programming Services but NCR may retain copies, disclose and further use the product of the services. Customer's programs (except those furnished by NCR), reports, printouts and other data generated by a program (except a compiler) are not products of Programming Services for purposes of this subsection.

11.   OWNERSHIP OF EQUIPMENT AND RiSK OF LOSS — If the equipment is rented, title shall remain in NCR. Customer shall not do anything prejudicing NCR's ownership; nor fail to do anything reasonably necessary to protect NCR's ownership. Customer agrees to execute any document necessary or desirable, in NCR's opinion, to ensure its title and ownership. This agreement, any contract, and any unit of equipment may not be assigned, sublet or transferred by Customer without NCR's prior written consent. If the equipment is purchased, title to the equipment shall pass to the Customer only upon NCR's receipt of payment of the full purchase price balance. NCR warrants title to be clear, free and unencumbered. NCR reserves, and the Customer hereby grants to NCR, a purchase money security interest in each unit of the equipment in the amount of its purchase price, and such security interest shall be satisfied by payment of the purchase price balance in full. NCR may file a financing statement (NCR being constituted an agent of Customer to sign on Customer's behalf or Customer shall execute if requested by NCR) with appropriate state and/or local authorities in order to perfect NCR's security interest. Any such filing shall not constitute acceptance of a contract by NCR.

Until delivery, NCR assumes all risk of loss. Upon delivery Customer assumes the risk of loss or damage for purchased equipment except such as caused willfully or negligently by NCR. NCR shall retain the risk of loss or damage for rented equipment except such as caused willfully or negligently by Customer.

12.   EXCUSED PERFORMANCE — Neither party shall be deemed to be in default of any provision hereof or be liable for any delay, failure in performance, or interruption of service resulting directly or indirectly from acts of God, civil or military authority, civil disturbance, war, strikes, fires, other catastrophies, or other cause beyond its reasonable control.

13.   MAINTENANCE OF EQUIPMENT — NCR shall perform remedial maintenance during the applicable maintenance period:

a. for rented equipment

b. for purchased equipment (except purchase of rented equipment)

(1) for a 90-day warranty period beginning on delivery or certification, and

(2) after the 90-day warranty period at NCR's then current rates, unless Customer notifies NCR on or before the 60th day of the warranty period that it does not desire continued maintenance coverage. The coverage shall continue until terminated pursuant to Section 18(a).

4

Remedial maintenance during other periods may be available at either a scheduled or hourly basis at NCR's then current wages. Use of equipment above designated levels may require additional charges for equipment on rent or maintenance.

Customer shall prepare prior to delivery of equipment, and thereafter maintain at its expense, the site of the equipment in accordance with NCR specifications. Customer shall provide at the site adequate and suitable working facilities and space for maintenance personnel. As to equipment maintained by NCR, only NCR shall perform service on it. Replaced parts shall become or remain the property of NCR. With respect to any alteration or attachment, as defined in section 17, to NCR equipment, NCR will provide maintenance and repair service for the unaltered portion of the equipment unless an alteration or attachment creates a safety hazard or renders maintenance and repair impractical. If an alteration, attachment, use of supplies not meeting NCR specifications, use of unsupported software, use of software not furnished by NCR, or modifications to NCR supported software not performed by NCR results in an increase in NCR's maintenance of NCR equipment, such increased maintenance will be billed at the appropriate increased rate.

Repair or replacement of purchased equipment on maintenance or warranty necessitated by fire originating outside of NCR furnished equipment, water, other casualty, acts of God, Customer's movement or negligence or acts of a third party is not included in the warranty or maintenance service charge and shall be provided at Customer's expense. Repair or replacement of rental equipment necessitated by Customer's movement or negligence is not included in the rent and shall be provided at Customer's expense.

NCR's liability to the Customer resulting from the performance of maintenance service shall be limited to restoring the equipment covered by this agreement to good operating condition. NCR shall have no obligation to perform any service outside the United States unless otherwise agreed.

14. **OPERATION —**

a. General — The equipment will comply with applicable safety and other governmental regulations in effect at the time of manufacture. Units of equipment sold as new may be composed in whole or in part of used components which are warranted the equivalent of new.

b. Equipment Functioning — If the equipment is purchased (except for purchase of rented equipment), then for 90 days following certification or delivery, NCR warrants the equipment to be in good working order and will at its expense keep the equipment in good operating order and repair by performing maintenance in accordance with Section 13. If the equipment is rented, NCR agrees to keep the equipment in good operating order and repair by performing maintenance in accordance with Section 13. THERE ARE NO WARRANTIES OF MERCHANTABILITY OR FITNESS. NCR'S SOLE OBLIGATION UNDER ANY WARRANTY IS LIMITED TO SUCH MAINTENANCE.

c. Programs And Programming Services — A Warranted Program, when operating in conjunction with unaltered associated Programs and designated equipment and within required operational conditions, will comply with customer-level documentation in effect on the date the issue was furnished to Customer. Customer shall determine compliance during the applicable test period. If, during the test period, the Program is found to be not complying, i.e. a "Problem" exists, NCR shall effect a resolution (which may be a subsequent issue) or the license may be terminated. After acceptance (or delivery when the Program is not warranted), NCR will furnish, and its obligation shall be limited to furnishing, software services under its then current policies and rates. Software services for Programs may be chargeable (even as to Problems inherent in the Program when furnished, but not occurring during the test period) and for Programming Services will be chargeable. NCR may change its policies on Programming Services and software services and reclassify software services on six months notice given by general publication. Some reclassifications may constitute a discontinuation of services. NCR assumes no responsibility for programs which have been altered or modified. THERE ARE NO WARRANTIES OR MERCHANTABILITY OR FITNESS. NCR'S SOLE OBLIGATION IS LIMITED TO FURNISHING SOFTWARE SERVICES UNDER ITS THEN CURRENT POLICIES AND CHARGES.

d. Limitations — Customer shall arrange for back-up equipment or service. Customer shall be solely responsible for proper audit and recovery routines and procedures. NCR shall not be liable for any expense or damages incurred by Customer, whether internal to Customer or paid by Customer to any third party, which may arise out of failure of the equipment to function or due to any malfunction of equipment or program upon whatever cause of action any claim is based except that NCR shall be liable for only bodily injury occasioned solely by the negligence or willful acts of NCR in design, manufacture, installation or servicing of the equipment. IT IS ACKNOWLEDGED THAT THESE LIMITATIONS PERMIT NCR TO PROVIDE EQUIPMENT, PROGRAMS AND SERVICES AT LOWER RATES THAN IT OTHERWISE COULD AND SUCH LIMITATIONS ON LIABILITY ARE REASONABLE.

5

e. Equipment Rental Credit — If the equipment is rented and if a component of the equipment being maintained becomes inoperative and remains inoperative for a period of twenty-four (24) scheduled maintenance hours or more from the time Customer notifies NCR until it is returned to good operating condition (48 hours in Alaska and Hawaii), NCR shall grant a credit to Customer for each inoperative hour at the rate of 1/720th of the basic monthly rental charge for such component. A like credit shall be granted for each interconnected NCR component being maintained which is not usable as a result of the breakdown. Customer shall not be entitled to the credit if the cause of inoperation is due to the fault or negligence of Customer, fire originating outside of NCR furnished equipment, water, and other acts of God, civil or military authority or the act of any third party.

15.   **SYSTEM IMPLEMENTATION** — "System" shall mean an integrated group of equipment supplied or specified by NCR and the NCR furnished programs utilized with it. "Installation Service" is installation and operational training and assistance. NCR's liability resulting from performance of Installation Service shall be limited to re-performing any such services. Customer has the responsibility for implementing and operating the System. Installation Services furnished to Customer are to facilitate implementation of the System by Customer and are not to be construed as evidencing any obligation of NCR for implementing or operating the System.

16.   **SYSTEM CAPABILITY** — Any proposal or recommendation by NCR for the equipment or programs ordered respecting the capability of the System to perform applications of, or produce certain results for, Customer is based on NCR's best efforts to provide an operational system for Customer. It shall constitute a commitment on the part of NCR only if a) it is attached to the Order or specifically incorporated by reference AND b) Customer cannot itself verify system capability in advance of equipment delivery.

CUSTOMER ACKNOWLEDGES ITS OBLIGATION TO NCR TO VERIFY SYSTEM CAPABILITY IN ADVANCE OR DELIVERY WHENEVER REASONABLY POSSIBLE.

When programming is to be performed by Customer prior to delivery of the equipment, Customer agrees that it has, as of the date of the order or will have prior to delivery, a suffcient number of competent and adequately trained personnel to accomplish evaluation and implementation and thereafter to operate the system efficiently. Because of this capability and because it has the better knowledge of its operations, methods and volumes, Customer has, or will have prior to delivery of the equipment, the better expertise to itself evaluate system capability.

If Customer can verify system capability in advance of delivery, failure to inform NCR in writing prior to delivery that the system will not perform as specified will be conclusively deemed to be an agreement by the Customer that it is suitable for the intended applications and will produce the anticipated results and no claim of reliance on any NCR recommendation or proposal will be made.

In the event that prior to delivery it is mutually determined that the system will not perform in accordance with specifications previously furnished to Customer or substantially as represented, Customer may at its option accept revised performance criteria or terminate the contract without liability of either party except for return of any advance payment when equitable.

In the event that compliance with specifications cannot be verified by Customer in advance of delivery, and on delivery it appears that the system cannot perform as specified, then the contract 1) may be terminated by either party without liability except any payments previously made to NCR shall be refunded, less the reasonable value of services received from the system or 2) may be amended to provide equipment and/or programs necessary to perform as represented.

17.   **OTHER EQUIPMENT AND PROGRAMS** — Customer may not make any alteration (any change made to the physical, mechanical or electrical arrangements of the equipment whether or not additional devices or parts are required) or attachment (the mechanical, electrical or electronic interconnection of non-NCR equipment marketed by others) to rented equipment unless specifically authorized in writing by NCR. In the event of any attachment or alteration to NCR equipment or in the event that a program not serviced by NCR is used or any modification is made to any NCR serviced program, or any program is used not furnished by NCR, NCR assumes no responsibility and shall not be liable for a) the proper functioning of the system or of any unit of equipment except for maintenance service under Section 13 or b) the capability of the system or c) infringement of any patent resulting from the combination. Notwithstanding anything to the contrary, Customer assumes all risk of loss or damage to NCR furnished equipment arising out of such attachment or alteration.

18.   **TERMINATION** — A contract for specific equipment, programs or services resulting from an accepted order may be terminated under the following conditions:

a. Either party may terminate a program license at the expiration of the term, or thereafter, on 30 days prior written notice. Either party may terminate a rental contract by written notice given 30 days before the expiration of the

6

initial term or any yearly extension; otherwise the term shall be extended yearly. Software service and equipment maintenance shall be continued on the expiration of the period set forth on the invoice for yearly periods unless (i) either party gives written notice to the other 30 days prior to the anniversary date of its intention to terminate service, (ii) as to equipment maintenance, the equipment is not in good condition on the effective date of any renewal period. Any equipment maintenance contract may be terminated by either party on 30 days notice.

Until terminated, Customer agrees to pay the applicable rent, license fee, equipment maintenance, software service fee or other charges. No program license shall be considered terminated until customer either returns or certifies destruction of the program.

b. Either party may, at its election and without prejudice to any other right or remedy, terminate the contract upon the filing of a petition in bankruptcy by or against the other, or should the other make an assignment for the benefit of creditors, or should a receiver be appointed or applied for by the other.

c. NCR may, at its election, and without prejudice to any other right or remedy available by law or under this Agreement unless pursuant to Section 16, treat any contract as terminated by Customer in the event the Customer cancels or attempts to cancel the contract prior to delivery, refuses delivery, fails to pay after 10 days prior written notice any payment due, or wilfully violates the confidentiality provisions of Section 10b. In such event, NCR may without further notice enter Customer's premises without liability for trespass or damage and reclaim and/or repossess the equipment and any NCR furnished program and the media they are on. In the case of a rental contract, program license or software services contract, NCR shall be entitled to the total amount due under it less amounts previously paid and costs which will not be incurred thereafter by NCR.

d. In accordance with Section 16.

19.   **DISPUTES** — Any controversy or claim, including any claim of misrepresentation, arising out of or related to this Agreement and/or any contract hereafter entered into between NCR and Customer, or the breach thereof, or the furnishing of any equipment or service by NCR to Customer, shall be settled by arbitration. The arbitration shall be conducted by a single arbitrator under the then current rules of the American Arbitration Association. The arbitrator shall be chosen from a panel of persons knowledgeable in business information and data processing systems. The decision and award of the arbitrator shall be final and binding and the award so rendered may be entered in any court having jurisdiction thereof. The aribtration shall be held and the award shall be deemed to be made in the city where the NCR district office procuring the order is located.

7

APPLICATION FOR CX SERVICE CONTRACT

Please Print or Type

CX Insurance Policy #_____

Contractor/Dealer	Address	City	State	Zip

Equipment Owner	Address	City	State	Zip

Original Installation Date	Address of Installation if Different Than Purchaser-User

COMPLETE THE FOLLOWING—4 YEAR PLAN NEW EQUIPMENT ONLY   Use Rate Schedule #1 or #4

AC or HEAT PUMP MAKE	MODEL NUMBER	H P	SERIAL NUMBER

HEATING EQUIPMENT MAKE	MODEL NUMBER		SERIAL NUMBER

Type of Heating Equipment Standing Pilot ___   Electric Ignition and/or Vent Damper ___   Recuperative/Condensing Furnace ___   Strip Heat ___   Electric Furnace ___   Oil Furnace ___

Extended 4 Year Contract Effective From _____ TO _____

Heat Pump Yes   No   Number of Compressors _____ CONTRACT COST (Schedule 1 or 4) _____

COMPLETE THE FOLLOWING—1 YEAR PLAN NEW OR EXISTING EQUIPMENT   Use Rate Schedule #2 or #3

AC or HEAT PUMP MAKE	MODEL NUMBER	H P	SERIAL NUMBER

HEATING EQUIPMENT MAKE	MODEL NUMBER		SERIAL NUMBER

Type of Heating Equipment Standing Pilot ___   Electric Ignition and/or Vent Damper ___   Recuperative/Condensing Furnace ___   Strip Heat ___   Electric Furnace ___   Oil Furnace ___

One Year Contract Effective From (Minimum of 30 Days From Date of Application)_____ TO _____

Heat Pump Yes   No   Number of Compressors _____ CONTRACT COST (Schedule 2 or 3) _____

IF COMPRESSOR COVERAGE IS DESIRED UNDER 1 YEAR PLAN COMPLETE THE FOLLOWING:

1) MOTOR COMPRESSOR MAKE	MODEL NUMBER	H P	SERIAL NUMBER

2) MOTOR COMPRESSOR MAKE	MODEL NUMBER	H P	SERIAL NUMBER

The undersigned agrees and understands that under the conditions of the CX contract the per occurrence and cumulative limits of liability appearing on the reverse side of this application are applicable to this contract.

DATE_____ CONTRACTOR/DEALER SIGNATURE_____

MAKE CHECK PAYABLE TO: Marsh & McLennan Group Associates.

Mail this completed application with contract payment to: MARSH & McLENNAN GROUP ASSOCIATES
PRODUCT WARRANTY DEPARTMENT
222 S. Riverside Plaza
Chicago, IL 60606

Appendix Three
Magnuson-Moss Warranty Act

Public Law 93-637
93rd Congress, S. 356
January 4, 1975

An Act

To provide minimum disclosure standards for written consumer product warranties; to define minimum Federal content standards for such warranties; to amend the Federal Trade Commission Act in order to improve its consumer protection activities; and for other purposes.

Be it enacted by the Senate and House of Representatives of the United States of America in Congress assembled, That this act may be cited as the "Magnuson-Moss Warranty—Federal Trade Commission Improvement Act".

Magnuson-Moss Warranty-- Federal Trade Commission Improvement Act. 15 USC 2301 note.

TITLE I—CONSUMER PRODUCT WARRANTIES

DEFINITIONS

15 USC 2301.

SEC. 101. For the purposes of this title:

(1) The term "consumer product" means any tangible personal property which is distributed in commerce and which is normally used for personal, family, or household purposes (including any such property intended to be attached to or installed in any real property without regard to whether it is so attached or installed).

(2) The term "Commission" means the Federal Trade Commission.

88 STAT. 2183
88 STAT. 2184

(3) The term "consumer" means a buyer (other than for purposes of resale) of any consumer product, any person to whom such product is transferred during the duration of an implied or written warranty (or service contract) applicable to the product, and any other person who is entitled by the terms of such warranty (or service contract) or under applicable State law to enforce against the warrantor (or service contractor) the obligations of the warranty (or service contract).

(4) The term "supplier" means any person engaged in the business of making a consumer product directly or indirectly available to consumers.

(5) The term "warrantor" means any supplier or other person who gives or offers to give a written warranty or who is or may be obligated under an implied warranty.

(6) The term "written warranty" means—

(A) any written affirmation of fact or written promise made in connection with the sale of a consumer product by a supplier to a buyer which relates to the nature of the material or workmanship and affirms or promises that such material or workmanship is defect free or will meet a specified level of performance over a specified period of time, or

(B) any undertaking in writing in connection with the sale by a supplier of a consumer product to refund, repair, replace, or take other remedial action with respect to such product in the event that such product fails to meet the specifications set forth in the undertaking,

which written affirmation, promise, or undertaking becomes part of the basis of the bargain between a supplier and a buyer for purposes other than resale of such product.

(7) The term "implied warranty" means an implied warranty arising under State law (as modified by sections 108 and 104(a)) in connection with the sale by a supplier of a consumer product.

(8) The term "service contract" means a contract in writing to perform, over a fixed period of time or for a specified duration,

services relating to the maintenance or repair (or both) of a consumer product.

(9) The term "reasonable and necessary maintenance" consists of those operations (A) which the consumer reasonably can be expected to perform or have performed and (B) which are necessary to keep any consumer product performing its intended function and operating at a reasonable level of performance.

(10) The term "remedy" means whichever of the following actions the warrantor elects:

    (A) repair,

    (B) replacement, or

    (C) refund;

except that the warrantor may not elect refund unless (i) the warrantor is unable to provide replacement and repair is not commercially practicable or cannot be timely made, or (ii) the consumer is willing to accept such refund.

88 STAT. 2184
88 STAT. 2185

(11) The term "replacement" means furnishing a new consumer product which is identical or reasonably equivalent to the warranted consumer product.

(12) The term "refund" means refunding the actual purchase price (less reasonable depreciation based on actual use where permitted by rules of the Commission).

(13) The term "distributed in commerce" means sold in commerce, introduced or delivered for introduction into commerce, or held for sale or distribution after introduction into commerce.

(14) The term "commerce" means trade, traffic, commerce, or transportation—

    (A) between a place in a State and any place outside thereof, or

    (B) which affects trade, traffic, commerce, or transportation described in subparagraph (A).

(15) The term "State" means a State, the District of Columbia, the Commonwealth of Puerto Rico, the Virgin Islands, Guam, the Canal Zone, or American Samoa. The term "State law" includes a law of the United States applicable only to the District of Columbia or only to a territory or possession of the United States; and the term "Federal law" excludes any State law.

WARRANTY PROVISIONS

15 USC 2302.

SEC. 102. (a) In order to improve the adequacy of information available to consumers, prevent deception, and improve competition in the marketing of consumer products, any warrantor warranting a consumer product to a consumer by means of a written warranty shall, to the extent required by rules of the Commission, fully and conspicuously disclose in simple and readily understood language the terms and conditions of such warranty. Such rules may require inclusion in the written warranty of any of the following items among others:

(1) The clear identification of the names and addresses of the warrantors.

(2) The identity of the party or parties to whom the warranty is extended.

(3) The products or parts covered.

(4) A statement of what the warrantor will do in the event of a defect, malfunction, or failure to conform with such written warranty—at whose expense—and for what period of time.

(5) A statement of what the consumer must do and expenses he must bear.

(6) Exceptions and exclusions from the terms of the warranty.

(7) The step-by-step procedure which the consumer should take in order to obtain performance of any obligation under the warranty, including the identification of any person or class of persons authorized to perform the obligations set forth in the warranty.

(8) Information respecting the availability of any informal dispute settlement procedure offered by the warrantor and a recital, where the warranty so provides, that the purchaser may be required to resort to such procedure before pursuing any legal remedies in the courts.

88 STAT. 2185
88 STAT. 2186

(9) A brief, general description of the legal remedies available to the consumer.

(10) The time at which the warrantor will perform any obligations under the warranty.

(11) The period of time within which, after notice of a defect, malfunction, or failure to conform with the warranty, the warrantor will perform any obligations under the warranty.

(12) The characteristics or properties of the products, or parts thereof, that are not covered by the warranty.

(13) The elements of the warranty in words or phrases which would not mislead a reasonable, average consumer as to the nature or scope of the warranty.

(b)(1)(A) The Commission shall prescribe rules requiring that the terms of any written warranty on a consumer product be made available to the consumer (or prospective consumer) prior to the sale of the product to him.

Availability prior to sale.

(B) The Commission may prescribe rules for determining the manner and form in which information with respect to any written warranty of a consumer product shall be clearly and conspicuously presented or displayed so as not to mislead the reasonable, average consumer, when such information is contained in advertising, labeling, point-of-sale material, or other representations in writing.

Information, presentation.

(2) Nothing in this title (other than paragraph (3) of this subsection) shall be deemed to authorize the Commission to prescribe the duration of written warranties given or to require that a consumer product or any of its components be warranted.

(3) The Commission may prescribe rules for extending the period of time a written warranty or service contract is in effect to correspond with any period of time in excess of a reasonable period (not less than 10 days) during which the consumer is deprived of the use of such consumer product by reason of failure of the product to conform with the written warranty or by reason of the failure of the warrantor (or service contractor) to carry out such warranty (or service contract) within the period specified in the warranty (or service contract).

Time extension.

(c) No warrantor of a consumer product may condition his written or implied warranty of such product on the consumer's using, in connection with such product, any article or service (other than article or service provided without charge under the terms of the warranty) which is identified by brand, trade, or corporate name; except that the prohibition of this subsection may be waived by the Commission if—

Conditions.

(1) the warrantor satisfies the Commission that the warranted product will function properly only if the article or service so identified is used in connection with the warranted product, and

(2) the Commission finds that such a waiver is in the public interest.

The Commission shall identify in the Federal Register, and permit public comment on, all applications for waiver of the prohibition of this subsection, and shall publish in the Federal Register its disposition of any such application, including the reasons therefor.

Publication in Federal Register.

88 STAT. 2187

(d) The Commission may by rule devise detailed substantive warranty provisions which warrantors may incorporate by reference in their warranties.

(e) The provisions of this section apply only to warranties which pertain to consumer products actually costing the consumer more than $5.

DESIGNATION OF WARRANTIES

15 USC 2303.

SEC. 103. (a) Any warrantor warranting a consumer product by means of a written warranty shall clearly and conspicuously designate such warranty in the following manner, unless exempted from doing so by the Commission pursuant to subsection (c) of this section:

"Full warranty."

(1) If the written warranty meets the Federal minimum standards for warranty set forth in section 104 of this Act, then it shall be conspicuously designated a "full (statement of duration) warranty".

"Limited warranty."

(2) If the written warranty does not meet the Federal minimum standards for warranty set forth in section 104 of this Act, then it shall be conspicuously designated a "limited warranty".

(b) Sections 102, 103, and 104 shall not apply to statements or representations which are similar to expressions of general policy concerning customer satisfaction and which are not subject to any specific limitations.

(c) In addition to exercising the authority pertaining to disclosure granted in section 102 of this Act, the Commission may by rule determine when a written warranty does not have to be designated either "full (statement of duration)" or "limited" in accordance with this section.

(d) The provisions of subsections (a) and (c) of this section apply only to warranties which pertain to consumer products actually costing the consumer more than $10 and which are not designated "full (statement of duration) warranties".

FEDERAL MINIMUM STANDARDS FOR WARRANTY

15 USC 2304.

SEC. 104. (a) In order for a warrantor warranting a consumer product by means of a written warranty to meet the Federal minimum standards for warranty—

(1) such warrantor must as a minimum remedy such consumer product within a reasonable time and without charge, in the case of a defect, malfunction, or failure to conform with such written warranty;

(2) notwithstanding section 108(b), such warrantor may not impose any limitation on the duration of any implied warranty on the product;

(3) such warrantor may not exclude or limit consequential damages for breach of any written or implied warranty on such product, unless such exclusion or limitation conspicuously appears on the face of the warranty; and

(4) if the product (or a component part thereof) contains a defect or malfunction after a reasonable number of attempts by the warrantor to remedy defects or malfunctions in such product, such warrantor must permit the consumer to elect either a refund for, or replacement without charge of, such product or part (as the case may be). The Commission may by rule specify for purposes of this paragraph, what constitutes a reasonable number of attempts to remedy particular kinds of defects or malfunctions under different circumstances. If the warrantor replaces a component part of a consumer product, such replacement shall include installing the part in the product without charge.

(b)(1) In fulfilling the duties under subsection (a) respecting a written warranty, the warrantor shall not impose any duty other than notification upon any consumer as a condition of securing remedy of any consumer product which malfunctions, is defective, or does not conform to the written warranty, unless the warrantor has demonstrated in a rulemaking proceeding, or can demonstrate in an administrative or judicial enforcement proceeding (including private enforcement), or in an informal dispute settlement proceeding, that such a duty is reasonable.

(2) Notwithstanding paragraph (1), a warrantor may require, as a condition to replacement of, or refund for, any consumer product under subsection (a), that such consumer product shall be made available to the warrantor free and clear of liens and other encumbrances, except as otherwise provided by rule or order of the Commission in cases in which such a requirement would not be practicable.

(3) The Commission may, by rule define in detail the duties set forth in section 104(a) of this Act and the applicability of such duties to warrantors of different categories of consumer products with "full (statement of duration)" warranties.

(4) The duties under subsection (a) extend from the warrantor to each person who is a consumer with respect to the consumer product.

(c) The performance of the duties under subsection (a) of this section shall not be required of the warrantor if he can show that the defect, malfunction, or failure of any warranted consumer product to conform with a written warranty, was caused by damage (not resulting from defect or malfunction) while in the possession of the consumer, or unreasonable use (including failure to provide reasonable and necessary maintenance).

(d) For purposes of this section and of section 102(c), the term "without charge" means that the warrantor may not assess the consumer for any costs the warrantor or his representatives incur in connection with the required remedy of a warranted consumer product. An obligation under subsection (a)(1)(A) to remedy without charge does not necessarily require the warrantor to compensate the consumer for incidental expenses; however, if any incidental expenses are incurred because the remedy is not made within a reasonable time or because the warrantor imposed an unreasonable duty upon the consumer as a condition of securing remedy, then the consumer shall be entitled to recover reasonable incidental expenses which are so incurred in any action against the warrantor.

"Without charge."

(e) If a supplier designates a warranty applicable to a consumer product as a "full (statement of duration)" warranty, then the warranty on such product shall, for purposes of any action under section 110(d) or under any State law, be deemed to incorporate at least the minimum requirements of this section and rules prescribed under this section.

FULL AND LIMITED WARRANTING OF A CONSUMER PRODUCT

SEC. 105. Nothing in this title shall prohibit the selling of a consumer product which has both full and limited warranties if such warranties are clearly and conspicuously differentiated.

15 USC 2305.

SERVICE CONTRACTS

SEC. 106. (a) The Commission may prescribe by rule the manner and form in which the terms and conditions of service contracts shall be fully, clearly, and conspicuously disclosed.

15 USC 2306.

(b) Nothing in this title shall be construed to prevent a supplier or warrantor from entering into a service contract with the consumer

88 STAT. 2189

in addition to or in lieu of a written warranty if such contract fully, clearly, and conspicuously discloses its terms and conditions in simple and readily understood language.

DESIGNATION OF REPRESENTATIVES

15 USC 2307.

SEC. 107. Nothing in this title shall be construed to prevent any warrantor from designating representatives to perform duties under the written or implied warranty: *Provided,* That such warrantor shall make reasonable arrangements for compensation of such designated representatives, but no such designation shall relieve the warrantor of his direct responsibilities to the consumer or make the representative a cowarrantor.

LIMITATION ON DISCLAIMER OF IMPLIED WARRANTIES

15 USC 2308.

SEC. 108. (a) No supplier may disclaim or modify (except as provided in subsection (b)) any implied warranty to a consumer with respect to such consumer product if (1) such supplier makes any written warranty to the consumer with respect to such consumer product, or (2) at the time of sale, or within 90 days thereafter, such supplier enters into a service contract with the consumer which applies to such consumer product.

(b) For purposes of this title (other than section 104(a)(2)), implied warranties may be limited in duration to the duration of a written warranty of reasonable duration, if such limitation is conscionable and is set forth in clear and unmistakable language and prominently displayed on the face of the warranty.

(c) A disclaimer, modification, or limitation made in violation of this section shall be ineffective for purposes of this title and State law.

COMMISSION RULES

15 USC 2309.

SEC. 109. (a) Any rule prescribed under this title shall be prescribed in accordance with section 553 of title 5, United States Code; except that the Commission shall give interested persons an opportunity for oral presentations of data, views, and arguments, in addition to written submissions. A transcript shall be kept of any oral presentation. Any such rule shall be subject to judicial review under section 18(e) of the Federal Trade Commission Act (as amended by section 202 of this

Ante, p. 2193.

Act) in the same manner as rules prescribed under section 18(a)(1) (B) of such Act, except that section 18(e)(3)(B) of such Act shall not apply.

Used motor vehicles.

(b) The Commission shall initiate within one year after the date of enactment of this Act a rulemaking proceeding dealing with warranties and warranty practices in connection with the sale of used motor vehicles; and, to the extent necessary to supplement the protections offered the consumer by this title, shall prescribe rules dealing with such warranties and practices. In prescribing rules under this subsection, the Commission may exercise any authority it may have under this title, or other law, and in addition it may require disclosure that a used motor vehicle is sold without any warranty and specify the form and content of such disclosure.

REMEDIES

Informal
dispute
settlements.
15 USC 2310.

SEC. 110. (a)(1) Congress hereby declares it to be its policy to encourage warrantors to establish procedures whereby consumer disputes are fairly and expeditiously settled through informal dispute settlement mechanisms.

(2) The Commission shall prescribe rules setting forth minimum requirements for any informal dispute settlement procedure which is incorporated into the terms of a written warranty to which any provision of this title applies. Such rules shall provide for participation in such procedure by independent or governmental entities.

(3) One or more warrantors may establish an informal dispute settlement procedure which meets the requirements of the Commission's rules under paragraph (2). If—

(A) a warrantor establishes such a procedure,

(B) such procedure, and its implementation, meets the requirements of such rules, and

(C) he incorporates in a written warranty a requirement that the consumer resort to such procedure before pursuing any legal remedy under this section respecting such warranty,

then (i) the consumer may not commence a civil action (other than a class action) under subsection (d) of this section unless he initially resorts to such procedure; and (ii) a class of consumers may not proceed in a class action under subsection (d) except to the extent the court determines necessary to establish the representative capacity of the named plaintiffs, unless the named plaintiffs (upon notifying the defendant that they are named plaintiffs in a class action with respect to a warranty obligation) initially resort to such procedure. In the case of such a class action which is brought in a district court of the United States, the representative capacity of the named plaintiffs shall be established in the application of rule 23 of the Federal Rules of Civil Procedure. In any civil action arising out of a warranty obligation and relating to a matter considered in such a procedure, any decision in such procedure shall be admissible in evidence.

28 USC app.

(4) The Commission on its own initiative may, or upon written complaint filed by any interested person shall, review the bona fide operation of any dispute settlement procedure resort to which is stated in a written warranty to be a prerequisite to pursuing a legal remedy under this section. If the Commission finds that such procedure or its implementation fails to comply with the requirements of the rules under paragraph (2), the Commission may take appropriate remedial action under any authority it may have under this title or any other provision of law.

Review of dispute settlement procedures.

(5) Until rules under paragraph (2) take effect, this subsection shall not affect the validity of any informal dispute settlement procedure respecting consumer warranties, but in any action under subsection (d), the court may invalidate any such procedure if it finds that such procedure is unfair.

(b) It shall be a violation of section 5(a)(1) of the Federal Trade Commission Act (15 U.S.C. 45(a)(1)) for any person to fail to comply with any requirement imposed on such person by this title (or a rule thereunder) or to violate any prohibition contained in this title (or a rule thereunder).

(c)(1) The district courts of the United States shall have jurisdiction of any action brought by the Attorney General (in his capacity as such), or by the Commission by any of its attorneys designated by it for such purpose, to restrain (A) any warrantor from making a deceptive warranty with respect to a consumer product, or (B) any person from failing to comply with any requirement imposed on such person by or pursuant to this title or from violating any prohibition contained in this title. Upon proper showing that, weighing the equities and considering the Commission's or Attorney General's likelihood of ultimate success, such action would be in the public interest and after notice to the defendant, a temporary restraining order or preliminary injunction may be granted without bond. In the case of an

Jurisdiction.

88 STAT. 2191

15 USC 45.

action brought by the Commission, if a complaint under section 5 of the Federal Trade Commission Act is not filed within such period (not exceeding 10 days) as may be specified by the court after the issuance of the temporary restraining order or preliminary injunction, the order or injunction shall be dissolved by the court and be of no further force and effect. Any suit shall be brought in the district in which such person resides or transacts business. Whenever it appears to the court that the ends of justice require that other persons should be parties in the action, the court may cause them to be summoned whether or not they reside in the district in which the court is held, and to that end process may be served in any district.

"Deceptive warranty."

(2) For the purposes of this subsection, the term "deceptive warranty" means (A) a written warranty which (i) contains an affirmation, promise, description, or representation which is either false or fraudulent, or which, in light of all of the circumstances, would mislead a reasonable individual exercising due care; or (ii) fails to contain information which is necessary in light of all of the circumstances, to make the warranty not misleading to a reasonable individual exercising due care; or (B) a written warranty created by the use of such terms as "guaranty" or "warranty", if the terms and conditions of such warranty so limit its scope and application as to deceive a reasonable individual.

Civil suit.

(d)(1) Subject to subsections (a)(3) and (e), a consumer who is damaged by the failure of a supplier, warrantor, or service contractor to comply with any obligation under this title, or under a written warranty, implied warranty, or service contract, may bring suit for damages and other legal and equitable relief—

(A) in any court of competent jurisdiction in any State or the District of Columbia; or

(B) in an appropriate district court of the United States, subject to paragraph (3) of this subsection.

(2) If a consumer finally prevails in any action brought under paragraph (1) of this subsection, he may be allowed by the court to recover as part of the judgment a sum equal to the aggregate amount of cost and expenses (including attorneys' fees based on actual time expended) determined by the court to have been reasonably incurred by the plaintiff for or in connection with the commencement and prosecution of such action, unless the court in its discretion shall determine that such an award of attorneys' fees would be inappropriate.

(3) No claim shall be cognizable in a suit brought under paragraph (1)(B) of this subsection—

(A) if the amount in controversy of any individual claim is less than the sum or value of $25;

(B) if the amount in controversy is less than the sum or value of $50,000 (exclusive of interests and costs) computed on the basis of all claims to be determined in this suit; or

(C) if the action is brought as a class action, and the number of named plaintiffs is less than one hundred.

(e) No action (other than a class action or an action respecting a warranty to which subsection (a)(3) applies) may be brought under subsection (d) for failure to comply with any obligation under any written or implied warranty or service contract, and a class of consumers may not proceed in a class action under such subsection with respect to such a failure except to the extent the court determines necessary to establish the representative capacity of the named plaintiffs, unless the person obligated under the warranty or service contract is afforded a reasonable opportunity to cure such failure to comply. In the case of such a class action (other than a class action respecting a warranty to which subsection (a)(3) applies) brought

310

83 STAT. 2192

under subsection (d) for breach of any written or implied warranty or service contract, such reasonable opportunity will be afforded by the named plaintiffs and they shall at that time notify the defendant that they are acting on behalf of the class. In the case of such a class action which is brought in a district court of the United States, the representative capacity of the named plaintiffs shall be established in the application of rule 23 of the Federal Rules of Civil Procedure.   28 USC app.

(f) For purposes of this section, only the warrantor actually making a written affirmation of fact, promise, or undertaking shall be deemed to have created a written warranty, and any rights arising thereunder may be enforced under this section only against such warrantor and no other person.

EFFECT ON OTHER LAWS

SEC. 111. (a)(1) Nothing contained in this title shall be construed   15 USC 2311.
to repeal, invalidate, or supersede the Federal Trade Commission Act (15 U.S.C. 41 et seq.) or any statute defined therein as an Antitrust Act.

(2) Nothing in this title shall be construed to repeal, invalidate, or supersede the Federal Seed Act (7 U.S.C. 1551–1611) and nothing in this title shall apply to seed for planting.

(b)(1) Nothing in this title shall invalidate or restrict any right or remedy of any consumer under State law or any other Federal law.

(2) Nothing in this title (other than sections 108 and 104(a) (2) and (4)) shall (A) affect the liability of, or impose liability on, any person for personal injury, or (B) supersede any provision of State law regarding consequential damages for injury to the person or other injury.

(c)(1) Except as provided in subsection (b) and in paragraph (2) of this subsection, a State requirement—

    (A) which relates to labeling or disclosure with respect to written warranties or performance thereunder;

    (B) which is within the scope of an applicable requirement of sections 102, 103, and 104 (and rules implementing such sections), and

    (C) which is not identical to a requirement of section 102, 103, or 104 (or a rule thereunder),

shall not be applicable to written warranties complying with such sections (or rules thereunder).

(2) If, upon application of an appropriate State agency, the Commission determines (pursuant to rules issued in accordance with section 109) that any requirement of such State covering any transaction to which this title applies (A) affords protection to consumers greater than the requirements of this title and (B) does not unduly burden interstate commerce, then such State requirement shall be applicable (notwithstanding the provisions of paragraph (1) of this subsection) to the extent specified in such determination for so long as the State administers and enforces effectively any such greater requirement.

(d) This title (other than section 102(c)) shall be inapplicable to any written warranty the making or content of which is otherwise governed by Federal law. If only a portion of a written warranty is so governed by Federal law, the remaining portion shall be subject to this title.

EFFECTIVE DATE

SEC. 112. (a) Except as provided in subsection (b) of this section,   15 USC 2312.
this title shall take effect 6 months after the date of its enactment but shall not apply to consumer products manufactured prior to such date.

88 STAT. 2193

(b) Section 102(a) shall take effect 6 months after the final publication of rules respecting such section; except that the Commission, for good cause shown, may postpone the applicability of such sections until one year after such final publication in order to permit any designated classes of suppliers to bring their written warranties into compliance with rules promulgated pursuant to this title.

Rules.

(c) The Commission shall promulgate rules for initial implementation of this title as soon as possible after the date of enactment of this Act but in no event later than one year after such date.

TITLE II—FEDERAL TRADE COMMISSION IMPROVEMENTS

JURISDICTION OF COMMISSION

SEC. 201. (a) Section 5 of the Federal Trade Commission Act (15 U.S.C. 45) is amended by striking out "in commerce" wherever it appears and inserting in lieu thereof "in or affecting commerce".

(b) Subsections (a) and (b) of section 6 of the Federal Trade Commission Act (15 U.S.C. 46(a), (b)) are each amended by striking out "in commerce" and inserting in lieu thereof "in or whose business affects commerce".

(c) Section 12 of the Federal Trade Commission Act (15 U.S.C. 52) is amended by striking out "in commerce" wherever it appears and inserting in lieu thereof in subsection (a) "in or having an effect upon commerce," and in lieu thereof in subsection (b) "in or affecting commerce".

RULEMAKING

SEC. 202. (a) The Federal Trade Commission Act (15 U.S.C. 41 et seq.) is amended by redesignating section 18 as section 21, and inserting after section 17 the following new section:

15 USC 58.

15 USC 57a.

"SEC. 18. (a)(1) The Commission may prescribe—

"(A) interpretive rules and general statements of policy with respect to unfair or deceptive acts or practices in or affecting commerce (within the meaning of section 5(a)(1) of this Act), and

"(B) rules which define with specificity acts or practices which are unfair or deceptive acts or practices in or affecting commerce (within the meaning of such section 5(a)(1)). Rules under this subparagraph may include requirements prescribed for the purpose of preventing such acts or practices.

"(2) The Commission shall have no authority under this Act, other than its authority under this section, to prescribe any rule with respect to unfair or deceptive acts or practices in or affecting commerce (within the meaning of section 5(a)(1)). The preceding sentence shall not affect any authority of the Commission to prescribe rules (including interpretive rules), and general statements of policy, with respect to unfair methods of competition in or affecting commerce.

"(b) When prescribing a rule under subsection (a)(1)(B) of this section, the Commission shall proceed in accordance with section 553 of title 5, United States Code (without regard to any reference in such section to sections 556 and 557 of such title), and shall also (1) publish a notice of proposed rulemaking stating with particularity the reason for the proposed rule; (2) allow interested persons to submit written data, views, and arguments, and make all such submissions publicly available; (3) provide an opportunity for an informal hearing in accordance with subsection (c); and (4) promul-

88 STAT. 2194

gate, if appropriate, a final rule based on the matter in the rulemaking record (as defined in subsection (e)(1)(B)), together with a statement of basis and purpose.

"(c) The Commission shall conduct any informal hearings required by subsection (b)(3) of this section in accordance with the following procedure:

Hearing procedures.

"(1) Subject to paragraph (2) of this subsection, an interested person is entitled—

"(A) to present his position orally or by documentary submissions (or both), and

"(B) if the Commission determines that there are disputed issues of material fact it is necessary to resolve, to present such rebuttal submissions and to conduct (or have conducted under paragraph (2)(B)) such cross-examination of persons as the Commission determines (i) to be appropriate, and (ii) to be required for a full and true disclosure with respect to such issues.

"(2) The Commission may prescribe such rules and make such rulings concerning proceedings in such hearings as may tend to avoid unnecessary costs or delay. Such rules or rulings may include (A) imposition of reasonable time limits on each interested person's oral presentations, and (B) requirements that any cross-examination to which a person may be entitled under paragraph (1) be conducted by the Commission on behalf of that person in such manner as the Commission determines (i) to be appropriate, and (ii) to be required for a full and true disclosure with respect to disputed issues of material fact.

"(3)(A) Except as provided in subparagraph (B), if a group of persons each of whom under paragraphs (1) and (2) would be entitled to conduct (or have conducted) cross-examination and who are determined by the Commission to have the same or similar interests in the proceeding cannot agree upon a single representative of such interests for purposes of cross-examination, the Commission may make rules and rulings (i) limiting the representation of such interest, for such purposes, and (ii) governing the manner in which such cross-examination shall be limited.

"(B) When any person who is a member of a group with respect to which the Commission has made a determination under subparagraph (A) is unable to agree upon group representation with the other members of the group, then such person shall not be denied under the authority of subparagraph (A) the opportunity to conduct (or have conducted) cross-examination as to issues affecting his particular interests if (i) he satisfies the Commission that he has made a reasonable and good faith effort to reach agreement upon group representation with the other members of the group and (ii) the Commission determines that there are substantial and relevant issues which are not adequately presented by the group representative.

"(4) A verbatim transcript shall be taken of any oral presentation, and cross-examination, in an informal hearing to which this subsection applies. Such transcript shall be available to the public.

"(d)(1) The Commission's statement of basis and purpose to accompany a rule promulgated under subsection (a)(1)(B) shall include (A) a statement as to the prevalence of the acts or practices treated by the rule; (B) a statement as to the manner and context in which such acts or practices are unfair or deceptive; and (C) a statement as to the economic effect of the rule, taking into account the effect on small business and consumers.

Statement of basis and purpose, requirements.

"Commission."   "(2) (A) The term 'Commission' as used in this subsection and subsections (b) and (c) includes any person authorized to act in behalf of the Commission in any part of the rulemaking proceeding.

"(B) A substantive amendment to, or repeal of, a rule promulgated under subsection (a)(1)(B) shall be prescribed, and subject to judicial review, in the same manner as a rule prescribed under such subsection. An exemption under subsection (g) shall not be treated as an amendment or repeal of a rule.

"(3) When any rule under subsection (a)(1)(B) takes effect a subsequent violation thereof shall constitute an unfair or deceptive act or practice in violation of section 5(a)(1) of this Act, unless the Commission otherwise expressly provides in such rule.

Judicial review.   "(e)(1)(A) Not later than 60 days after a rule is promulgated under subsection (a)(1)(B) by the Commission, any interested person (including a consumer or consumer organization) may file a petition, in the United States Court of Appeals for the District of Columbia circuit or for the circuit in which such person resides or has his principal place of business, for judicial review of such rule. Copies of the petition shall be forthwith transmitted by the clerk of the court to the Commission or other officer designated by it for that purpose. The provisions of section 2112 of title 28, United States Code, shall apply to the filing of the rulemaking record of proceedings on which the Commission based its rule and to the transfer of proceedings in the courts of appeals.

"Rulemaking record."   "(B) For purposes of this section, the term 'rulemaking record' means the rule, its statement of basis and purpose, the transcript required by subsection (c)(4), any written submissions, and any other information which the Commission considers relevant to such rule.

"(2) If the petitioner or the Commission applies to the court for leave to make additional oral submissions or written presentations and shows to the satisfaction of the court that such submissions and presentations would be material and that there were reasonable grounds for the submissions and failure to make such submissions and presentations in the proceeding before the Commission, the court may order the Commission to provide additional opportunity to make such submissions and presentations. The Commission may modify or set aside its rule or make a new rule by reason of the additional submissions and presentations and shall file such modified or new rule, and the rule's statement of basis of purpose, with the return of such submissions and presentations. The court shall thereafter review such new or modified rule.

5 USC 701.   "(3) Upon the filing of the petition under paragraph (1) of this subsection, the court shall have jurisdiction to review the rule in accordance with chapter 7 of title 5, United States Code, and to grant appropriate relief, including interim relief, as provided in such chapter. The court shall hold unlawful and set aside the rule on any ground specified in subparagraphs (A), (B), (C), or (D) of section 706(2) of title 5, United States Code (taking due account of the rule of prejudicial error), or if—

"(A) the court finds that the Commission's action is not supported by substantial evidence in the rulemaking record (as defined in paragraph (1)(B) of this subsection) taken as a whole, or

"(B) the court finds that—

"(i) a Commission determination under subsection (c) that the petitioner is not entitled to conduct cross-examination or make rebuttal submissions, or "(ii) a Commission rule or ruling under subsection (c) limiting the petitioner's cross-examination or rebuttal submissions,

has precluded disclosure of disputed material facts which was necessary for fair determination by the Commission of the rule-making proceeding taken as a whole.

The term 'evidence', as used in this paragraph, means any matter in the rulemaking record.   "Evidence."

"(4) The judgment of the court affirming or setting aside, in whole or in part, any such rule shall be final, subject to review by the Supreme Court of the United States upon certiorari or certification, as provided in section 1254 of title 28, United States Code.

"(5)(A) Remedies under the preceding paragraphs of this subsection are in addition to and not in lieu of any other remedies provided by law.

"(B) The United States Courts of Appeal shall have exclusive jurisdiction of any action to obtain judicial review (other than in an enforcement proceeding) of a rule prescribed under subsection (a)(1)(B), if any district court of the United States would have had jurisdiction of such action but for this subparagraph. Any such action shall be brought in the United States Court of Appeals for the District of Columbia circuit, or for any circuit which includes a judicial district in which the action could have been brought but for this subparagraph.

"(C) A determination, rule, or ruling of the Commission described in paragraph (3)(B)(i) or (ii) may be reviewed only in a proceeding under this subsection and only in accordance with paragraph (3)(B). Section 706(2)(E) of title 5, United States Code, shall not apply to any rule promulgated under subsection (a)(1)(B). The contents and adequacy of any statement required by subsection (b)(4) shall not be subject to judicial review in any respect.

"(f)(1) In order to prevent unfair or deceptive acts or practices   Banks. in or affecting commerce (including acts or practices which are unfair or deceptive to consumers) by banks, each agency specified in paragraph (2) of this subsection shall establish a separate division of consumer affairs which shall receive and take appropriate action upon complaints with respect to such acts or practices by banks subject to its jurisdiction. The Board of Governors of the Federal Reserve   Regulations. System shall prescribe regulations to carry out the purposes of this section, including regulations defining with specificity such unfair or deceptive acts or practices, and containing requirements prescribed for the purpose of preventing such acts or practices. Whenever the Commission prescribes a rule under subsection (a)(1)(B) of this section, then within 60 days after such rule takes effect such Board shall promulgate substantially similar regulations prohibiting acts or practices of banks which are substantially similar to those prohibited by rules of the Commission and which impose substantially similar requirements, unless such Board finds that (A) such acts or practices of banks are not unfair or deceptive, or (B) that implementation of similar regulations with respect to banks would seriously conflict with essential monetary and payments systems policies of the Board, and publishes any such finding, and the reasons therefor, in   Publication the Federal Register.   in Federal

"(2) Compliance with regulations prescribed under this subsection   Register. shall be enforced under section 8 of the Federal Deposit Insurance Act, in the case of—   12 USC 1818.

"(A) national banks and banks operating under the code of law for the District of Columbia, by the division of consumer affairs established by the Comptroller of the Currency;

"(B) member banks of the Federal Reserve System (other than banks referred to in subparagraph (A)) by the division of consumer affairs established by the Board of Governors of the Federal Reserve System; and

"(C) banks insured by the Federal Deposit Insurance Corporation (other than banks referred to in subparagraph (A) or (B)), by the division of consumer affairs established by the Board of Directors of the Federal Deposit Insurance Corporation.

"(3) For the purpose of the exercise by any agency referred to in paragraph (2) of its powers under any Act referred to in that paragraph, a violation of any regulation prescribed under this subsection shall be deemed to be a violation of a requirement imposed under that Act. In addition to its powers under any provision of law specifically referred to in paragraph (2), each of the agencies referred to in that paragraph may exercise, for the purpose of enforcing compliance with any regulation prescribed under this subsection, any other authority conferred on it by law.

"(4) The authority of the Board of Governors of the Federal Reserve System to issue regulations under this subsection does not impair the authority of any other agency designated in this subsection to make rules respecting its own procedures in enforcing compliance with regulations prescribed under this subsection.

Report to Congress. "(5) Each agency exercising authority under this subsection shall transmit to the Congress not later than March 15 of each year a detailed report on its activities under this paragraph during the preceding calendar year.

"(g)(1) Any person to whom a rule under subsection (a)(1)(B) of this section applies may petition the Commission for an exemption from such rule.

"(2) If, on its own motion or on the basis of a petition under paragraph (1), the Commission finds that the application of a rule prescribed under subsection (a)(1)(B) to any person or class or persons is not necessary to prevent the unfair or deceptive act or practice to which the rule relates, the Commission may exempt such person or class from all or part of such rule. Section 553 of title 5, United States Code, shall apply to action under this paragraph.

"(3) Neither the pendency of a proceeding under this subsection respecting an exemption from a rule, nor the pendency of judicial proceedings to review the Commission's action or failure to act under this subsection, shall stay the applicability of such rule under subsection (a)(1)(B).

Compensation. "(h)(1) The Commission may, pursuant to rules prescribed by it, provide compensation for reasonable attorneys fees, expert witness fees, and other costs of participating in a rulemaking proceeding under this section to any person (A) who has, or represents, an interest (i) which would not otherwise be adequately represented in such proceeding, and (ii) representation of which is necessary for a fair determination of the rulemaking proceeding taken as a whole, and (B) who is unable effectively to participate in such proceeding because such person cannot afford to pay costs of making oral presentations, conducting cross-examination, and making rebuttal submissions in such proceeding.

"(2) The aggregate amount of compensation paid under this subsection in any fiscal year to all persons who, in rulemaking proceedings in which they receive compensation, are persons who either (A) would be regulated by the proposed rule, or (B) represent persons who would be so regulated, may not exceed 25 percent of the aggregate amount paid as compensation under this subsection to all persons in such fiscal year.

"(3) The aggregate amount of compensation paid to all persons in any fiscal year under this subsection may not exceed $1,000,000."

(b) Section 6(g) of the Federal Trade Commission Act (15 U.S.C. 46(g)) is amended by inserting "(except as provided in section 18 (a)(2) of this Act)" before "to make rules and regulations".

(c)(1) The amendments made by subsections (a) and (b) of this section shall not affect the validity of any rule which was promulgated under section 6(g) of the Federal Trade Commission Act prior to the date of enactment of this section. Any proposed rule under section 6(g) of such Act with respect to which presentation of data, views, and arguments was substantially completed before such date may be promulgated in the same manner and with the same validity as such rule could have been promulgated had this section not been enacted. 15 USC 57a note.

(2) If a rule described in paragraph (1) of this subsection is valid and if section 18 of the Federal Trade Commission Act would have applied to such rule had such rule been promulgated after the date of enactment of this Act, any substantive change in the rule after it has been promulgated shall be made in accordance with such section 18. Ante, p. 2193.

(d) The Federal Trade Commission and the Administrative Conference of the United States shall each conduct a study and evaluation of the rulemaking procedures under section 18 of the Federal Trade Commission Act and each shall submit a report of its study (including any legislative recommendations) to the Congress not later than 18 months after the date of enactment of this Act. 15 USC 57a note. Study and evaluation. Report to Congress.

INVESTIGATIVE AUTHORITY

Sec. 203. (a)(1) Section 6(a) of the Federal Trade Commission Act (15 U.S.C. 46(a)) is amended by striking out "corporation" and inserting "person, partnership, or corporation"; and by striking out "corporations and to individuals, associations, and partnerships", and inserting in lieu thereof "persons, partnerships, and corporations".

(2) Section 6(b) of such Act is amended by striking out "corporations" where it first appears and inserting in lieu thereof "persons, partnerships, and corporations,"; and by striking out "respective corporations" and inserting in lieu thereof "respective persons, partnerships, and corporations".

(3) The proviso at the end of section 6 of such Act is amended by striking out "any such corporation to the extent that such action is necessary to the investigation of any corporation, group of corporations," and inserting in lieu thereof "any person, partnership, or corporation to the extent that such action is necessary to the investigation of any person, partnership, or corporation, group of persons, partnerships, or corporations,".

(b)(1) The first paragraph of section 9 of such Act (15 U.S.C. 49) is amended by striking out "corporation" where it first appears and inserting in lieu thereof "person, partnership, or corporation".

(2) The third paragraph of section 9 of such Act is amended by striking out "corporation or other person" both places where it appears and inserting in each such place "person, partnership, or corporation".

(3) The fourth paragraph of section 9 of such Act is amended by striking out "person or corporation" and inserting in lieu thereof "person, partnership, or corporation".

(c)(1) The second paragraph of section 10 (15 U.S.C. 50) of such Act is amended by striking out "corporation" each place where it appears and inserting in lieu thereof in each such place "person, partnership, or corporation".

(2) The third paragraph of section 10 of such Act is amended by striking out "corporation" where it first appears and inserting in lieu thereof "persons, partnership, or corporation"; and by striking out "in the district where the corporation has its principal office or in any district in which it shall do business" and inserting in lieu thereof "in the case of a corporation or partnership in the district where the corporation or partnership has its principal office or in any district in which it shall do business, and in the case of any person in the district where such person resides or has his principal place of business".

REPRESENTATION

15 USC 56.

SEC. 204. (a) Section 16 of the Federal Trade Commission Act is amended to read as follows:

"SEC. 16. (a)(1) Except as otherwise provided in paragraph (2) or (3), if—

"(A) before commencing, defending, or intervening in, any civil action involving this Act (including an action to collect a civil penalty) which the Commission, or the Attorney General on behalf of the Commission, is authorized to commence, defend, or intervene in, the Commission gives written notification and undertakes to consult with the Attorney General with respect to such action; and

"(B) the Attorney General fails within 45 days after receipt of such notification to commence, defend, or intervene in, such action;

the Commission may commence, defend, or intervene in, and supervise the litigation of, such action and any appeal of such action in its own name by any of its attorneys designated by it for such purpose.

"(2) Except as otherwise provided in paragraph (3), in any civil action—

15 USC 53.

"(A) under section 13 of this Act (relating to injunctive relief);

Post, p. 2201.

"(B) under section 19 of this Act (relating to consumer redress);

"(C) to obtain judicial review of a rule prescribed by the Commission, or a cease and desist order issued under section 5

15 USC 45.
15 USC 49.

of this Act; or

"(D) under the second paragraph of section 9 of this Act (relating to enforcement of a subpena) and under the fourth paragraph of such section (relating to compliance with section 6 of this Act);

the Commission shall have exclusive authority to commence or defend, and supervise the litigation of, such action and any appeal of such action in its own name by any of its attorneys designated by it for such purpose, unless the Commission authorizes the Attorney General to do so. The Commission shall inform the Attorney General of the exercise of such authority and such exercise shall not preclude the Attorney General from intervening on behalf of the United States in such action and any appeal of such action as may be otherwise provided by law.

"(3)(A) If the Commission makes a written request to the Attorney General, within the 10-day period which begins on the date of the entry of the judgment in any civil action in which the Commission represented itself pursuant to paragraph (1) or (2), to represent itself through any of its attorneys designated by it for such purpose before the Supreme Court in such action, it may do so, if—

"(i) the Attorney General concurs with such request; or

"(ii) the Attorney General, within the 60-day period which begins on the date of the entry of such judgment—

"(a) refuses to appeal or file a petition for writ of certiorari with respect to such civil action, in which case he shall give written notification to the Commission of the reasons for such refusal within such 60-day period; or

"(b) the Attorney General fails to take any action with respect to the Commission's request.

"(B) In any case where the Attorney General represents the Commission before the Supreme Court in any civil action in which the Commission represented itself pursuant to paragraph (1) or (2), the Attorney General may not agree to any settlement, compromise, or dismissal of such action, or confess error in the Supreme Court with respect to such action, unless the Commission concurs.

"(C) For purposes of this paragraph (with respect to representation before the Supreme Court), the term 'Attorney General' includes the Solicitor General.

"Attorney General."

"(4) If, prior to the expiration of the 45-day period specified in paragraph (1) of this section or a 60-day period specified in paragraph (3), any right of the Commission to commence, defend, or intervene in, any such action or appeal may be extinguished due to any procedural requirement of any court with respect to the time in which any pleadings, notice of appeal, or other acts pertaining to such action or appeal may be taken, the Attorney General shall have one-half of the time required to comply with any such procedural requirement of the court (including any extension of such time granted by the court) for the purpose of commencing, defending, or intervening in the civil action pursuant to paragraph (1) or for the purpose of refusing to appeal or file a petition for writ of certiorari and the written notification or failing to take any action pursuant to paragraph 3(A)(ii).

"(5) The provisions of this subsection shall apply notwithstanding chapter 31 of title 28, United States Code, or any other provision of law.

28 USC 501.

"(b) Whenever the Commission has reason to believe that any person, partnership, or corporation is liable for a criminal penalty under this Act, the Commission shall certify the facts to the Attorney General, whose duty it shall be to cause appropriate criminal proceedings to be brought."

(b) Section 5(m) of such Act is repealed.

15 USC 45.

(c) The amendment and repeal made by this section shall not apply to any civil action commenced before the date of enactment of this Act.

15 USC 56 note.

CIVIL PENALTIES FOR KNOWING VIOLATIONS

SEC. 205. (a) Section 5 of the Federal Trade Commission Act (15 U.S.C. 45(a)) is amended by inserting after subsection (l) the following new subsection:

"(m)(1)(A) The Commission may commence a civil action to recover a civil penalty in a district court of the United States against any person, partnership, or corporation which violates any rule under this Act respecting unfair or deceptive acts or practices (other than an interpretive rule or a rule violation of which the Commission has provided is not an unfair or deceptive act or practice in violation of

88 STAT. 2201

subsection (a)(1)) with actual knowledge or knowledge fairly implied on the basis of objective circumstances that such act is unfair or deceptive and is prohibited by such rule. In such action, such person, partnership, or corporation shall be liable for a civil penalty of not more than $10,000 for each violation.

"(B) If the Commission determines in a proceeding under subsection (b) that any act or practice is unfair or deceptive, and issues a final cease and desist order with respect to such act or practice, then the Commission may commence a civil action to obtain a civil penalty in a district court of the United States against any person, partnership, or corporation which engages in such act or practice—

"(1) after such cease and desist order becomes final (whether or not such person, partnership, or corporation was subject to such cease and desist order), and

"(2) with actual knowledge that such act or practice is unfair or deceptive and is unlawful under subsection (a)(1) of this section.

In such action, such person, partnership, or corporation shall be liable for a civil penalty of not more than $10,000 for each violation.

"(C) In the case of a violation through continuing failure to comply with a rule or with section 5(a)(1), each day of continuance of such failure shall be treated as a separate violation, for purposes of subparagraphs (A) and (B). In determining the amount of such a civil penalty, the court shall take into account the degree of culpability, any history of prior such conduct, ability to pay, effect on ability to continue to do business, and such other matters as justice may require.

"(2) If the cease and desist order establishing that the act or practice is unfair or deceptive was not issued against the defendant in a civil penalty action under paragraph (1)(B) the issues of fact in such action against such defendant shall be tried de novo.

"(3) The Commission may compromise or settle any action for a civil penalty if such compromise or settlement is accompanied by a public statement of its reasons and is approved by the court."

15 USC 45 note.

(b) The amendment made by subsection (a) of this section shall not apply to any violation, act, or practice to the extent that such violation, act, or practice occurred before the date of enactment of this Act.

CONSUMER REDRESS

Sec. 206. (a) The Federal Trade Commission Act (15 U.S.C. 45(a)) is amended by inserting after section 18 the following new section:

15 USC 57b.

"Sec. 19. (a)(1) If any person, partnership, or corporation violates any rule under this Act respecting unfair or deceptive acts or practices (other than an interpretive rule, or a rule violation of which the Commission has provided is not an unfair or deceptive act or practice in violation of section 5(a)), then the Commission may commence a civil action against such person, partnership, or corporation for relief under subsection (b) in a United States district court or in any court of competent jurisdiction of a State.

"(2) If any person, partnership, or corporation engages in any unfair or deceptive act or practice (within the meaning of section 5(a)(1)) with respect to which the Commission has issued a final cease and desist order which is applicable to such person, partnership, or corporation, then the Commission may commence a civil action against such person, partnership, or corporation in a United States district court or in any court of competent jurisdiction of a State. If the Commission satisfies the court that the act or practice to which the cease and desist order relates is one which a reasonable man would have known under the circumstances was dishonest or fraudulent, the court may grant relief under subsection (b).

"(b) The court in an action under subsection (a) shall have jurisdiction to grant such relief as the court finds necessary to redress injury to consumers or other persons, partnerships, and corporations resulting from the rule violation or the unfair or deceptive act or practice, as the case may be. Such relief may include, but shall not be limited to, rescission or reformation of contracts, the refund of money or return of property, the payment of damages, and public notification respecting the rule violation or the unfair or deceptive act or practice, as the case may be; except that nothing in this subsection is intended to authorize the imposition of any exemplary or punitive damages.

"(c)(1) If (A) a cease and desist order issued under section 5(b) has become final under section 5(g) with respect to any person's, partnership's, or corporation's rule violation or unfair or deceptive act or practice, and (B) an action under this section is brought with respect to such person's partnership's, or corporation's rule violation or act or practice, then the findings of the Commission as to the material facts in the proceeding under section 5(b) with respect to such person's, partnership's, or corporation's rule violation or act or practice, shall be conclusive unless (i) the terms of such cease and desist order expressly provide that the Commission's findings shall not be conclusive, or (ii) the order became final by reason of section 5(g)(1), in which case such finding shall be conclusive if supported by evidence.

"(2) The court shall cause notice of an action under this section to be given in a manner which is reasonably calculated, under all of the circumstances, to apprise the persons, partnerships, and corporations allegedly injured by the defendant's rule violation or act or practice of the pendency of such action. Such notice may, in the discretion of the court, be given by publication. Notice.

"(d) No action may be brought by the Commission under this section more than 3 years after the rule violation to which an action under subsection (a)(1) relates, or the unfair or deceptive act or practice to which an action under subsection (a)(2) relates; except that if a cease and desist order with respect to any person's, partnership's, or corporation's rule violation or unfair or deceptive act or practice has become final and such order was issued in a proceeding under section 5(b) which was commenced not later than 3 years after the rule violation or act or practice occurred, a civil action may be commenced under this section against such person, partnership, or corporation at any time before the expiration of one year after such order becomes final. Statute of limitations.

"(e) Remedies provided in this section are in addition to, and not in lieu of, any other remedy or right of action provided by State or Federal law. Nothing in this section shall be construed to affect any authority of the Commission under any other provision of law."

(b) The amendment made by subsection (a) of this section shall not apply to— 15 USC 57b note.

(1) any violation of a rule to the extent that such violation occurred before the date of enactment of this Act, or

(2) any act or practice with respect to which the Commission issues a cease-and-desist order, to the extent that such act or practice occurred before the date of enactment of this Act, unless such order was issued after such date and the person, partnership or corporation against whom such an order was issued had been notified in the complaint, or in the notice or order attached thereto, that consumer redress may be sought.

AUTHORIZATION OF APPROPRIATIONS

Ante, p. 2201.
15 USC 57c.

SEC. 207. The Federal Trade Commission Act (15 U.S.C. 41 et seq.) is amended by inserting after section 19 the following new section:

"SEC. 20. There are authorized to be appropriated to carry out the functions, powers, and duties of the Federal Trade Commission not to exceed $42,000,000 for the fiscal year ending June 30, 1975; not to exceed $46,000,000 for the fiscal year ending June 30, 1976; and not to exceed $50,000,000 for the fiscal year ending in 1977. For fiscal years ending after 1977, there may be appropriated to carry out such functions, powers, and duties, only such sums as the Congress may hereafter authorize by law."

Approved January 4, 1975.

LEGISLATIVE HISTORY:

HOUSE REPORTS: No. 93-1107 accompanying H.R. 7917 (Comm. on Interstate and Foreign Commerce) and No. 93-1606 (Comm. of Conference).
SENATE REPORTS: No. 93-151 (Comm. on Commerce) and No. 93-280 (Comm. on Banking, Housing and Urban Affairs) and No. 93-1408 (Comm. of Conference).
CONGRESSIONAL RECORD:
     Vol. 119 (1973): Sept. 12, considered and passed Senate.
     Vol. 120 (1974): Sept. 19, considered and passed House, amended, in lieu of H.R. 7917.
                      Dec. 18, Senate agreed to conference report.
                      Dec. 19, House agreed to conference report.

○

Appendix Four
Florida Service Warranty Kit

PART III. SERVICE WARRANTY ASSOCIATIONS

Repeal of Chapter 634, Part III

Laws 1983, c. 83–322, § 38, provides in effect for the repeal of §§ 634.401 to 634.444 (Chapter 634, Part III) on October 1, 1993, and review thereof pursuant to § 11.61, the Regulatory Sunset Law. For earlier provisions pertaining to regulatory review of these provisions, see the Historical Note under §§ 634.011, 634.301, and 634.401; and, for the provisions regulating the review and a listing of all statutes affected by the Regulatory Sunset Law and amendments thereto, see § 11.61.

634.401. Definitions

As used in this part, the term:

(1) "Consumer product" means tangible personal property primarily used for personal, family, or household purposes.

(2) "Department" means the Department of Insurance.

(3) "Gross income" means the total amount of revenue received in connection with business-related activity.

(4) "Gross written premiums" means the total amount of premiums, inclusive of commissions, for which the association is obligated under service warranties issued in this state.

(5) "Impaired" means having liabilities in excess of assets.

(6) "Indemnify" means to undertake repair or replacement of a consumer product, in return for the payment of a segregated premium, when such consumer product suffers operational failure.

(7) "Insolvent" means unable to pay debts as they become due in the usual course of business.

(8) "Insurance code" means the Florida Insurance Code as defined in s. 624.01.

(9) "Insurer" means any property or casualty insurer duly authorized to transact such business in this state.

(10) "Net assets" means the amount by which the total assets of an association, excluding goodwill, franchises, customer lists, patents or trademarks, and receivables from or advances to officers, directors,

employees, salesmen, and affiliated companies, exceed the total liabilities of the association. For purposes of this definition, the term "total liabilities" does not include the capital stock, paid-in capital, or retained earnings of an association.

(11) "Person" includes an individual, company, corporation, association, insurer, agent, and any other legal entity.

(12) "Premium" means the total consideration received or to be received by whatever name called, by an insurer or service warranty association for, or related to, the issuance and delivery of a service warranty, including any charges designated as assessments or fees for membership, policy, survey, inspection, or service or other charges. However, a repair charge is not a premium unless it exceeds the usual and customary repair fee charged by the association, provided the repair is made before the issuance and delivery of the warranty.

(13) "Sales representative" means any person utilized by an insurer or service warranty association for the purpose of selling or issuing service warranties and includes any individual possessing a certificate of competency who has the power to legally obligate the insurer or service warranty association or who merely acts as the qualifying agent to qualify the association in instances when a state statute or local ordinance requires a certificate of competency to engage in a particular business. However, in the case of service warranty associations selling service warranties from five or more business locations, the store manager or other person in charge of each such location shall be considered the sales representative.

(14) "Service warranty" means any warranty, guaranty, extended warranty or extended guaranty, contract agreement, or other written promise under the terms of which there is an undertaking to indemnify against the cost of repair or replacement of a consumer product in return for the payment of a segregated charge by the consumer; however, maintenance service contracts under the terms of which there are no provisions for such indemnification, motor vehicle service agreements, and home warranties subject to regulation under parts I and II of this chapter are expressly excluded from this definition. However, the term "service warranty" does not include service contracts entered into between consumers and nonprofit organizations or cooperatives the members of which consist of condominium associations and condominium owners, which contracts require the performance of repairs and maintenance of appliances or maintenance of the residential property.

(15) "Service warranty association" or "association" means any person, other than an authorized insurer, issuing service warranties.

(16) "Warrantor" means any person engaged in the sale of service warranties and deriving not more than 50 percent of its gross income from the sale of service warranties.

(17) "Warranty seller" means any person engaged in the sale of service warranties and deriving more than 50 percent of its gross income from the sale of service warranties.

Repeal

For repeal of this section, see the italicized note preceding § 634.401.

Historical Note

Derivation:

Laws 1983, c. 83–322, § 1.
Laws 1982, c. 82–234, § 34.
Laws 1980, c. 80–78, § 1.
Laws 1978, c. 78–255, § 5.

Prior Provisions for Legislative Review of Regulatory Statutes:

Laws 1981, c. 81–148, § 3, provided that "Parts II and III of Chapter 634, Florida Statutes, are repealed on July 1, 1983, and shall be reviewed by the Legislature pursuant to the Regulatory Reform Act of 1976, as amended"; and, Laws 1981, c. 81–318, the Regulatory Sunset Law, providing for legislative review of laws regulating professions, occupations, business, industry and other endeavors in Florida, provided for the repeal and the regulatory review of this chapter part on October 1, 1983. Laws 1983, c. 83–322, §§ 36, 37, provided that notwithstanding the Regulatory Sunset Act or provisions to the contrary that the provisions contained in part III, with the exception of §§ 634.410 and 634.418 are revived and readopted. Section 38 of the 1983 law enacted provisions discussed in the italicized note at the head of this chapter part.

Laws 1980, c. 80–78, § 1, added the second sentence to the definition of "service warranty".

Laws 1982, c. 82–234, § 34, in the definition of "Indemnity", substituted "payment" for "prepayment".

Laws 1983, c. 83–322, § 1, substituted "motor vehicle service agreements" for "automobile warranties" in the definition of "service warranty", redefined "premium" and "net assets", and added definition of "Insurance code". The definitions were alphabetized in Fla.St.1983.

Library References

Words and Phrases (Perm. Ed.)

Notes of Decisions

1. Construction and application

Record in proceeding before insurance commissioner to determine whether service warranty association had to post bond as warrantor of appliances sold in connection with realty, or as warranty seller of appliances sold for personal use, supported finding that the association was warranty seller, notwithstanding argument of association that such appliances became fixtures upon attachment in homes. Dependable Air Conditioning and Appliances, Inc. v. Office of Treasurer and Ins. Com'r, App., 400 So.2d 117 (1981).

Insurance commissioner's adoption of hearing officer's recommended order that appliances sold to consumers for personal use did not become fixtures for purposes of determining amount of bond that service warranty association was obligated to post was not invalid adoption of rule where hearing officer was adjudicating individual case that was refining incipient policy for the department of insurance. Id.

634.402. Powers of department; rules

The department shall administer this part, and to that end it may adopt and enforce rules necessary and proper to effectuate any provision of this part.

Repeal

For repeal of this section, see the italicized note preceding § 634.401.

Historical Note

Derivation:
  Laws 1978, c. 78–255, § 5.

634.403. License required

(1) No person in this state shall provide or offer to provide service warranties unless authorized therefor under a subsisting license issued by the department. The service warranty association shall pay to the department a license fee of $200 for such license for each license year, or part thereof, the license is in force.

(2) An insurer, while authorized to transact property or casualty insurance in this state, may also transact a service warranty business without additional qualifications or authority, but shall be otherwise subject to the applicable provisions of this part.

Repeal

For repeal of this section, see the italicized note preceding § 634.401.

Historical Note

Derivation:
  Laws 1978, c. 78–255, § 5.

Library References

Insurance ⬤7.
C.J.S. Insurance § 71.

634.404. Qualifications for license

The department may not issue or renew a license to any service warranty association unless the association:

(1) Is a solvent association.

(2) Furnishes the department with evidence satisfactory to it that the management of the association is competent and trustworthy and can successfully manage the affairs of the association in compliance with law.

(3) Proposes to use and uses in its business a name, together with a trademark or emblem, if any, which is distinctive and not so similar to the name or trademark of any other person already doing business in this state as will tend to mislead or confuse the public.

(4) Makes the deposit or files the bond required under s. 634.405.

(5) Is formed under the laws of this state or another state, district, territory, or possession of the United States, if the association is other than a natural person.

Repeal

For repeal of this section, see the italicized note preceding § 634.401.

Historical Note

Derivation:
Laws 1983, c. 83–322, § 2.
Laws 1978, c. 78–255, § 5.

Laws 1983, c. 83–322, § 2, inserted "or renew" in the introduction and deleted "or letter of credit" in subsec. (4).

Library References

Insurance ⊕7.
C.J.S. Insurance § 71.

634.405. Required deposit or bond

(1) To assure the faithful performance of its obligations to its members or subscribers in the event of insolvency, each service warranty association shall, before the issuance of its license by the department and during such time as the association may have premiums in force in this state, deposit and maintain securities of the type eligible for deposit by insurers under s. 625.52. Whenever the market value of the securities deposited with the department is less than 95 percent of the amount required, the association shall deposit additional securities or otherwise increase the deposit to the amount required. Such securities shall have at all times a market value as follows:

(a) *Warrantors.—*

1. Any warrantor which:

a. Was licensed under this part before October 1, 1983;

b. Was transacting service warranty business in this state before June 14, 1978;

c. Has continuously transacted service warranty business in this state since June 14, 1978; and

d. Has not during any year since June 14, 1978, written more than $100,000 of gross written premiums,

shall place and maintain in trust with the department an amount equal to 50 percent of the gross written premiums in force.

2. A warrantor which has $300,000 or less of gross written premiums in this state and to which the provisions of subparagraph 1. do not apply shall place and maintain in trust with the department an amount not less than $50,000. A new warrantor, before the issuance of its license and

before receiving any premiums, shall place and maintain in trust with the department the amount of $50,000.

3. A warrantor which has more than $300,000 but less than $750,000 of gross written premiums in this state shall place and maintain in trust with the department an amount not less than $75,000.

4. A warrantor which has $750,000 or more of gross written premiums in this state shall place and maintain in trust with the department an amount equal to $100,000.

5. All warrantors, upon receipt of written notice from the department, shall have 30 calendar days in which to make additional deposits.

(b) *Warranty sellers.*—A warranty seller shall, before the issuance of its license, place in trust with the department an amount not less than $100,000.

(2) In lieu of any deposit of securities required under subsection (1) and subject to the approval of the department, the service warranty association may file with the department a surety bond issued by an authorized surety insurer. The bond shall be for the same purpose as the deposit in lieu of which it is filed. The department may not approve any bond under the terms of which the protection afforded against insolvency is not equivalent to the protection afforded by those securities provided for in subsection (1). When a bond is deposited in lieu of the required securities, no warranties may be written which provide coverage for a time period beyond the duration of such bond. The bond shall guarantee that the service warranty association will faithfully and truly perform all the conditions of any service warranty contract. No such bond may be canceled or subject to cancellation unless at least 60 days' advance notice thereof, in writing, is filed with the department. In the event that notice of termination of the bond is filed with the department, the service warranty association insured thereunder shall, within 30 days of the filing of notice of termination, provide the department with a replacement bond meeting the requirements of this part or deposit additional securities as required under subsection (1). The cancellation of a bond will not relieve the obligation of the issuer of the bond for claims arising out of contracts issued before cancellation of the bond unless a replacement bond or securities are filed. In no event may the liability of the issuer under the bond exceed the face amount of the bond. If within 30 days of filing the notice of termination no replacement bond or additional security is provided, the department shall suspend the license of the association until the deposit requirements are satisfied.

(3) In lieu of any deposit of securities required under subsection (1) or the bond required under subsection (2) and subject to the approval of the department, a warrantor which has less than $50,000 in gross written premiums as reflected in its most recent financial statement may maintain an escrow trust account with a bank or other recognized depository

in this state into which shall be deposited unearned service warranty premiums. Seventy-five percent of the first-year premiums and 100 percent of the subsequent-year premiums paid for multiyear contracts shall be deposited. No more than one-twelfth of the total amount of first-year premiums on deposit may be withdrawn in any one calendar month. No more than one-twelfth of the total annual unearned premium for the current contract year may be withdrawn in any one calendar month.

(4) Securities and bonds posted by an association pursuant to this section are for the benefit of, and subject to action thereon in the event of insolvency or impairment of any association or insurer by, any person or persons sustaining an actionable injury due to the failure of the association to faithfully perform its obligations to its warranty holders.

(5) The state is responsible for the safekeeping of all securities deposited with the department under this part. Such securities are not, on account of being in this state, subject to taxation, but shall be held exclusively and solely to guarantee the faithful performance by the association of its obligations to its members or subscribers.

(6) The depositing association shall, during its solvency, have the right to exchange or substitute other securities of like quality and value for securities on deposit, to receive the interest and other income accruing to such securities, and to inspect the deposit at all reasonable times.

(7) Such deposit or bond shall be maintained unimpaired as long as the association continues in business in this state. Whenever the association ceases to do business in this state and furnishes the department proof satisfactory to the department that it has discharged or otherwise adequately provided for all its obligations to its members or subscribers in this state, the department shall release the deposited securities to the parties entitled thereto, on presentation of the receipts of the department for such securities, or shall release any bond filed with it in lieu of such deposit.

(8) A service warranty association utilizing a letter of credit on October 1, 1982, entirely or in part for the deposit required by this section may continue to utilize the letter of credit entirely or in part for the deposit only until the letter of credit expires or until July 1, 1984, whichever occurs first.

Repeal

For repeal of this section, see the italicized note preceding § 634.401.

Historical Note

Derivation:
Laws 1983, c. 83–322, § 3.

Laws 1978, c. 78–255, § 5.

Prior to the 1983 amendment, this section provided:

"(1) To assure the faithful performance of its obligations to its members or subscribers in the event of insolvency, each service warranty association shall, prior to the issuance of its license by the department and during such time as the association may have premiums in force in this state, deposit and maintain securities of the type eligible for deposit by insurers under s. 625.52, which securities shall have at all times a market value as follows:

"(a) *Warrantors.—*

"1. Any warrantor which has transacted no service warranty business in this state prior to June 14, 1978, shall, prior to the issuance of its license and before receiving any premiums, place in trust with the department an initial amount of $50,000.

"2. A warrantor which has less than $300,000 of gross written premiums shall place in trust with the department an amount equal to 50 percent of the gross premiums in force or $50,000, whichever is less.

"3. A warrantor which has more than $300,000 but less than $750,000 of gross written premiums in this state shall place in trust with the department an amount not less than $75,000.

"4. A warrantor which has $750,000 or more of gross written premiums in this state shall place in trust with the department an amount equal to $100,000.

"5. All warrantors, upon receipt of written notice from the department, shall have 30 calendar days in which to make additional deposits.

"(b) *Warranty sellers.—*

"1. A warranty seller licensed after June 14, 1978, shall, prior to the issuance of its license, place in trust with the department an amount not less than $100,000.

"2. Any warranty seller licensed under part II of this chapter prior to June 14, 1978, shall be required to deposit an amount equal to $75,000 by October 1, 1978, and $100,000 by October 1, 1979.

"(2) In lieu of any deposit of securities required under subsection (1) and subject to the department's approval, the service warranty association may file with the department a surety bond issued by an authorized surety insurer or an irrevocable letter of credit from a state or federally chartered bank located in this state. The letter of credit or bond shall be for the same purpose as the deposit in lieu of which it is filed. The department shall not approve any bond or letter of credit under the terms of which the protection afforded against insolvency is not equivalent to the protection afforded by those securities provided for in subsection (1). When a letter of credit or bond is deposited in lieu of the required securities, no warranties may be written which provide coverage for a time period beyond the duration of such letter of credit or bond.

"(3) Securities, bonds, and letters of credit posted by an association pursuant to this section shall be for the benefit of and subject to action thereon, in the event of insolvency or impairment of any association or insurer, by any person or persons sustaining an actionable injury due to the failure of the association to faithfully perform its obligations to its warranty holders.

"(4) The state shall be responsible for the safekeeping of all securities deposited with the department under this part. Such securities shall not, on account of being in this state, be subject to taxation, but shall be held exclusively and solely to guarantee the association's faithful performance of its obligations to its members or subscribers.

"(5) The depositing association shall, during its solvency, have the right to exchange or substitute other securities of like quality and value for securities on deposit, to receive the interest and other income accruing to such securities, and to inspect the deposit at all reasonable times.

"(6) Such deposit, bond, or letter of credit shall be maintained unimpaired as long as the association continues in business in this state. Whenever the association ceases to do business in this state and furnishes the department proof satisfactory to the department that it has discharged or otherwise adequately provided for all its obligations to its members or subscribers in this state, the department shall release the deposited securities to the parties entitled thereto, on presentation of the department's receipts for such securities, or shall release any bond or letter of credit filed with it in lieu of such deposit."

Laws 1983, c. 83–322, § 3, substantially rewrote this section.

Library References

Insurance ⊚7.
C.J.S. Insurance § 71.

Notes of Decisions

1. In general

Insurance commissioner's adoption of hearing officer's recommended order that appliances sold to consumers for personal use did not become fixtures for purposes of determining amount of bond that service warranty association was obligated to post was not invalid adoption of rule where hearing officer was adjudicating individual case that was refining incipient policy for the department of insurance. Dependable Air Conditioning and Appliances, Inc. v. Office of Treasurer and Ins. Com'r, App., 400 So.2d 117 (1981).

Record in proceeding before insurance commissioner to determine whether service warranty association had to post bond as warrantor of appliances sold in connection with realty, or as warranty seller of appliances sold for personal use, supported finding that the association was warranty seller, notwithstanding argument of association that such appliances became fixtures upon attachment in homes. Id.

Determination of whether major household appliances were fixtures or personal property for purposes of determining service warranty association's requirement to post bond and furnish evidence of solvency under this section was not dependent upon intention of parties to sale or the ease with which appliances might be removed from realty, but instead was dependent upon purpose of this part. Id.

634.406. Financial requirements

(1) An association licensed under this part shall maintain a funded, unearned premium reserve account, consisting of unencumbered assets, equal to a minimum of 25 percent of the gross written premiums received on all warranty contracts in force, wherever written. Such assets shall be held as prescribed under ss. 625.301–625.340. In the case of multiyear contracts which are offered by associations having net assets of less than $500,000 and for which premiums are collected in advance for coverage in a subsequent year, 100 percent of the premiums for such subsequent years shall be placed in the funded, unearned premium reserve account.

(2) An association will not be required to establish an unearned premium reserve if it has purchased contractual liability insurance which demonstrates to the satisfaction of the department that 100 percent of its claim exposure is covered by such policy. The contractual liability insurance shall be obtained from an insurer that holds a certificate of authority to do business within the state or from an insurer approved by the department as financially capable of meeting the obligations incurred pursuant to the policy. For the purposes of this subsection, the contractual liability policy shall contain the following provisions:

(a) In the event that the service warranty association is unable to fulfill its obligation under contracts issued in this state for any reason, including insolvency, bankruptcy, or dissolution, the contract liability insurer will pay losses and unearned premiums under such plans directly to the person making a claim under the contract.

(b) The insurer issuing the contractual liability policy shall assume full responsibility for the administration of claims in the event of the inability of the association to do so.

(c) The policy may not be canceled or not renewed by either the insurer or the association unless 60 days' written notice thereof has been given to the department by the insurer before the date of such cancellation or nonrenewal.

(3) No warrantor may allow its gross written premiums to exceed a 7 to 1 ratio to net assets.

(4) No warranty seller may allow its gross written premiums to exceed a 5 to 1 ratio to net assets.

Repeal

For repeal of this section, see the italicized note preceding § 634.401.

Historical Note

Derivation:

Laws 1983, c. 83–322, § 4.

Laws 1978, c. 78–255, § 5.

Laws 1983, c. 83–322, § 4, rewrote the first and added the second sentence of subsec. (1), interpolated a new subsec. (2), and redesignated former subsecs. (2) and (3) as subsecs. (3) and (4).

Prior to the 1983 amendment, the first sentence of subsec. (1) provided:

"An association licensed under this part shall maintain a funded, unearned premium reserve account equal to a minimum of 25 percent of the gross written premiums."

634.407. Application for and issuance of license

(1) An application for license as a service warranty association shall be made to, and filed with, the department on printed forms as prescribed and furnished by it.

(2) In addition to information relative to its qualifications as required under s. 634.404, the department may require that the application show:

(a) The location of the applicant's home office.

(b) The name and residence address of each director or officer of the applicant.

(c) Such other pertinent information as may be required by the department.

(3) The department may require that the application, when filed, be accompanied by:

(a) A copy of the applicant's articles of incorporation, certified by the public official having custody of the original, and a copy of the applicant's bylaws, certified by the applicant's secretary.

(b) A copy of the most recent financial statement of the applicant, verified under oath of at least two of its principal officers.

(c) A license fee in the amount of $200, as required under s. 634.403.

(4) Upon completion of the application for license, the department shall examine the application and make such further investigation of the applicant as it deems advisable. If it finds that the applicant is qualified therefor, the department shall issue to the applicant a license as a service warranty association. If the department does not find the applicant to be qualified, it shall refuse to issue the license and shall give the applicant written notice of such refusal, setting forth the grounds therefor.

Repeal

For repeal of this section, see the italicized note preceding § 634.401.

Historical Note

Derivation:

Laws 1983, c. 83–322, § 5.
Laws 1978, c. 78–255, § 5.

Laws 1983, c. 83–322, § 5, deleted the fourth sentence of subsec. (4) requiring that

notice of refusal be accompanied by refund of the license fee.

Library References

Insurance ☞7.
C.J.S. Insurance § 71.

634.408. License expiration; renewal

Each license issued to a service warranty association under this part shall expire on June 1 next following the date of issuance. If the association is then qualified therefor under the provisions of this part, its license may be renewed annually, upon its request, and upon payment to the department of the license fee in the amount of $200 in advance for each such license year.

Repeal

For repeal of this section, see the italicized note preceding § 634.401.

Historical Note

Derivation:

Laws 1983, c. 83–322, § 6.
Laws 1978, c. 78–255, § 5.

Laws 1983, c. 83–322, § 6, substituted "June 1" for "September 30" near the beginning of the section.

Library References

Insurance ☞7.
C.J.S. Insurance § 71.

634.4085.   Acquisition of association

No person may merge or consolidate with, or obtain control of, a service warranty association unless prior documentation is filed with the department demonstrating that the requirements for issuance of a license under this part will be satisfied.

Repeal

For repeal of this section, see the italicized note preceding § 634.401.

Historical Note

Derivation:

Laws 1983, c. 83–322, § 24.

Library References

Insurance ☞72.3.

C.J.S. Insurance § 115 et seq.

634.409.   Grounds for suspension or revocation of license

(1) The license of any service warranty association may be revoked or suspended, or the department may refuse to renew any such license, if it is determined that the association has violated any lawful rule or order of the department or any provision of this part.

(2) The license of any service warranty association shall be suspended or revoked if it is determined that such association:

(a) Is in an unsound financial condition, or is in such condition as would render its further transaction of service warranties in this state hazardous or injurious to its warranty holders or to the public.

(b) Has refused to be examined or to produce its accounts, records, and files for examination, or if any of its officers have refused to give information with respect to its affairs or have refused to perform any other legal obligation as to such examination, when required by the department.

(c) Has failed to pay any final judgment rendered against it in this state within 60 days after the judgment became final.

(d) Has, without just cause, refused to pay proper claims arising under its service warranties or, without just cause, has compelled warranty holders to accept less than the amount due them, or to employ attorneys, or to bring suit against the association to secure full payment or settlement of such claims.

(e) Is affiliated with, and under the same general management or interlocking directorate or ownership as, another service warranty association which transacts direct warranties in this state without having a license therefor.

(f) Is using such methods or practices in the conduct of its business as would render its further transaction of service warranties in this state hazardous or injurious to its warranty holders or to the public.

(3) The department may, pursuant to s. 120.60, in its discretion and without advance notice or hearing thereon, immediately suspend the license of any service warranty association if it finds that one or more of the following circumstances exist:

(a) The association is insolvent or impaired.

(b) The reserve account required by s. 634.406(1) is not being maintained.

(c) A proceeding for receivership, conservatorship, or rehabilitation or any other delinquency proceeding regarding the association has been commenced in any state.

(d) The financial condition or business practices of the association otherwise pose an imminent threat to the public health, safety, or welfare of the residents of this state.

(4) A violation of this part by an insurer is grounds for suspension or revocation of the insurer's certificate of authority in this state.

Repeal

For repeal of this section, see the italicized note preceding § 634.401.

Historical Note

Derivation:

Laws 1983, c. 83–322, § 7.

Laws 1978, c. 78–255, § 5.

Laws 1983, c. 83–322, § 7, inserted "rule or" preceding "order" in subsec. (1), inserted "financial" and deleted "or using such methods and practices in the conduct of its business," following "such condition" in subsec. (2)(a), deleted "with such frequency as to indicate its general business practice in this state, and" following "Has," in subsec. (2)(d) and added subsec. (2)(f).

634.410. Repealed by Laws 1981, c. 81–148, § 3, eff. Oct. 1, 1983; Laws 1981, c. 81–318, § 2, eff. Oct. 1, 1983 (See § 11.61); Laws 1983, c. 83–322, §§ 36, 37, eff. Oct. 1, 1983

Historical Note

The repealed section, which provided the procedure to suspend or revoke a license, was derived from Laws 1978, c. 78–255, § 5.

634.411. Order; notice of suspension or revocation of license; effect; publication

(1) Suspension or revocation of a service warranty association's license shall be by order of the department mailed to the association by registered or certified mail. The department shall also promptly give notice

of such suspension or revocation to the association's sales representatives in this state which are of record in the department's office. The association shall not solicit or write any new service warranties in this state during the period of any such suspension or revocation.

(2) In its discretion, the department may cause notice of any such revocation or suspension to be published in one or more newspapers of general circulation published in this state.

Repeal

For repeal of this section, see the italicized note preceding § 634.401.

Historical Note

Derivation:
Laws 1978, c. 78–255, § 5.

634.412. Duration of suspension; obligations of association during suspension; reinstatement

(1) A suspension of the license of a service warranty association shall be for such period, not to exceed 1 year, as is fixed in the order of suspension, unless such suspension or the order upon which the suspension is based is modified, rescinded, or reversed.

(2) During the period of suspension, the association shall file its annual statement and pay fees, licenses, and taxes as required under this part as if the license had continued in full force.

(3) Upon expiration of the suspension period, if within such period the license has not otherwise terminated, the license of the association shall automatically be reinstated, unless the causes of the suspension have not been removed or the association is otherwise not in compliance with the requirements of this part.

(4) Upon reinstatement of the license of an association, or upon reinstatement of the certificate of authority of an insurer, following suspension, the authority of the sales representatives of the association in this state to represent the association or insurer shall likewise be reinstated.

Repeal

For repeal of this section, see the italicized note preceding § 634.401.

Historical Note

Derivation:
Laws 1983, c. 83–322, § 8.
Laws 1978, c. 78–255, § 5.

Laws 1983, c. 83–322, § 8, deleted in subsec. (3) "it is determined, upon notice and hearing, that the" preceding "causes of the suspension", and deleted the second sen- tence of subsec. (4) pertaining to prompt notice of reinstatement to certain persons.

Library References

Insurance ☞7.
C.J.S. Insurance § 71.

634.413. Administrative fine in lieu of suspension or revocation

If the department finds that one or more grounds exist for the discretionary revocation or suspension of a certificate of authority issued under this part, the department may, in lieu of such suspension or revocation, impose a fine upon the insurer or service warranty associa- tion in an amount not to exceed $1,000 per violation; however, if it is found that an insurer or service warranty association has knowingly and willfully violated a lawful rule or order of the department or a provision of this part, the department may impose a fine upon the insurer or association in an amount not to exceed $10,000 for each violation.

Repeal

For repeal of this section, see the italicized note preceding § 634.401.

Historical Note

Derivation:
Laws 1983, c. 83–322, § 9.
Laws 1978, c. 78–255, § 5.

Laws 1983, c. 83–322, § 9, deleted ", upon notice and hearing as provided for in s.

634.410," following "If," at the beginning of the section.

Library References

Insurance ☞7, 27.
C.J.S. Insurance §§ 71, 86.

634.414. Filing; approval of forms

(1) No service warranty form or related form shall be issued or used in this state unless it has been filed with and approved by the department.

(2) Each filing shall be made not less than 30 days in advance of its issuance or use. At the expiration of 30 days from date of filing, a form so filed shall be deemed approved unless prior thereto it has been affirmatively disapproved by written order of the department.

(3) Each service warranty contract shall contain a cancellation provi- sion. In the event the contract is canceled by the warranty holder, return of premium shall be based upon 90 percent of unearned pro-rata premium less any claims that have been paid. In the event the contract is canceled by the association, return of premium shall be based upon 100 percent of unearned pro-rata premium.

Repeal

For repeal of this section, see the italicized note preceding § 634.401.

Historical Note

Derivation:

Laws 1978, c. 78–255, § 5.

Library References

Insurance ⊕133(1).
C.J.S. Insurance § 227 et seq.

634.4145. Grounds for disapproval of forms

The department shall disapprove any form filed under s. 634.312 if the form:

(1) Violates this part;

(2) Is misleading in any respect; or

(3) Is reproduced so that any material provision is substantially illegible.

Repeal

For repeal of this section, see the italicized note preceding § 634.401.

Historical Note

Derivation:

Laws 1983, c. 83–322, § 10.

Library References

Insurance ⊕124 et seq.
C.J.S. Insurance § 223 et seq.

634.415. Tax on premiums; annual statement; reports; quarterly statements

(1) In addition to the license fees provided in this part for service warranty associations and license taxes as provided in the insurance code as to insurers, each such association and insurer shall, annually on or before March 1, file with the department its annual statement, in the form prescribed by the department, showing all premiums or assessments received by it in connection with the issuance of service warranties in this state during the preceding calendar year and using accounting principles which will enable the department to ascertain whether the financial requirements set forth in s. 634.406 have been satisfied. If, after notice and hearing as provided for in chapter 120, the department demonstrates that the income derived from the license fees provided for

herein is insufficient to pay the costs of administering this part, the department may impose a premium tax of not more than 0.5 percent of the gross written premiums of all service warranty associations licensed to do business in this state.

(2) Premiums and assessments received by insurers are subject to any premium tax provided for in the insurance code.

(3) The department may levy a fine of up to $100 a day for each day an association neglects to file the annual statement in the form and within the time provided by this part. The department shall deposit all sums collected by it under this section to the credit of the Insurance Commissioner's Regulatory Trust Fund.

(4) In addition to an annual statement, the department may require of licensees, under oath and in the form prescribed by it, quarterly statements or special reports which it deems necessary to the proper supervision of licensees under this part.

Repeal

For repeal of this section, see the italicized note preceding § 634.401.

Historical Note

Derivation:

Laws 1983, c. 83–322, § 11.

Laws 1978, c. 78–255, § 5.

Laws 1983, c. 83–322, § 11, rewrote the first sentence of subsec. (3) which read:

"Any association or insurer neglecting to file the annual statement in the form and within the time provided by this section shall forfeit $100 for each day during which such neglect continues, and, upon notice by the department to that effect, its authority to do business in this state shall cease while such default continues."

634.416. Examination of associations

(1) Service warranty associations licensed under this part are subject to periodic examination by the department, in the same manner and subject to the same terms and conditions that apply to insurers under part II of chapter 624. However, the rate charged a service warranty association by the department for examination may be adjusted to reflect the amount collected for the Form 10-K filing fee as provided in this section. On or before May 1 of each year, an association may submit to the department the Form 10-K, as filed with the United States Securities and Exchange Commission pursuant to the Securities Exchange Act of 1934, as amended. Upon receipt and review of the most current Form 10-K, the department may waive the examination requirement; if the department determines not to waive the examination, such examination will be limited to that examination necessary to ensure compliance with this part. The Form 10-K shall be accompanied by a filing fee of $2,000 to be deposited into the Insurance Commissioner's Regulatory Trust Fund.

(2) The department is not required to examine an association that has less than $20,000 in gross written premiums as reflected in its most recent annual statement. The department may examine such an association if it has reason to believe that the association may be in violation of this part or is otherwise in an unsound financial condition. If the department examines an association that has less than $20,000 in gross written premiums, the examination fee may not exceed 5 percent of the gross written premiums of the association.

Repeal

For repeal of this section, see the italicized note preceding § 634.401.

Historical Note

Derivation:
Laws 1983, c. 83–322, § 12.
Laws 1978, c. 78–255, § 5.

Laws 1983, c. 83–322, § 12, added the second and subsequent sentences in subsec. (1) and added subsec. (2).

Library References

Insurance ☜4.2.
C.J.S. Insurance § 57.

634.4165.   Office records required

As a minimum requirement for permanent office records, each licensed service warranty association shall maintain:

(1) A complete set of accounting records, including, but not limited to, a general ledger, cash receipts and disbursements journals, accounts receivable registers, and accounts payable registers.

(2) A detailed warranty register of warranties in force, by unique identifier. The register shall include the unique identifier, date of issue, issuing sales representative, name of warranty holder, location of the property, warranty period, gross premium, commission to sales representative, and net premium.

(3) A detailed centralized claims or service records register which includes the unique identifier, date of issue, date of claim, issuing service representative, amount of claim or service, date claim paid, and, if applicable, disposition other than payment and reason therefor.

Repeal

For repeal of this section, see the italicized note preceding § 634.401.

Historical Note

Derivation:
Laws 1983, c. 83–322, § 13.

634.417. Service of process

Service warranty associations are subject to service of process in the same manner and subject to the same terms, conditions, and fees as apply to insurers under chapter 624.

Repeal

For repeal of this section, see the italicized note preceding § 634.401.

Historical Note

Derivation:

Laws 1983, c. 83–322, § 14.
Laws 1978, c. 78–255, § 5.

Prior to the 1983 amendment, this section provided:

"(1) Each service warranty association applying for authority to transact business in this state, whether domestic or foreign, shall file with the department, on a form furnished by the department, its appointment of the Insurance Commissioner and Treasurer, and his successors in office, as its attorney to receive service of all legal process issued against it in any civil action or proceeding in this state, and shall agree that process so served shall be valid and binding upon the association. The appointment shall be irrevocable, shall bind the association and any successor in interest as to the assets or liabilities of the association, and shall remain in effect as long as there are outstanding in this state any obligations or liabilities of the association resulting from its warranty transactions therein.

"(2) At the time of appointment of the Insurance Commissioner and Treasurer as its process agent, the association shall file with the department a designation of the name and address of the person to whom process against it, served upon the Insurance Commissioner and Treasurer, is to be forwarded. The association may change the designation at any time by a new filing."

Laws 1983, c. 83–322, § 14, rewrote this section.

Cross References

Insurance commissioner and treasurer, appointment as agent to receive service of process, see § 624.422.
Service of process generally, see § 48.031.

634.418. Repealed by Laws 1981, c. 81–148, § 3, eff. Oct. 1, 1983; Laws 1981, c. 81–318, § 2, eff. Oct. 1, 1983 (See § 11.61); Laws 1983, c. 83–322, §§ 36, 37, eff. Oct. 1, 1983

Historical Note

The repealed section, which pertained to serving process, was derived from Laws 1978, c. 78–255, § 5.

634.419. Registration required

No person shall solicit, negotiate, advertise, or effectuate service warranty contracts in this state unless such person is registered as a sales representative or acts under the supervision of a sales representative. Sales representatives shall be responsible for the actions of persons under their supervision.

Repeal

For repeal of this section, see the italicized note preceding § 634.401.

Historical Note

Derivation:

Laws 1978, c. 78–255, § 5.

Library References

Insurance ⚓7.
C.J.S. Insurance § 71.

634.420. Registration of sales representatives

Each service warranty association or insurer shall, on forms prescribed by the department, register, on or before October 1 of each even-numbered year, the name and business address of each sales representative utilized by it in this state and shall, within 30 days after termination of the contract, notify the department of such termination. At the time of biennial registration, a $40 filing fee for each sales representative shall be paid by the service warranty association or insurer to the department. Any sales representative utilized subsequent to the October 1 filing date shall be registered with the department within 10 days after such utilization. No employee or sales representative of a service warranty association or insurer may directly or indirectly solicit or negotiate insurance contracts, or hold himself out in any manner to be an insurance agent or solicitor, unless so qualified and licensed therefor under the insurance code.

Repeal

For repeal of this section, see the italicized note preceding § 634.401.

Historical Note

Derivation:

Laws 1983, c. 83–322, § 15.
Laws 1978, c. 78–255, § 5.

Laws 1983, c. 83–322, § 15, provided biennial registration on even-numbered years in lieu of annual registration and doubled the registration fee.

634.421. Reporting and accounting for funds

(1) All funds belonging to insurers, service warranty associations, or others received by a sales representative in transactions under his registration are trust funds so received by such agent in a fiduciary capacity; and the agent, in the applicable regular course of business, shall account for and pay such funds to the insurer, association, warranty holder, or other person entitled thereto.

(2) Any sales representative who, not being entitled thereto, diverts or appropriates such funds or any portion thereof to his own use is guilty of theft as provided in s. 812.014.

Repeal

For repeal of this section, see the italicized note preceding § 634.401.

Historical Note

Derivation:
Laws 1983, c. 83–322, § 16.
Laws 1978, c. 78–255, § 5.
Laws 1983, c. 83–322, § 16, substituted reference to theft as provided for in

§ 812.014 for larceny as provided for in § 812.021 in subsec. (2).

634.422. Grounds for compulsory refusal, suspension, or revocation of registration of sales representatives

The department shall deny, suspend, revoke, or refuse to renew or continue the registration of any sales representative if it is found that any one or more of the following grounds applicable to the sales representative exist:

(1) Material misstatement, misrepresentation, or fraud in registration.

(2) The registration is willfully used, or to be used, to circumvent any of the requirements or prohibitions of this part.

(3) Willful misrepresentation of any service warranty contract or willful deception with regard to any such contract, done either in person or by any form of dissemination of information or advertising.

(4) In the adjustment of claims arising out of warranties, material misrepresentation to a service warranty holder or other interested party of the terms and coverage of a contract with the intent and for the purpose of effecting settlement of such claim on less favorable terms than those provided in and contemplated by the contract.

(5) Demonstrated lack of fitness or trustworthiness to engage in the business of service warranty.

(6) Demonstrated lack of adequate knowledge and technical competence to engage in the transactions authorized by the registration.

(7) Fraudulent or dishonest practices in the conduct of business under the registration.

(8) Misappropriation, conversion, or unlawful withholding of moneys belonging to an association, insurer, or warranty holder, or to others, and received in the conduct of business under the registration.

(9) Rebating, or attempting to rebate, or unlawfully dividing, or offering to divide, his commission with another.

(10) Willful failure to comply with, or willful violation of, any proper order or rule of the department, or willful violation of any provision of this part.

(11) Being found guilty of or pleading nolo contendere to a felony involving moral turpitude, in this state or any other state, without regard to whether judgment of conviction has been entered by the court having jurisdiction of such case.

Repeal

For repeal of this section, see the italicized note preceding § 634.401.

Historical Note

Derivation:
Laws 1983, c. 83–322, § 17.
Laws 1978, c. 78–255, § 5.

Laws 1983, c. 83–322, § 17, added subsec. (11).

Library References

Insurance ⟐7, 12.
C.J.S. Insurance §§ 71, 85.

634.423. Grounds for discretionary refusal, suspension, or revocation of registration of sales representatives

The department may deny, suspend, revoke, or refuse to renew or continue the registration of any sales representative if it is found that any one or more of the following grounds applicable to the sales representative exist under circumstances for which such denial, suspension, revocation, or refusal is not mandatory under s. 634.422:

(1) Any cause for which granting of the registration could have been refused had it then existed and been known to the department.

(2) Violation of any provision of this part, or of any other law applicable to the business of service warranties, in the course of dealings under the registration.

(3) Violation of any lawful order or rule of the department.

(4) Failure or refusal to pay over, upon demand, to any service warranty association or insurer he represents or has represented any money coming into his hands which belongs to the association or insurer.

(5) In the conduct of business under the registration, engaging in unfair methods of competition or in unfair or deceptive acts or practices, as such methods, acts, or practices are or may be defined under this part, or otherwise showing himself to be a source of injury or loss to the public or detriment to the public interest.

(6) Being found guilty of or pleading guilty or nolo contendere to a felony, in this state or any other state, without regard to whether judgment of conviction has been entered by the court having jurisdiction of such case.

Repeal

For repeal of this section, see the italicized note preceding § 634.401.

Historical Note

Derivation:

Laws 1983, c. 83–322, § 18.
Laws 1978, c. 78–255, § 5.
Laws 1983, c. 83–322, § 18, deleted "after notice and hearing thereon as provided in s.

634.424" following "if it is found" in the introduction and rewrote subsec. (6) which read "conviction of a felony".

Library References

Insurance ⬚7, 12 et seq.
C.J.S. Insurance §§ 71, 85.

634.424. Procedure for refusal, suspension, or revocation of registration of sales representatives

(1) If any sales representative is convicted by a court of a violation of any provision of this part, the registration of such individual shall thereby be deemed to be immediately revoked without any further procedure relative thereto by the department.

(2) If, after an investigation or upon other evidence, the department has reason to believe that there may exist any one or more grounds for the suspension, revocation, or refusal to renew or continue the registration of any sales representative, as such grounds are specified in ss. 634.422 and 634.423, the department may proceed to suspend, revoke, or refuse to renew or continue the registration, as the case may be.

(3) If such registered sales representative also holds a license to perform professional services of the type covered by the service warranty issued, the department shall file with the regulatory authority that issued such license a recommendation that such license be suspended or revoked. Such regulatory authority shall promptly review the recom-

mendation and take appropriate action in accordance with its laws and rules to suspend or revoke such license.

(4) Whenever it appears that any licensed insurance agent has violated the provisions of this part, the department may take such action relative thereto as is authorized by the insurance code for a violation of the insurance code by such agent.

Repeal

For repeal of this section, see the italicized note preceding § 634.401.

Historical Note

Derivation:

Laws 1983, c. 83–322, § 19.
Laws 1978, c. 78–255, § 5.

Laws 1983, c. 83–322, § 19, deleted former subsec. (2) pertaining to right to hear-

ing, added a new subsec. (3), and renumbered other provisions accordingly.

634.425. Duration of suspension or revocation

(1) The department shall, in its order suspending a registration, specify the time period during which the suspension is to be in effect. Such period may not exceed 1 year. The registration shall remain suspended during the period so specified, subject to any rescission or modification of the order by the department before the expiration of the suspension period. A registration which has been suspended may not be reinstated except upon request, but the department may not grant such reinstatement if it finds that the circumstances for which the registration was suspended still exist or are likely to recur.

(2) No person whose registration has been revoked by the department has the right to apply for another registration within 2 years from the effective date of such revocation or, if judicial review of such revocation is sought, within 2 years from the date of the final court order or decree affirming the revocation. The department, however, may not grant a new registration if it finds that the circumstance or circumstances for which the previous registration was revoked still exist or are likely to recur.

(3) The department may not grant or issue any registration to any individual whose registration has been revoked twice.

(4) During the period of suspension, or after revocation of the registration, the former registrant may not engage in or attempt to engage in any transaction or business for which a registration is required under this part.

Repeal

For repeal of this section, see the italicized note preceding § 634.401.

Historical Note

Derivation:
Laws 1983, c. 83–322, § 20.
Laws 1978, c. 78–255, § 5.

Laws 1983, c. 83–322, § 20, made nonsubstantive changes throughout subsec. (1), and reworded subsec. (3).

Library References

Insurance ☞7, 12 et seq.
C.J.S. Insurance §§ 71, 85.

634.426. Administrative fine in lieu of suspension or revocation of registration

(1) If, pursuant to procedures provided for in this part, it is found that one or more grounds exist for the suspension, revocation, or refusal to renew or continue any registration issued under this act, on a first offense and except when such suspension, revocation, or refusal is mandatory, an order may be entered imposing upon the registrant, in lieu of such suspension, revocation, or refusal, an administrative penalty for each violation in the amount of $100, or in the event of willful misconduct or willful violation on the part of the registrant, an administrative fine not to exceed $1,000 for each violation. The administrative penalty may be augmented by an amount equal to any commissions received by or accruing to the credit of the registrant in connection with any transaction to which the grounds for suspension, revocation, or refusal are related.

(2) The order may allow the registrant a reasonable period, not to exceed 30 days, within which to pay to the department the amount of the penalty so imposed. If the registrant fails to pay the penalty in its entirety to the department at its office in Tallahassee within the period so allowed, the registration of the registrant shall stand suspended or revoked or renewal or continuation may be refused, as the case may be, upon expiration of such period and without any further proceedings.

Repeal

For repeal of this section, see the italicized note preceding § 634.401.

Historical Note

Derivation:
Laws 1983, c. 83–322, § 21.
Laws 1978, c. 78–255, § 5.

Laws 1983, c. 83–322, § 21, substituted "not to exceed $1,000" for "of $500" in the first sentence of subsec. (1).

Library References

Insurance ☞27.
C.J.S. Insurance § 86.

634.427. Disposition of taxes and fees

All license fees, taxes on premiums, registration fees, and administrative fines and penalties collected under this part from service warranty associations and sales representatives shall be deposited to the credit of the Insurance Commissioner's Regulatory Trust Fund.

Repeal

For repeal of this section, see the italicized note preceding § 634.401.

Historical Note

Derivation:
Laws 1983, c. 83–322, § 22.
Laws 1978, c. 78–255, § 5.

Laws 1983, c. 83–322, § 22, deleted "and assessments" following "premiums".

Library References

Insurance ⬥7.
C.J.S. Insurance § 71.

634.428. Insurance business not authorized

Nothing in this part shall be deemed to authorize any service warranty association to transact any business other than that of service warranty as herein defined, or otherwise to engage in the business of insurance unless such association is authorized therefor as an insurer under a certificate of authority issued by the department under the insurance code.

Repeal

For repeal of this section, see the italicized note preceding § 634.401.

Historical Note

Derivation:
Laws 1978, c. 78–255, § 5.

Cross References

Certificate of authority requirement, see § 624.401.

Library References

Insurance ⬥4.5 et seq.
C.J.S. Insurance §§ 59, 70.

634.429. Fronting not permitted

No authorized insurer or licensed service warranty association may act as a fronting company for any unauthorized insurer or unlicensed service warranty association. A "fronting company" is an authorized insurer or licensed service warranty association which, by reinsurance or otherwise, generally transfers to one or more unauthorized insurers or unlicensed service warranty associations the risk of loss under warranties written by it in this state.

Repeal

For repeal of this section, see the italicized note preceding § 634.401.

Historical Note

Derivation:
Laws 1983, c. 83–322, § 23.
Laws 1978, c. 78–255, § 5.

Laws 1983, c. 83–322, § 23, deleted "substantially all of" preceding "the risk".

Library References

Insurance ⚖6, 29.
C.J.S. Insurance §§ 70, 88.

634.430. Dissolution or liquidation

Any dissolution or liquidation of an association subject to the provisions of this part shall be under the supervision of the department, which shall have all powers with respect thereto granted to it under the laws of the state with respect to the dissolution and liquidation of property and casualty companies pursuant to chapter 631.

Repeal

For repeal of this section, see the italicized note preceding § 634.401.

Historical Note

Derivation:
Laws 1978, c. 78–255, § 5.

Library References

Insurance ⚖72.4, 72.5.
C.J.S. Insurance §§ 124 et seq., 133.

634.431. Penalty for violation

Except as otherwise provided in this part, any person who knowingly makes a false or otherwise fraudulent application for license or registration under this part, or who knowingly violates any provision hereof, in addition to being subject to any applicable denial, suspension, revocation, or refusal to renew or continue any license or registration, is guilty of a misdemeanor of the second degree, punishable as provided in s. 775.082, s. 775.083, or s. 775.084. Each instance of violation shall be considered a separate offense.

Repeal

For repeal of this section, see the italicized note preceding § 634.401.

Historical Note

Derivation:
Laws 1978, c. 78–255, § 5.

Library References

Insurance ⟐27.
C.J.S. Insurance § 86.

634.433.   Civil remedy

(1) Any person damaged by a violation of the provisions of this part may bring a civil action against a person violating such provisions in the circuit court of the county in which the alleged violator resides or has his principal place of business or in the county in which the alleged violation occurred.   Upon adverse adjudication, the defendant will be liable for actual damages or $500, whichever is greater, together with court costs and reasonable attorney's fees incurred by the plaintiff.

(2) No punitive damages may be awarded under this section unless the acts giving rise to the violation occur with such frequency as to indicate a general business practice and these acts are:

(a) Willful, wanton, and malicious; or

(b) In reckless disregard for the rights of any insured.

Any person who pursues a claim under this subsection shall post in advance the costs of discovery.   Such costs shall be awarded to the insurer if no punitive damages are awarded to the plaintiff.

(3) As a condition precedent to bringing an action under this section, the department and the insurer shall be given written notice of the violation.   The notice shall state with specificity the facts which allegedly constitute the violation and the law upon which the plaintiff is relying and shall state that such notice is given in order to perfect the right to pursue the civil remedy authorized by this section.   No action will lie if, within 30 days thereafter, the damages are paid or the circumstances giving rise to the violation are corrected.

(4) This section shall not be construed to authorize a class action suit against a service warranty association or a civil action against the department, its employees, or the Insurance Commissioner.

Repeal

For repeal of this section, see the italicized note preceding § 634.401.

Historical Note

Derivation:

Laws 1983, c. 83–322, § 25.

Library References

Insurance ☞27.
C.J.S. Insurance § 86.

634.435. Unfair methods of competition and unfair or deceptive acts or practices prohibited

No person may engage in this state in any trade practice which is defined in this part as, or determined pursuant to s. 634.437 to be, an unfair method of competition or an unfair or deceptive act or practice involving the business of service warranty.

Repeal

For repeal of this section, see the italicized note preceding § 634.401.

Historical Note

Derivation:

Laws 1983, c. 83–322, § 27.

Library References

Insurance ☞11.
Trade Regulation ☞861 et seq.
C.J.S. Insurance § 60 et seq.

C.J.S. Trade-Marks, Trade-Names, and Unfair Competition § 237.

634.436. Unfair methods of competition and unfair or deceptive acts or practices defined

The following methods, acts, or practices are defined as unfair methods of competition and unfair or deceptive acts or practices:

(1) Misrepresentation and false advertising of insurance policies.— Knowingly making, issuing, circulating, or causing to be made, issued, or circulated, any estimate, illustration, circular, statement, sales presentation, omission, or comparison which:

(a) Misrepresents the benefits, advantages, conditions, or terms of any service warranty contract.

(b) Is misleading or is a misrepresentation as to the financial condition of any person.

(c) Uses any name or title of any contract misrepresenting the true nature thereof.

(d) Is a misrepresentation for the purpose of inducing, or tending to induce, the lapse, forfeiture, exchange, conversion, or surrender of any service warranty contract.

(2) False information and advertising generally.—Knowingly making, publishing, disseminating, circulating, or placing before the public, or causing, directly or indirectly, to be made, published, disseminated, circulated, or placed before the public:

(a) In a newspaper, magazine, or other publication;

(b) In the form of a notice, circular, pamphlet, letter, or poster;

(c) Over any radio or television station; or

(d) In any other way,

an advertisement, announcement, or statement containing any assertion, representation, or statement with respect to the business of service warranty, which assertion, representation, or statement is untrue, deceptive, or misleading.

(3) Defamation.—Knowingly making, publishing, disseminating, or circulating, directly or indirectly, or aiding, abetting, or encouraging the making, publishing, disseminating, or circulating of, any oral or written statement, or any pamphlet, circular, article, or literature, which is false or maliciously critical of, or derogatory to, any person and which is calculated to injure such person.

(4) False statements and entries.—

(a) Knowingly:

1. Filing with any supervisory or other public official;

2. Making, publishing, disseminating, or circulating;

3. Delivering to any person;

4. Placing before the public; or

5. Causing, directly or indirectly, to be made, published, disseminated, circulated, delivered to any person, or placed before the public, any false statement.

(b) Knowingly making any false entry of a material fact in any book, report, or statement of any person.

(5) Unfair claim settlement practices.—

(a) Attempting to settle claims on the basis of an application or any other material document which was altered without notice to, or knowledge or consent of, the warranty holder;

(b) Making a material misrepresentation to the warranty holder for the purpose and with the intent of effecting settlement of such claims, loss, or damage under such contract on less favorable terms than those provided in, and contemplated by, such contract; or

(c) Committing or performing with such frequency as to indicate a general business practice any of the following practices:

1. Failure properly to investigate claims;

2. Misrepresentation of pertinent facts or contract provisions relating to coverages at issue;

3. Failure to acknowledge and act promptly upon communications with respect to claims;

4. Denial of claims without conducting reasonable investigations based upon available information;

5. Failure to affirm or deny coverage of claims upon written request of the warranty holder within a reasonable time after proof-of-loss statements have been completed; or

6. Failure to promptly provide a reasonable explanation to the warranty holder of the basis in the contract in relation to the facts or applicable law for denial of a claim or for the offer of a compromise settlement.

(6) Failure to maintain procedures for handling complaints.—Failing to maintain a record of each complaint received for a 3-year period after the date of the receipt of the written complaint.

(7) Discriminatory refusal to issue a contract.—Refusing to issue a contract solely because of an individual's race, color, creed, marital status, sex, or national origin.

Repeal

For repeal of this section, see the italicized note preceding § 634.401.

Historical Note

Derivation:
Laws 1983, c. 83–322, § 28.

Cross References

Unfair trade practices, see § 626.951 et seq.

Library References

Insurance ⟐11.
Trade Regulation ⟐861 et seq.
C.J.S. Insurance § 60 et seq.

C.J.S. Trade-Marks, Trade-Names, and Unfair Competition § 237.

634.437. Power of department to examine and investigate

The department has the power to examine and investigate the affairs of every person involved in the business of service warranty in this state in order to determine whether such person has been or is engaged in any unfair method of competition or in any unfair or deceptive act or practice prohibited by s. 634.435.

Repeal

For repeal of this section, see the italicized note preceding
§ 634.401.

Historical Note

Derivation:

   Laws 1983, c. 83–322, § 29.

Library References

Insurance ☞9, 11.
C.J.S. Insurance § 60 et seq.

634.438. Prohibited practices; hearings, witnesses, appearances, production of books, and service of process

(1) Whenever the department has reason to believe that any person has engaged, or is engaging, in this state in any unfair method of competition or any unfair or deceptive act or practice as defined in s. 634.436, or is engaging in the business of service warranty without being properly licensed as required by this part, and that a proceeding by the department in respect thereto would be in the interest of the public, the department shall conduct or cause to have conducted a hearing in accordance with chapter 120.

(2) The department or a duly empowered hearing officer shall, during the conduct of such hearing, have those powers enumerated in s. 120.58; however, the penalty for failure to comply with a subpoena or with an order directing discovery is limited to a fine not to exceed $1,000 per violation.

(3) A statement of charges, notice, or order under this part may be served by anyone duly authorized by the department, either in the manner provided by law for service of process in civil actions or by certifying and mailing a copy thereof to the person affected by such statement, notice, order, or other process at his or its residence or principal office or place of business. The verified return by the person so serving such statement, notice, order, or other process, setting forth the manner of the service, is proof of the same; and the return postcard receipt for such statement, notice, order, or other process, certified and mailed as provided in this subsection, is proof of service of the same.

Repeal

For repeal of this section, see the italicized note preceding
§ 634.401.

Historical Note

Derivation:

   Laws 1983, c. 83–322, § 30.

634.439. Cease and desist and penalty orders

After the hearing provided for in s. 634.438, the department shall enter a final order in accordance with s. 120.59. If it is determined that the person charged has engaged in an unfair or deceptive act or practice or the unlawful transaction of service warranty business, the department also shall issue an order requiring the violator to cease and desist from engaging in such method of competition, act, or practice or the unlawful transaction of service warranty business. Further, the department may, at its discretion, order any one or more of the following penalties:

(1) The suspension or revocation of such person's license, or eligibility for any license, if he knew, or reasonably should have known, he was in violation of this part.

(2) If it is determined that the person charged has provided or offered to provide service warranties without proper licensure, the imposition of [1] an administrative penalty not to exceed $1,000 for each service warranty contract offered or effectuated.

[1] The words "the imposition of" were inserted by the division of statutory revision.

Repeal

For repeal of this section, see the italicized note preceding § 634.401.

Historical Note

Derivation:
Laws 1983, c. 83–322, § 31.

634.44. Appeals from orders of the department

Any person subject to an order of the department under s. 634.439 may obtain a review of such order by filing an appeal therefrom in accordance with the provisions and procedures for appeal from the orders of the department in general under s. 120.68.

Repeal

For repeal of this section, see the italicized note preceding § 634.401.

Historical Note

Derivation:
  Laws 1983, c. 83–322, § 32.

634.441. Penalty for violation of cease and desist order

Any person who violates a cease and desist order of the department under s. 634.439 while such order is in effect, after notice and hearing as provided in s. 634.438, is subject, at the discretion of the department, to any one or more of the following penalties:

(1) A monetary penalty of not more than $50,000 as to all matters determined in such hearing.

(2) The suspension or revocation of such person's license or eligibility to hold a license.

Repeal

For repeal of this section, see the italicized note preceding § 634.401.

Historical Note

Derivation:
  Laws 1983, c. 83–322, § 33.

634.442. Injunctive proceedings

In addition to the penalties and other enforcement provisions of this part, if any person violates s. 634.403 or s. 634.420 or any rule adopted pursuant thereto, the department may resort to a proceeding for injunction in the circuit court of the county where such person resides or has his or its principal place of business, and therein apply for such temporary and permanent orders as the department may deem necessary to restrain such person from engaging in any such activities, until such person has complied with such provision or rule.

Repeal

For repeal of this section, see the italicized note preceding § 634.401.

Historical Note

Derivation:
Laws 1983, c. 83–322, § 34.

Cross References

Fines in lieu of suspension or revocation, generally, see § 624.4211.
Injunctions, see Civil Procedure Rule 1.610.

Library References

Injunction ⚷64 et seq.
Insurance ⚷11, 27.

C.J.S. Injunctions § 106.
C.J.S. Insurance §§ 60 et seq., 86.

634.443. Civil liability

The provisions of this part are cumulative to rights under the general civil and common law, and no action of the department will abrogate such rights to damages or other relief in any court.

Repeal

For repeal of this section, see the italicized note preceding § 634.401.

Historical Note

Derivation:
Laws 1983, c. 83–322, § 35.

Library References

Insurance ⚷11, 27.
C.J.S. Insurance §§ 60 et seq., 86.

634.444. Investigatory records

All active examination or investigatory records of the department made or received pursuant to this part shall be deemed privileged and confidential and are not subject to public inspection under the provisions of chapter 119 for so long as is reasonably necessary to complete the examination or investigation.

Repeal

For repeal of this section, see the italicized note preceding § 634.401.

Historical Note

Derivation:
Laws 1983, c. 83–322, § 26.

Library References

Insurance ⚷9.
C.J.S. Insurance § 73.

Index

acceptance of offer, characteristics of, 94–95

A-Copy, Inc., 247–258
  benefits of program of, 257–258
  collection procedures of, 258
  contract administration by, 248–249, 251–253, 255–257
  history of, 247
  inventory control by, 254–255
  marketing strategies of, 248–249
  organizational structure of, 247
  pricing strategies of, 249
  sales strategies of, 250

Adesco, Inc., 239–246
  benefits of program of, 245–246
  contract administration by, 240–241
  history of, 239–240
  marketing strategies of, 240–243
  pricing strategies of, 243–245

administration, *see* contract administration procedures

administrative reports, 185–189
  formats for, 189
  objectives of, 185
  types of, 185–189

advertising
  testing of, 143
  use of, 141–142

Americare program, *see* Xerox Americare

automatic renewal provision, specifications of, 106–107

benefits of contracts
  to customers, 6–7
  to servicing organization, 5–6
  see also feature-benefit analysis

billing procedures
  of NCR Corporation, 233–234
  types of, 190–191, 193

body language, sales presentations and, 156–157

breach of contract
  billing and, 193
  characteristics of, 96

break-even analysis, 76–91
  calculation of, 79–84
  data for, 76
  by formula, 79
  by graph, 76–79, 80–84
  sales volume and, 85–91

break-even chart
  construction of, 76–79
  elements on, 76
  for profitability analysis, 85–89
  for sales volume, 85
  uses of, 79–84

break-even point (BEP), calculation of, 79, 85–91

business ethics, 194–197
  importance of, 194, 196–197
  violations of, 194–196

cancellation, of contracts, 114–115
Canon U.S.A., Inc., 259–271
  benefits of program of, 266–267
  contract administration by, 267–271
  contract options of, 261–262
  dealership organization of, 259–261
  inventory control by, 265–266
  pricing strategies of, 262–265
casualty insurance, customer need for,
  109
collection procedures, 192–193
  of A-Copy, Inc., 258
  for late payments, 191
computers, uses of:
  calculating time standards, 169–177
  classifying and prioritizing service
    calls, 168–169
  contract administration, 179–180, 257
  inventory, 199, 204–205, 207, 235
  service orders, 181–185
  telemarketing, 153
  see also data base programs
Conditions section, purpose and items
  of, 109–111
consideration, in binding contract,
  95–96
contract administration procedures:
  A-Copy, Inc., 248–249, 251–253,
    255–257
  Adesco, Inc., 240–241
  billing, 189–192
  Canon U.S.A., 267–271
  collection, 189, 192
  data base programs, 179–180
  Marsh & McLennan, 229–230
  NCR Corporation, 235–237
  personnel, 166–179
  reports, 185–189
  service forms, 181–185
  Xerox Americare, 223–224
contract laws, elements of:
  acceptance of offer, 94–95
  breach of contract, 96

consideration, 95–96
discharge of contract, 96
offer, 94
see also Magnuson-Moss Warranty
  Act; state law, on service contracts;
  written contracts
contract pre-inspection, policy
  requirements for, 56–58
contract service
  benefits of, 20
  characteristics of, 19–20
  length of, 19–20
contract service, types of:
  cost-plus, 29–30
  deductible, 29
  full repair and maintenance, 24–27
  maintenance only, 21–24
  rebate, 29
  repair only, 27–29
  wrap-around, 30
  see also contract service
customer profiles
  for commercial and industrial
    products, 129–131
  for consumer products, 131–132

data base programs
  for contract administration, 179–180
  for profitability analysis, 49–50
  for repair hours analysis, 41–42
  see also computers, uses of
dealer(s)
  as Adesco, Inc. market, 242–243
  of Canon U.S.A., Inc., 259–261
  as sales personnel, 163–164
  third party, 211, 237
  warranty obligations of, 13–14
  see also distributors
deceptive practices, forms of, 194–196
Delphi panel, uses of, 134
direct mail
  as research tool, 134–135
  selection criteria for, 160
  techniques used in, 142–143
  testing of, 143
distributors
  as sales personnel, 163–164

third-party, 211
see also dealers
double dipping, prevention of, 111

Economic Order Quantity (EOQ)
    formula, use of, 201–204
ethics, *see* business ethics
Exclusions section, purpose and items
    of, 109, 111–112

failure rate
    external factors affecting, 109
    pricing and, 68
feature, of contract, 135
feature-benefit analysis, 135–141
    customer objections to, 141
    definitions in, 135
    outline for, 137–138
    sales use of, 135–141
federal laws, *see* Magnuson-Moss
    Warranty Act
Federal Trade Commission, warranty
    regulation by, 98–101
Florida, service contract regulation by,
    101–103
focus groups, characteristics of, 134
franchise firms, characteristics of,
    211–212
Full Repair and Maintenance contracts,
    24–27
    benefits of, 24–25
    liabilities of, 25–27
    pricing of, 39–51, 54
    statement of provisions in, 108

General and Administrative (G&A)
    expenses, calculation of, 62–65

Income Statement, preparation of,
    45–48
inspection of equipment, 56–58
insurance, casualty, 109
insurance (contract), 31–37
    benefits of, 33–34, 36
    characteristics of, 32–33
    factors determining, 36–37
    limitations and restrictions of, 33

negotiating of, 34–36
premiums for, 33–34
purpose of, 31–32
regulations governing, 33
insured contract(s)
    benefits of, 228–229
    by Marsh & McLennan Group
        Associates, 227–229
    pricing of, 228
inventory controls
    by A-Copy, Inc., 254–255
    by Canon U.S.A., Inc, 265–266
    of existing products, 199–200
    by NCR Corporation, 235
    of new products, 200–201
    by Xerox Americare, 223
inventory controls, types of:
    computers, 199, 204–205, 207
    Economic Order Quantity (EOQ)
        formula, 201–204
    safety stock, 204
    service vehicle stock, 205–207
    see also parts and materials

labor costs
    anticipation of demand and, 167–168
    billable versus unbillable, 74–76
    calculation of, 42, 59–61, 67–68,
        70–75
labor hours, calculation of, 70–72
legal considerations, *see* contract law,
    elements of; Magnuson-Moss
    Warranty Act; state law, on service
    contracts; written contracts
legal rights, contractual notification of,
    114
liability
    limitations on servicing organization,
        112
    for production losses, 111
L/PM (labor to parts and materials ratio),
    uses of, 61, 63–65

MAB Maintenance Agreement, terms of,
    233–234
Magnuson-Moss Warranty Act
    requirements of, 97–101, 128–129

Magnuson-Moss Warranty Act (*continued*)
    violations of, 128–129
maintenance cost analysis, data
        requirements for:
    failure rates, 68–70
    inspection costs, 56–58
    job-site factors, 54
    labor, 59–61, 63–65, 67–68, 70–72
    location, 54
    multiplicity of units, 54
    overhead, 59
    parts and materials, 61–62, 65–68
    profit goals, 63
    replacement costs, 70–71
    sales volume, 58–66
    surcharges, 54–55
    travel time, 54–55
Maintenance Only contracts, 21–24
    benefits of, 21–23
    break-even analysis of, 76
    liabilities of, 24
    monitoring of, 24
    pricing of, 52–76
    provisions of, 107
marketing plan, steps in:
    analyze situation, 120–122
    develop strategies, 124
    draw up timetable, 124
    establish monitoring and control
        procedures, 125
    establish objectives, 123–124
    evaluate assumptions, 122–123
    prepare budget, 125
    survey problems and opportunities,
        122
    write action plans, 125, 126
    write contingency plans, 125–127
marketing strategies
    of A-Copy, Inc., 248–249
    development of, 124
    of Adesco, Inc., 240–243
market research, sources for, 132–135
    primary, 133–135
    secondary, 132–133
Marsh & McLennan Group Associates,
        226–230
    benefits of program of, 228–229

contract administration procedures of,
        229–230
    contract options of, 227–228
    history of, 226
    pricing strategies of, 228
    Product Warranty Department of, 227
    support programs of, 230
Minnehoma Insurance Company, *see*
        Adesco, Inc.

NCR Corporation, 231–238
    contract administration procedures of,
        235–237
    history of, 231–232
    maintenance agreement of, 233–234
    parts and materials management by,
        235
    service organization of, 232–233

offer, in contract, 94–95
overhead costs, calculation of, 59, 62

parties to agreement, characteristics of,
        105
parts and materials
    cost calculation of, 43–44, 61–62,
        74–75
    failure rates of, 68
    grouping of, 66
    management of, 198–207, 223, 235,
        265–266
    pricing of, 66–68, 72
    rate calculation for, 65–66
    replacement costs of, 43–44
    service life of, 68–70
    usage and disbursement controls for,
        207
    see also inventory controls
payment(s), late, 190–191
    see also collection procedures
payment terms
    in advance, 190
    contractual statement of, 114
    at time of service, 190
    see also billing procedures; collection
        procedures
period of contract, written specification
        of, 106

personnel administration, elements of:
  anticipation of demand, 167–168
  prioritizing calls, 168–169
  productivity, 166–167
  scheduling, 166, 168–169, 178–179
  time standards, 169–177
person-to-person sales
  advantages of, 156–157
  disadvantages of, 158
  training for, 157
pricing
  calculation of, 73–75
  contractual specification of, 113–114
  of Full Repair and Maintenance
    contracts, 54
  of Maintenance Only contracts, 52–76
  of Repair Only contracts, 39–51
pricing factors:
  age of equipment, 41
  competition, 48
  failure rate, 41, 68–70
  inspection costs, 56–58
  job-site, 54
  labor, 42, 48, 59–61, 63–65, 67–68,
    70–72
  location, 54
  multiplicity of units, 54
  overhead, 59
  parts and material, 40–44, 48, 61–62,
    65–68
  profit goals, 44–51, 63
  repair hours, 41–42
  replacement costs, 70–71
  sales goals, 44–51, 58–66
  surcharges, 41, 55–56
  travel time, 42–43, 54–55
pricing strategies, corporate:
  A-Copy, Inc., 249
  Canon U.S.A., Inc., 262–265
  Marsh & McLennan, 228
  Xerox Americare, 221–222
profits, uses of, 91–92
profitability analysis, 45–51
  break-even analysis and, 79–89
  calculation of, 44–51, 59, 63, 65–66,
    73–76
  elements in, 53

  importance of, 51
  report form for, 185–187
Pro Forma Income Statement,
  preparation of, 45–48

repair(s)
  cost of, 70–72
  replacement versus, 40
  time requirements for, 39, 41–43
repair analysis, 39
  calculation of, 41–43
  model of, 40
Repair Only contracts, 27–29
  pricing of, 39–51
  risks of, 27–28
  sales and profitability analysis of,
    45–51
  statement of provisions in, 108–109
replacements
  contractual terms of, 110
  costs of, 70–71
reports, *see* administrative reports

safety stock, levels of, 204
sales analysis
  elements of, 48–51, 52
  importance of, 51
sales goals
  business ethics and, 195–196
  calculation of, 44–51
sales personnel
  selection of, 159–163
  training of, 157–158, 159, 162
sales strategies:
  advertising, 141–142
  customer profiles, 129–132
  direct mail, 142–143
  feature-benefit analysis, 135–138
  marketing plan, 120–127, 158–164
  market research, 132–135
  person-to-person, 156–158
  telemarketing, 144–156
  time purchase, 127–129
sales strategies, corporate:
  A-Copy, Inc., 205
  Xerox Americare, 222–223

sales techniques, *see* person-to-person
  sales; telemarketing
sales volume
  break-even analysis and, 85–89
  calculation of, 58–66
service calls
  classifying and prioritizing of,
    168–169
  scheduling of, 178–179
  time standards for, 169–177
service centers
  customer use of, 113
  of NCR Corporation, 232–233
service life, 68, 109
service order forms, 181–185
service time standards, 169–177
service vehicle, parts stock on, 205–207
Service Warranty Association, functions
  of, 102
Standard Industrial Classification (SIC)
  code, 130–131
state law, on service contracts, 101–103
surcharges
  calculation of, 55–56
  determination of, 41–42
  sales and profitability goals and, 51

telemarketing, 143–158
  by A-Copy, Inc., 248
  advantages of, 146
  automated, 153
  business ethics and, 195–196
  compensation plan for, 153–154
  customer account cards for, 155–156
  monitoring of, 153–156
  nature of, 144–145
  objectives of, 146, 153–154
  person-to-person sales versus,
    156–158
  selection criteria for, 159–160
  training sales personnel for, 152
  see also person-to-person sales
telemarketing script, elements of:
  close, 149, 150
  competitive analysis, 148
  customer objections, 146, 148
  customer reassurance, 151

feature-benefit analysis, 148
  grabber, 147
  opening statement, 146–147
  questioning phase, 147–148
  trial close, 148
telephone consultation, trends in, 17
third-party service, 208–214
  contractual exclusion of, 109
  customer benefits of, 212–213
  opportunities for, 209–210, 213–214
  types of, 210–212
Time and Material service, 18–19
time-of-purchase sales, 127–129
title of agreement, 104
trade publications, advertising in,
  141–142
travel time
  calculations of, 42–43
  pricing and, 54–55
  scheduling of, 178
trend reports, 187–189

warranty cards, customer profiles and,
  131–132
warranty(ies), 10–16
  cost of fulfilling, 11, 14–16
  federal regulation of, 97–101
  manufacturer versus dealer
    obligations for, 13–14
  profits from, 16
  type and extent of, 11–13
  violations of, 128–129
Warranty Reserve Account, function of,
  15
warranty reserves, calculation of, 14–16
wrap-around contract, 128–129
written contracts, 104, 116–118
written contracts, preliminary steps of:
  procure legal counsel, 115–118
  review contract law, 94–96
  review existing contract forms and
    content, 103
  review federal and state laws, 96–103
written contracts, provisions of:
  attachments, 113
  automatic renewal clause, 106–107
  cancellability, 114–115

conditions, 109–111
definitions, 109
equipment covered, 105
exclusions, 109, 111-112
"How to Obtain Service" clause,
   112–113
legal rights notification, 114
parties to agreement, 105
payment terms, 113–114
period of contract, 106
price, 113–114
provisions, 107–109
signatures, 115

special conditions, 112
title of agreement, 104

Xerox Americare, 217–225
benefits of program of, 224–225
contract administration procedures of,
   223–224
contract options offered by, 219–220
history of, 217–219
parts and materials management by,
   223
pricing strategies of, 221–222
sales strategies of, 222–223